USING MICROSOFT EXCEL

A How-To-Do-It Manual
for Librarians

ROBERT MACHALOW

HOW-TO-DO-IT MANUALS
FOR LIBRARIES
Number 11

Series Editor: Bill Katz

NEAL-SCHUMAN PUBLISHERS, INC.
New York, London

Microsoft Excel is a trademark or registered
trademark of the Microsoft Corporation.

Published by Neal-Schuman Publishers, Inc.
23 Leonard Street
New York, NY 10013

Copyright © 1991 Robert Machalow.

All rights reserved. Reproduction of this book, in whole or in
part, without written permission of the publisher is prohibited.

Printed and bound in the United States of America

Library of Congress Cataloging-in-Publication Data

Machalow, Robert.
   Using Microsoft Excel : a how-to-do-it manual for librarians /
Robert Machalow.
     p.   cm. — (How-to-do-it manuals for libraries ; no. 11)
   Includes index.
   ISBN 1-55570-075-6
   1. Microcomputers — Library applications — Handbooks, manuals, etc.
2. Libraries — Automation — Handbooks, manuals, etc. 3. Microsoft
Excel (Computer programs) I. Title. II. Series.
Z678.93.M53M29   1990
025'.00285'536—dc20
                                                           90-21524
                                                            CIP

TO ROSALIE AND DEBORAH

CONTENTS

		Preface	vii
Part I		How it Works	1
	1	Microsoft Excel	3
	2	A Worksheet	12
	3	Customizing the Display	26
	4	Linking	35
	5	Printing	50
	6	Databases	57
	7	Formulas and Functions	71
	8	Excel Features I	82
	9	Excel Features II	90
	10	Charting	105
	11	Macros	118
	12	Further Customization	140
Part II		Library Applications	163
	13	Periodicals List	165
	14	Time	173
	15	Maps	182
	16	Catalog Cards	193
	17	Quizzes	207
		Index	233

PREFACE

As librarians become more computer literate, they realize that off-the-shelf software can be adapted to library needs. One of the more powerful software packages is Microsoft Excel. This program combines powerful spreadsheet, database, and graphics capabilities.

Microsoft Excel works in a graphical user interface (GUI) environment. A GUI permits users to learn quicker, work faster, make fewer mistakes, and become less frustrated and less fatigued than working in alternative environments. Excel's displays can be customized to an almost limitless degree. Because Excel is user-friendly, its use is simple and its mastery well within reach. Because it is a new generation program, its functions can be automated through the use of macros.

Excel is the only WYSIWYG (what you see is what you get) spreadsheet available. Due to this feature and the ability to preview printouts, printing is more efficient. Excel's charts are presentation graphics quality.

This book gives you the experience to use Excel in library situations. By working through the examples presented, you will master the commands and functions of Excel. In addition, you will be guided through several library situations, including the compilation and graphing of budget worksheets and databases, the linking of files, and the use of functions, formulas, and macros. The second portion of the book illustrates several advanced library applications of Microsoft Excel, including the use of Excel for time keeping, the production of an online periodicals list, creating maps of a library, an example of its use in bibliographic instruction, and interactive quizzes.

ACKNOWLEDGMENTS

Several people at York College of the City University of New York have aided me in my efforts to write this book. They include Edward Kalaydjian, the Business Manager, David Goetz, of the Academic Computing and Educational Technology Department, and Cindy Pederson-Goetz, the Property Manager. Of course, the person who has helped me most has been my wife, Rosalie Machalow.

PART I

HOW IT WORKS

1 MICROSOFT EXCEL

Microsoft Excel is a powerful new generation program that allows the manipulation of numbers and text in worksheets and databases. Excel also represents data as charts which can be customized by the user. Unlike older generation packages, Excel permits the user to display worksheets and charts simultaneously. In addition, Excel can be customized by the user in many ways, including the size and type of font, and the colors, size and shape in which information is displayed. Furthermore, worksheets can be linked together easily, permitting the user to update several worksheets simultaneously.

Some of the more interesting features of Excel include:

- up to four different type fonts can be used on a worksheet;
- the heights of rows and the size of fonts can be varied;
- the gridlines can be displayed and/or printed as desired;
- text and number formats can be created by the user;
- notes (either viewed or printed) can be added to displayed information.

Excel can read and write Lotus 1-2-3, dBase, and Multiplan files.

Because Microsoft Excel is such a powerful program, it requires powerful equipment. The program requires an IBM Personal System/2 or compatible, an IBM AT or compatible, or a Compaq 386 Deskpro or compatible. The computer must have an IBM VGA or EGA or compatible graphics board, a Hercules Graphics card or compatible, or another graphics card compatible with Microsoft Windows version 2.0 or higher. In addition, the computer must have a hard disk with at least 5 megabytes of free space. Microsoft Excel must be installed on a hard disk: it cannot be run from floppy disks. The computer must have 640K of random access memory (RAM). It must also use an operating system of DOS 3.0 or higher.

In addition to the required equipment, optional equipment can be added. A printer can be added to obtain a hard copy of your work on Excel. Laser printers such as the IBM Pageprinter and Hewlett-Packard Laserjet can be used with Excel; other printers such as the IBM Proprinter, IBM graphics printers, and EPSON FX 80 printers can be used. Expanded memory cards can be added to expand memory beyond the required 640K; this will permit the building of larger worksheets as well as the simultaneous manipulation of several worksheets.

Two of the most useful optional system components are a mouse and Microsoft Windows. A mouse can be used to easily make menu selections, work in a dialog box and indicate ranges; all these can be done with a keyboard, but some people find using a mouse easier. Microsoft Windows permits the user to run multiple applications simultaneously; for example, while running Excel in a Windows environment, you could also run a word processing program and switch between the two easily. In addition, you could transfer information from your word processing program to Excel and from Excel to your word processing program. To do any of this, you would have to install Excel under Windows (version 2.0 or higher). In addition, you would probably need expanded memory to keep both of the applications in memory.

With all that in mind, you install Microsoft Excel by placing the setup disk in the A drive, getting the A: prompt (type A: and depress the ENTER key) and then type setup. Follow the on screen instructions to install Excel.

To begin using Microsoft Excel once it has been installed, get to the directory containing the Excel program (you can do this by typing cd\windows and depressing the ENTER key if you have installed Excel in the subdirectory of your hard disk named Windows). Then type Excel at the prompt and depress the ENTER key. You will see a blank worksheet that looks like Figure 1.1.

Before using the worksheet in Figure 1.1, notice several important features.

MENU BAR

The available menus are toward the top of the display in the menu bar. The first menu bar that you see is the worksheet menu bar which includes the following menu choices: File, Edit, Formula, Format, Data, Options, Macro, Window, and Help. Notice that one letter of each of the selections is underlined: if you are using the keyboard, to gain access to the menu choices you depress the key marked ALT and then the underlined letter of the selection you are interested in. Alternatively, if you are using the keyboard, you can depress the / key to gain access to the menu bar; this alternative makes the use of Excel easier for those users who have used Lotus 1-2-3. Instead of depressing the letter of the menu choice, you could, after gaining access to the menu bar by depressing either the ALT or / key, simply use the ARROW keys to move the highlighting to your desired choice and then depress the ENTER key. At the beginning, you will probably use the latter technique of selecting

FIGURE 1-1 Blank Worksheet

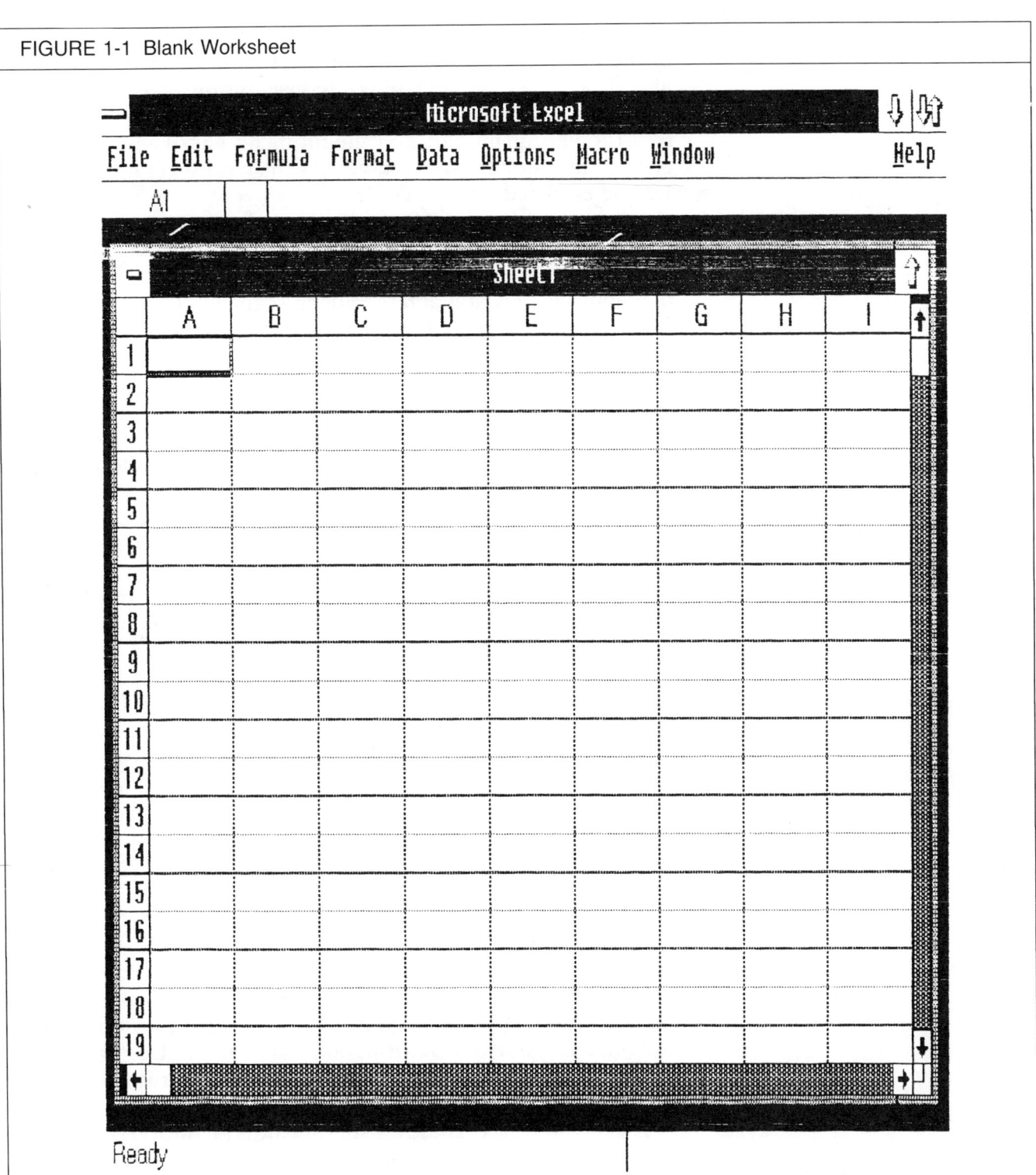

menus because the underlined letters are not always the first letter of the menu choice. Using the optional mouse, move the pointer and click (press and release the mouse button).

There are three other major menu bars in Excel: the chart menu bar, the info menu bar, and the nil menu bar. These menu bars contain many of the same choices as the worksheet menu bar and will be explored later in this book.

Once one of the menus is selected, a pull-down menu appears. A typical pull-down menu looks like Figure 1.2. To choose one of the items from a pull-down menu, you can use the ARROW keys to highlight the selection and then depress the ENTER key. Alternatively, you can depress the underlined letter of the choice. To select a command using the optional mouse, point at the command and click (press and release the mouse button). Some items from the pull-down menus are followed by ellipses (. . .); the selection of one of these items leads to another set of options, displayed in a dialog box. If a menu choice is grayed, it is not available at the time the pull-down menu is selected.

FORMULA BAR

Under the menu bar is the formula bar. This line consists of three parts: the current cell address, the enter and cancel boxes, and a blank area.

The formula bar begins with a cell address such as A1. This is the cell address of the currently active cell; cells are described in terms of column (designated by a letter of the alphabet) followed by row (designated by a number). You will notice the display of the column heads, near the top of the blank worksheet, and the row heads, along the left side of the worksheet.

Next to the address of the currently active cell there are two small boxes which are used when using a mouse. These are the enter box and the cancel box.

Finally there is a blank area on the formula bar. As you type anything into the worksheet, it will appear in this part of the formula bar. Once you depress the ENTER key, what you have typed in the formula bar will appear in the currently active cell on the worksheet. If you make a mistake while typing in the formula bar, you can edit the information using the ARROW, BACKSPACE and DELETE keys. If you want to cancel the entire entry, simply depress the ESCAPE key.

The name of the currently displayed file is on the top of the blank worksheet, under the formula bar but above the column heads. Excel will suggest a name such as Sheet1 for a new worksheet.

FIGURE 1-2 Pull-down menu

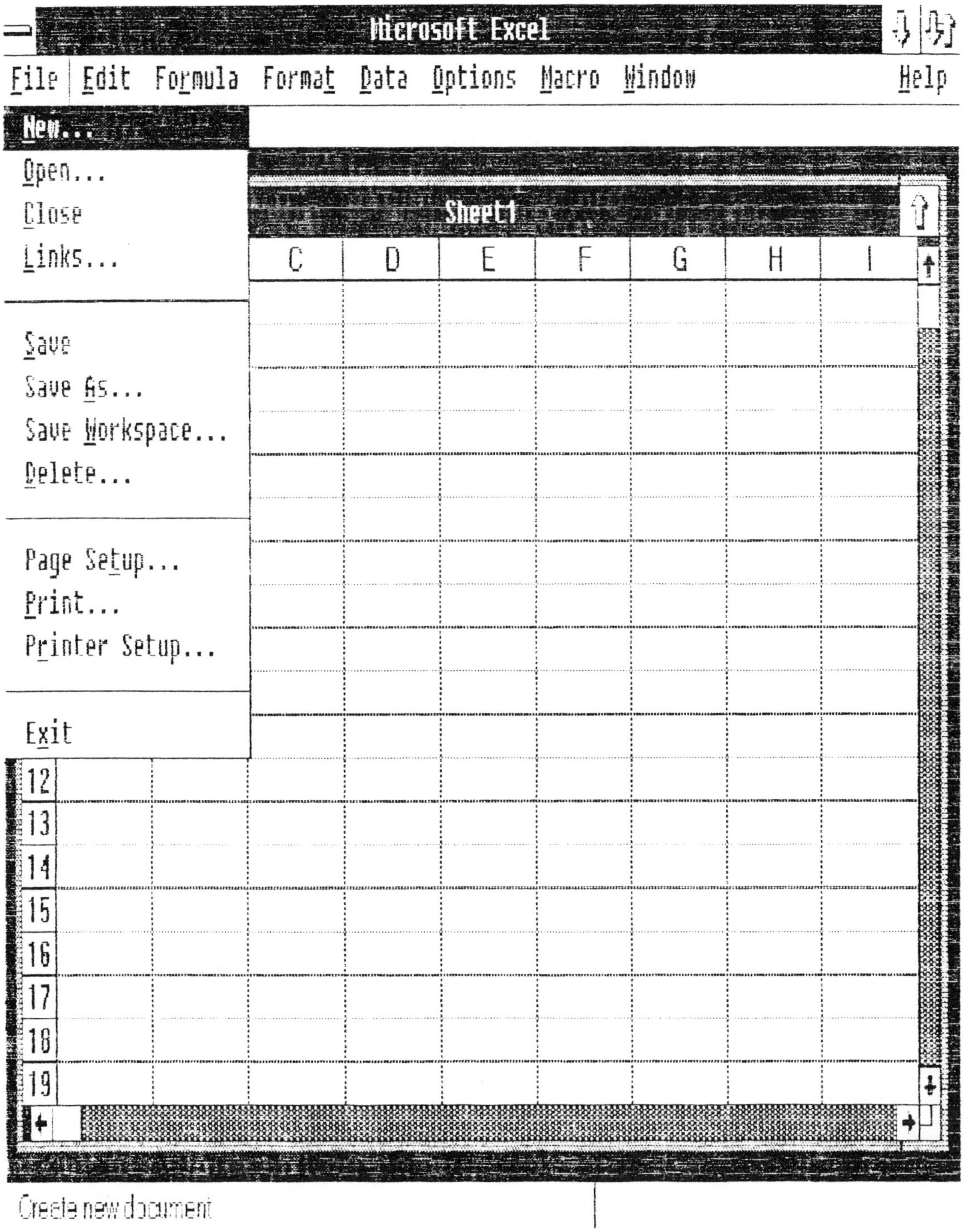

Once you save a worksheet, you can give it a name and the name you designate will be displayed here when you retrieve the worksheet.

STATUS BAR

At the bottom of the display is the status bar. The status bar has two parts: the message area and the keyboard indicator area. The message area displays information about commands and current mode of Excel. The keyboard indicator area includes information on standard keys of your keyboard, such as whether the capslock, numlock, and scroll lock are turned on.

SCROLL BARS

On the perimeter of the worksheet are scroll bars. These scroll bars are used to move around the worksheet if you are using the optional mouse.

On the blank worksheet, you will see one cell highlighted: this is the currently active cell; its address can be seen in the formula bar. As you move around the worksheet, the highlighting will move from one cell to the next and the address in the formula bar will change to reflect the currently active cell.

MOVING AROUND AN EXCEL WORKSHEET

To move around an Excel document, you can use either the keyboard or the optional mouse.

With the keyboard, to move the active cell one cell in any direction, you can use the ARROW keys. If you are using a keyboard that has ARROW keys only on the numeric keyboard, the numlock must be off; otherwise, you will type numbers instead of moving the currently active cell. If you are moving a few cells, using the ARROW keys is easy, but if you are moving larger distances, there are other techniques that can be used.

If you are anywhere on the worksheet and need to get to cell A1, depress the CONTROL and HOME keys simultaneously. The currently active cell will then be A1.

Instead of going to cell A1, you may want to go to another specific cell. To do this, simply depress the function key F5 and enter the cell reference. When you depress the ENTER key, the currently active cell will be the one you have entered.

If you want to move to the beginning of a row, simply depress the HOME key. You will then be in the A column of whatever row you are working on.

If you want to move to the end of a row, simply depress the END key. You will then be at the last occupied column of the current worksheet.

Since a Microsoft Excel worksheet can have up to 16,384 rows and 256 columns, you may find it necessary to move horizontally and vertically one screen at a time. To move up one screen, depress the PAGE UP key; to move down one screen, depress the PAGE DOWN key; to move left one screen, depress the CONTROL and PAGE UP keys simultaneously; to move right one screen, depress the CONTROL and PAGE DOWN keys simultaneously.

Using the optional mouse, moving around a document is often faster. To make a different cell the active one, simply move the mouse pointer to the new cell and click (press and release) the mouse button. In a similar manner, to scroll a line or column, you can click on the scroll arrow.

MENU CHOICES AND DIALOG BOXES

After you have depressed the ALT or / key and the underlined letter of the menu choice or have used the ARROW key to highlight the menu selection desired and depressed the ENTER key, you will see a pull-down menu. Each of the menu choices on the menu bar has several commands which can be accessed through pull-down menus.

Some of the choices on the pull-down menus have ellipses (...) after them: this means that there will be further choices to be made regarding this command. The further choices will appear in a dialog box. A sample dialog box looks like Figure 1.3.

To move within a dialog box, depress the ALT and underlined letter key simultaneously. Alternatively, you can use the TAB key to go from one portion of the dialog box to the next. Within a list box, you can use the UP and DOWN ARROW keys. If the list in the list box is long, you can depress the key that corresponds to the first letter of the choice you are seeking and then use the ARROW keys. Within a list of options, you can turn an option on or off by depressing the ALT and underlined letter keys simultaneously. Alternatively, you can use the ARROW key to highlight the choice and then depress the SPACEBAR; if the option box is blank, depressing the SPACEBAR will place an x in the box; if the box is filled, depressing the SPACEBAR will erase the x. To carry out the changes made in the dialog box, depress the ENTER key; to cancel the changes, simply depress the ESCAPE key.

If you are using a mouse, select an item by clicking (depressing the mouse button and releasing it) once. You can choose an option by clicking on it with the mouse. To carry out changes made, click

10 USING MICROSOFT EXCEL

FIGURE 1-3 Typical Dialog Box

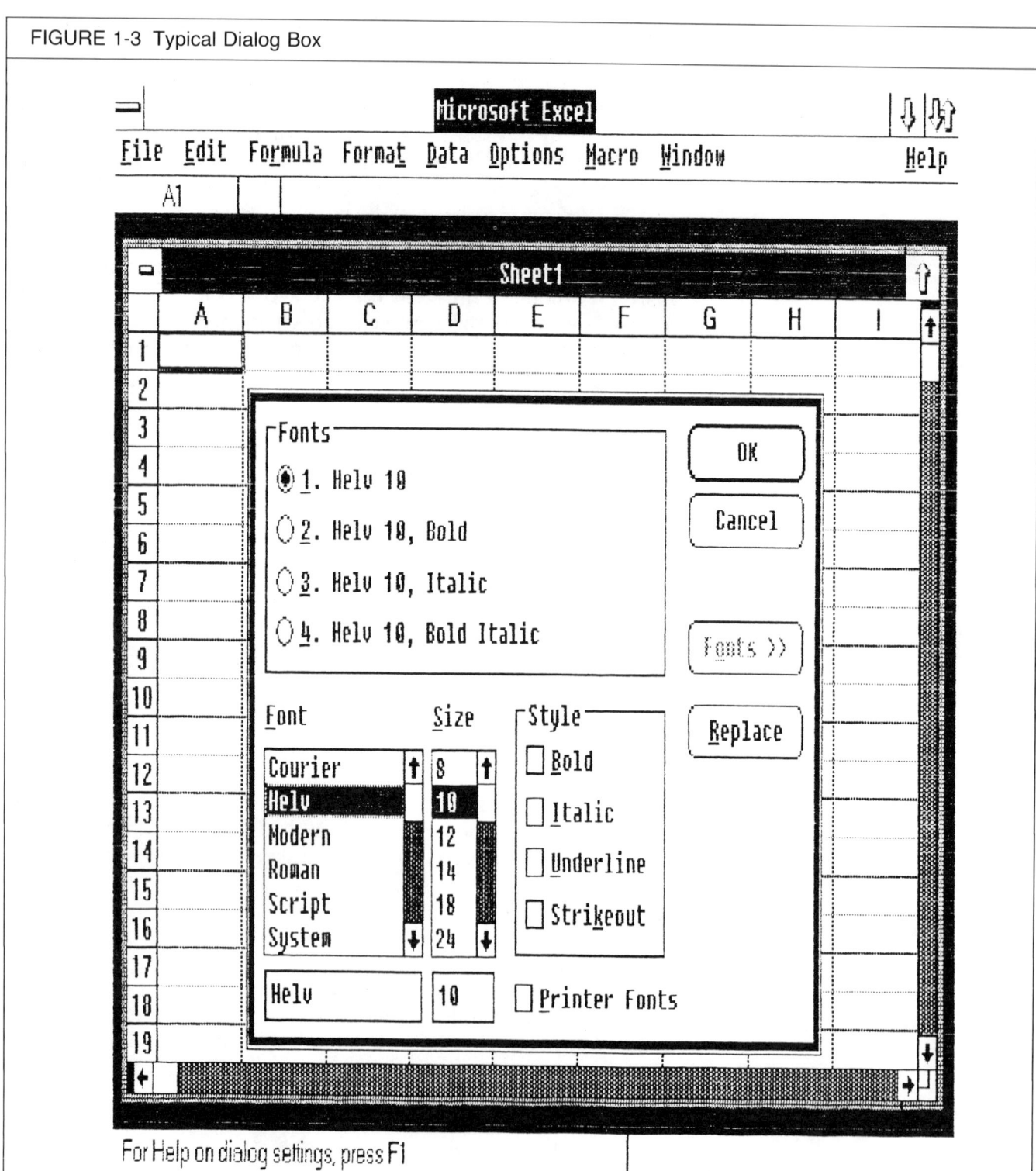

on the OK button; to cancel changes made, click on the cancel button.

In some dialog boxes, some of the choices may also be followed by ellipses (. . .). Once again, this means that another dialog box will follow if that option is chosen.

HELP

Excel offers many different types of online help. By depressing the function key F1 you get current context help. On the other hand, you can depress the function key F1 while holding down the SHIFT key to receive help and then choose a command. You can also receive online help by depressing the ALT or / key and choosing the help pull-down menu. From this pull-down menu, you can select the help index and find the topic with which you need help.

Excel also offers special help for users who are familiar with Lotus 1-2-3 or Multiplan. You can find the equivalent of a command from either of these programs by getting to the help menu, choosing one of the programs as the help topic and then typing in the command as you would on either of these programs. Excel will give you the equivalent Excel command.

In addition, Excel offers a help tutorial and a help feature guide command. Each of these can be used as a guided tour of the features of this program.

2 A WORKSHEET

The first worksheet we will construct will be a simple department budget for a library. It will be very helpful if you work along and construct the Excel worksheet as described. This worksheet will be modified as the first part of the book continues.

At first, this worksheet will have only five columns. If the currently active cell is not A1, get to that cell by either using the ARROW keys, depressing the CONTROL and HOME keys simultaneously, or by using the function key F5, typing the cell address A1, and depressing the ENTER key.

In this worksheet we will use the first row for the column headings. With cell A1 active, type Ordered. As you type it, you will notice that nothing appears in the cell; instead, what you have typed appears in the formula bar. When you depress the ENTER key, the word is placed in cell A1 and the currently active cell remains cell A1. If you notice an error in typing before depressing the ENTER key, you could edit in the formula bar. If you notice an error after typing, make the currently active cell the cell with the error, and then depress the EDIT key, the function key F2. Then make the necessary corrections and depress the ENTER key.

Instead of depressing the ENTER key after typing Ordered when the currently active cell was A1, you could have depressed the RIGHT ARROW key once. This will move the currently active cell to the right one cell, to cell B1. The word Ordered will now be in cell A1. This technique can be seen as a small but significant shortcut.

With cell B1 active, type Vendor; when the ENTER key or RIGHT ARROW key is depressed, Vendor will appear in cell B1. Repeat the procedure to place the word Amount in cell C1, Received in cell D1, and Invoice in cell E1. At this point, the worksheet should look like Figure 2.1.

Now we will use the worksheet to enter information. Entering information on a worksheet can be done exactly as the column headings were entered: move the active cell to where you want the information to appear on the worksheet, type the information which initially appears in the formula bar, and then either depress the ENTER or ARROW key. The information will appear on the worksheet in the formerly active cell. Repeat the process several times to enter all the information in Figure 2.2.

CHANGING COLUMN WIDTHS

On the next available line, enter the date 10/22/89 in the Ordered column; in the Vendor column type Neal-Schuman. You will notice that the name of the vendor is longer than the amount of space in the column. When you type an amount in the third

FIGURE 2-1 Department budget worksheet with five column headings

	A	B	C	D	E	F
1	Ordered	Vendor	Amount	Received	Invoice	
2						
3						
4						
5						
6						
7						
8						
9						
10						
11						
12						
13						
14						
15						
16						
17						
18						

FIGURE 2-2 Worksheet with some information

	A	B	C	D	E	F
1	Ordered	Vendor	Amount	Received	Invoice	
2	9/9/89	Longman	$125.50	10/10/89	$132.80	
3	9/10/89	EBS	$245.00	9/30/89	$200.10	
4	9/21/89	Holt	$589.75	11/1/89	$478.90	
5	10/2/89	Viking	$333.65	11/1/89	$345.98	
6	10/3/89	Que	$32.95	11/3/89	$32.95	
7	10/5/89	Microsoft	$32.00	10/20/89	$32.00	
8	10/12/89	Microsoft	$22.95	10/20/89	$22.95	
9						
10						
11						
12						
13						
14						
15						
16						
17						
18						

column, you will see that the name Neal-Schuman has been truncated. The default column width can be easily varied. First make the active cell one in the column that you want to widen. Then gain access to the menu bar by depressing either the ALT or / key and then selecting format from the menu choices. Then select column width from the pull-down menu. To select from the pull-down menu, you can either use the ARROW keys to highlight the selection and then depress the ENTER key or you can depress the underlined letter for the choice you desire. Alternatively, you could point and click using the optional mouse. In the column width dialog box, type the desired column width. In this case, you may want to make the column width 15 to be sure that there will be enough space for long names. Then depress the ENTER key or choose the OK button, and the column width will be modified as desired.

If you want to change the column widths of two adjacent columns at one time, you can select the two columns by placing the highlighting in the first column selected and, while depressing the SHIFT key, move the highlighting to the adjacent column. As you do this, you will notice that the display shows that the two cells are selected. Then, as above, depress the ALT or / key to gain access to the menu bar, select format, and from the pull-down menu choose column width. When you change the column width in the dialog box, you will change the column widths of the selected columns.

This technique works well for adjacent columns, no matter the number of columns involved. Another technique is to employ the EXTEND key, the function key F8. Select the first column. Then, turn on the EXTEND key by depressing the function key F8. With the EXTEND key on, you will see EXT in the message area of the status bar at the bottom of the display. Then select all the adjacent cells. This may be easier than trying to keep the SHIFT key down while using the ARROW keys.

Using the EXTEND key also permits you to select nonadjacent cells. With the EXTEND key on, after selecting the adjacent cells, if any, depress the SHIFT key and function key F8 simultaneously to keep the selection. Then move to the next cell that you want to select and follow the above procedure.

With a mouse, you can also select adjacent and/or nonadjacent cells. Click (press and release the mouse button) on the first cell and drag (press the mouse button and move the mouse pointer) through the first range that you want to select. Then move to the next cell or range of cells to be selected; hold down the CONTROL key while selecting additional cells or ranges.

INSERTING COLUMNS

At this point, you may decide that you really need to know the amount of money that has been encumbered. To do this, you will have to add the amounts listed in column C (see Figure 2.2). Before adding, it would be neater to insert a blank column next to column C for the running total.

To add a column, select the column that you want to have blank. In this case, since you want to have a blank column next to column C, select column D. To select an entire column, place the highlighting at the top of column D and then depress the CONTROL key and SPACEBAR simultaneously. To select a column with the mouse, click on the column head (the letter identifying the column). At this point, you will see the entire column highlighted.

Depress the ALT or / key to gain access to the menu bar and then select the edit pull-down menu. From the pull-down menu, choose insert. Since the column has been selected, Excel knows that you want to insert a column and shifts all the information from columns D and E over one column to the right. You now have an empty column D with which to work.

TOTALS

In cell D1 place the column heading Total. In cell D2 you simply want to copy the amount from cell C2; to do this, simply type +C2 or = +C2. If you do not type the =, Excel will automatically supply it.

In cell D3, you will want to add the amounts from cell C2 and C3. You could simply type +C2+C3 or = +C2+C3. Although this will work fine for adding two numbers together, when you want to add a complete column of numbers it will be more difficult and time consuming. Instead, you can use an Excel formula.

Formulas in Excel begin with an equal (=) sign. To add cells C2 and C3, you could write the formula:

=SUM(C2:C3)

The = sign tells Excel that what follows is a formula. The SUM tells Excel what formula is being used, in this case obtaining a sum. The range (C2:C3) tells Excel what to add, in this case from cell C2 to C3. If the formula had been written:

=SUM(C2:C9)

Excel would have added up all the values in all the cells from cell C2 through cell C9.

CELL ADDRESSES: RELATIVE, ABSOLUTE AND MIXED

You could type a separate formula for each of the cells in column D, but Excel offers an easier way of obtaining a running total. Before discussing this technique, it is necessary to understand that there are three types of cell addresses in Excel: relative, absolute, and mixed.

When a relative address is used in a formula, it will automatically change as it is copied. Thus, if we had the formula:

=SUM(C2:C3)

in cell D3 and then copied it to cell D4, the new formula would be:

=SUM(C3:C4)

This is not what we need to obtain a running total. Instead, we want to anchor the first part of the range at C2 and let the other part of the range be modified as it is copied. To do this, we have to make the first cell reference absolute.

The above formula with an absolute address would be written:

=SUM($C$2:C3)

When this formula is copied, only the second part of the range will be modified. Thus, in cell D4 the formula will be:

=SUM($C$2:C4)

The first part of the range is fixed; it is called absolute.

In this case, we could have used a mixed address for the first part of the range. A mixed address anchors one part of the address while allowing the other to change. Since we are only going to copy the formula down the column, the column reference will not be changed. Thus, we could have written the formula as:

=SUM(C$2:C3)

When copied down the column, this formula will produce the same results as the formula with the absolute address in the first part of the formula.

COPYING

To copy the formula down column D, first select the cell that is to be copied. Since it is only one cell in this case, you can simply highlight that cell. Then depress the ALT or / key and select edit. From the edit pull-down menu, choose copy. Notice that the highlighting around the selected cell looks different.

Select the cells to be copied to. Since there are several cells involved, place the highlighting in cell C4 and then either depress the function key F8 (the EXTEND key) and move the highlighting down the column or depress the SHIFT key while using the ARROW key to highlight the column's cells.

Once the selecting has been completed, depress the ALT or / key and select the edit pull-down menu. Choose paste. The formula will be pasted into the selected cells, and the total will be shown for each of the cells selected. Alternatively, after using edit copy, you could simply select the cells into which you want the selection copied and depress the ENTER key. The copying will be accomplished. This technique only works for copying information into a continuous range of cells (see Figure 2-3).

Edit Fill: Instead of copying the formula from one cell to the others, you could use edit fill. First type the formula in the first cell. Then select the entire range which will have the formulas, including the first cell. To select the range, hold down the SHIFT key

FIGURE 2-3 Worksheet with totals

	A	B	C	D	E	F	G
1	Ordered	Vendor	Amount	Total	Received	Invoice	
2	9/9/89	Longman	$125.50	$125.50	10/10/89	$132.80	
3	9/10/89	EBS	$245.00	$370.50	9/30/89	$200.10	
4	9/21/89	Holt	$589.75	$960.25	11/1/89	$478.90	
5	10/2/89	Viking	$333.65	#######	11/1/89	$345.98	
6	10/3/89	Que	$32.95	#######	11/3/89	$32.95	
7	10/5/89	Microsoft	$32.00	#######	10/20/89	$32.00	
8	10/12/89	Microsoft	$22.95	#######	10/20/89	$22.95	
9	10/22/89	Neal-Schuman	$310.50	#######	11/5/89	$300.55	
10							
11							
12							
13							
14							
15							
16							
17							
18							

while using the ARROW key or use the EXTEND key (the function key F8) and the ARROW key to highlight the appropriate cells. Then depress the ALT or / key, select the edit pull-down menu, and choose fill down. The mixed cell address in the formula will be modified appropriately in the entire column selected and a running total will be produced. Using edit fill saves a few steps.

Another Shortcut: Excel offers another way to copy a formula into adjacent cells. First select the entire range. Then in the first cell type the formula. Instead of invoking the edit copy and edit paste commands or the edit fill command, simply depress the CONTROL and ENTER keys simultaneously. The formula will be copied, and the addresses will be adjusted automatically.

VIEWING FORMULAS

If you want to see the formulas that Excel has written, you can place the highlighting in any of the cells in column D and look at the formula bar. Alternatively, you could display formulas by depressing the ALT or / key, selecting options, and choosing display from the pull-down menu. Then select formulas. The formulas will now be displayed (see Figure 2.4).

SELECTION TECHNIQUES

WITH THE KEYBOARD

Microsoft Excel offers a number of techniques to select cells, both with the keyboard and the optional mouse. With the keyboard, you can:

- Select one cell by depressing the ARROW keys.
- Extend a continuous selection by depressing the SHIFT and ARROW keys.
- Extend a selection by one block of data by depressing the CONTROL, SHIFT and ARROW keys.
- Extend a selection to the start of a row by depressing the SHIFT and HOME keys.
- Extend a selection to the last occupied column in the row by depressing the SHIFT and END keys.
- Extend a selection to the entire row containing the active cell by depressing the SHIFT and SPACEBAR keys.

A WORKSHEET 19

FIGURE 2-4 Worksheet displaying formulas

	A	B	C
1	Ordered	Vendor	Amount
2	32760	Longman	125.5
3	32761	EBS	245
4	32772	Holt	589.75
5	32783	Viking	333.65
6	32784	Que	32.95
7	32786	Microsoft	32
8	32793	Microsoft	22.95
9	32803	Neal-Schuman	310.5

	D	E	F	G
1	Total	Received	Invoice	
2	=+C2	32791	132.8	
3	=SUM($C$2:C3)	32781	200.1	
4	=SUM($C$2:C4)	32813	478.9	
5	=SUM($C$2:C5)	32813	345.90	
6	=SUM($C$2:C6)	32815	32.95	
7	=SUM($C$2:C7)	32801	32	
8	=SUM($C$2:C8)	32801	22.95	
9	=SUM($C$2:C9)	32817	300.55	

- Extend a selection to the entire column containing the active cell by depressing the CONTROL and SPACEBAR keys.
- Extend a selection to the end of data by depressing the CONTROL, SHIFT, and END keys.
- Select an entire worksheet by depressing the CONTROL, SHIFT, and SPACEBAR keys.
- Select non-continuous cells by using the EXTEND key, the function key F8.

SELECTION TECHNIQUES WITH A MOUSE

You can use the optional mouse to select cells in Microsoft Excel:

- To select a single cell, click the cell.
- To select a row or column, click the row or column heading.
- To select many rows or columns, click a heading and then drag in the headings.
- To select the entire worksheet, click the rectangle below the control menu icon.
- To make a non-continuous multiple selection, drag the first selection and then hold the CONTROL key as you drag through each additional selection.

When using a mouse, the following terms should be understood:

- Point: move until the tip of the mouse pointer indicates what is being pointed at.
- Press: hold down the mouse button.
- Click: press and release the mouse button.
- Drag: press the mouse button and move mouse pointer.
- Double click: click twice rapidly.
- Choose: pick a command by pointing and clicking.
- Scroll: click the scroll ARROW or drag the scroll bar which will move the document so that another portion can be seen.
- Select: point and click or drag to identify the portion of the worksheet selected.
- Turn on/off: click a checkbox in a dialog box.

SAVING A WORKSHEET

It is necessary to save a worksheet before exiting Excel if you plan to use the worksheet again. In this book, we will be using the worksheet. To save this worksheet, depress the ALT or / key and select file. From the file pull-down menu, choose save as; if you have not previously saved a worksheet and select save, Excel will automatically select save as from the pull-down menu. If you attempt to select exit from the file pull-down menu before saving a worksheet, Excel will ask if you want to save the worksheet.

When you select save as, a dialog box appears. You use the name area to type the name you want to assign to this worksheet. Any acceptable DOS name is acceptable to Excel. Save this worksheet as circbud, since it represents the budget of the circulating collection. When saving a worksheet, Excel automatically supplies an extension: .xls. If you do not specify a directory, Excel will save your worksheet in the same directory as Excel. To specify a

SUMMARY

In this chapter, you have

1. set up a worksheet;
2. changed column widths;
3. selected cells;
4. used the EXTEND key;
5. inserted a column;
6. written and copied a simple formula;
7. studied relative, absolute, and mixed cell addresses;
8. displayed formulas;
9. learned selection techniques using the keyboard and mouse;
10. learned mouse terminology;
11. saved a worksheet.

different directory, begin the name with the letter of the drive followed by a COLON (such as a:).

REVIEW

To review what has been discussed in this chapter, you will set up two worksheets. The first will be a worksheet that details a library's book budget; the second will be a database of individuals who have requested the purchase of specific books.

The library book budget worksheet will have five columns. The first will be for the date of the last update, the second for the department, the third for the budgeted amount, the fourth for the encumbered amount, and the final for the invoiced amount. There will be five departments: serials, reference, circulation, special collection one and special collection two. The final line for the worksheet will have totals for the last three columns.

The worksheet should look like Figure 2.5.

Remember to change the column widths. To do this, select the columns and gain access to the menu bar by depressing the ALT or / key. Then select the format menu and choose column width.

Did you select only one column to widen? If you did, you could have used the EXTEND key (the function key F8) and selected multiple columns.

To obtain totals, you should have written a formula such as:

=SUM(C2:C6)

Notice that in this case the cell addresses are relative. When you copy this formula to cells D7 and E7, the relative addresses are changed to obtain a total for each of the columns (see Figure 2.6). If you want to check that the relative formulas have been changed appropriately, you can either highlight each cell and study the formula bar or modify the worksheet to display formulas. To display the formulas, depress the ALT or / key, select the options pull-down menu, and choose display.

Save this worksheet; it will be used again. Use the name books. Then close the file by depressing the ALT or / key, selecting file, and then choose close. This will clear the display. You will now be ready to open a new worksheet.

To open a new worksheet, depress the ALT or / key and then select the file pull-down menu. Choose new from the pull-down

FIGURE 2-5 Library book budget spreadsheet (blank)

	A	B	C	D	E	F
1	Date	Department	Budgeted	Encumbered	Invoiced	
2		Serials				
3		Reference				
4		Circulation				
5		Sp. Collection 1				
6		Sp. Collection 2				
7		Totals				
8						
9						
10						
11						
12						
13						
14						
15						
16						
17						
18						

FIGURE 2-6 Library book budget spreadsheet with totals

	A	B	C	D	E	F
1	Date	Department	Budgeted	Encumbered	Invoiced	
2	Nov-89	Serials	$30,000	$950.00	$800.75	
3	Nov-89	Reference	$10,000	$2,000.45	$1,999.75	
4	Nov-89	Circulation	$35,000	$13,555.75	$15,750.95	
5	Nov-90	Sp. Collection 1	$15,000	$750.95	$888.90	
6	Nov-89	Sp. Collection 2	$10,000	$889.45	$917.75	
7		Totals	100000	18146.6	20358.1	
8						
9						
10						
11						
12						
13						
14						
15						
16						
17						
18						

menu. From the dialog box select worksheet and a new worksheet will appear.

This worksheet will be used to construct the database to keep track of which patron has requested that the library purchase a specific book. This worksheet will have eight columns: date of request, name of requester, street address of requester, city/state/zip code, author of book requested, title of book requested, vendor from whom book was ordered, and whether or not the patron was notified. The worksheet will look like Figure 2.7.

Once again, to construct this worksheet, you will have to adjust the column widths of several columns. You could enlarge all of the necessary columns to the same width by first selecting the appropriate columns using the EXTEND key (the function key F8). After selecting, depress the ALT or / key to gain access to the menu bar and select the format pull-down menu. Choose column width and type in a number. If, on the other hand, you decide that certain columns have to be wider than others, repeat the format column width command several times.

Add the following information to your worksheet. You may want to add the information in a non-routine manner to practice moving the highlighting around the worksheet. This will be good practice. When you get to column D, you may want to copy the information from the second row to the other rows in this column, since the information is the same for each of the requesters. Since the information is text rather than cell addresses, it will be copied without any changes (see Figure 2.8).

Save the worksheet. Depress the ALT or / key, select the file pull-down menu and choose save as. The name of this worksheet should be request. This worksheet will also be used again.

24 USING MICROSOFT EXCEL

FIGURE 2-7 Worksheet for requesters (blank)

	A	B	C	D
1	Date	Requester	Address	City/State/Zip
2				
3				
4				
5				
6				
7				
8				
9				
10				
11				
12				
13				
14				
15				
16				
17				
18				

	E	F	G	H
1	Author	Title	Vendor	Notified?
2				
3				
4				
5				
6				
7				
8				
9				
10				
11				
12				
13				
14				
15				
16				
17				
18				

A WORKSHEET 25

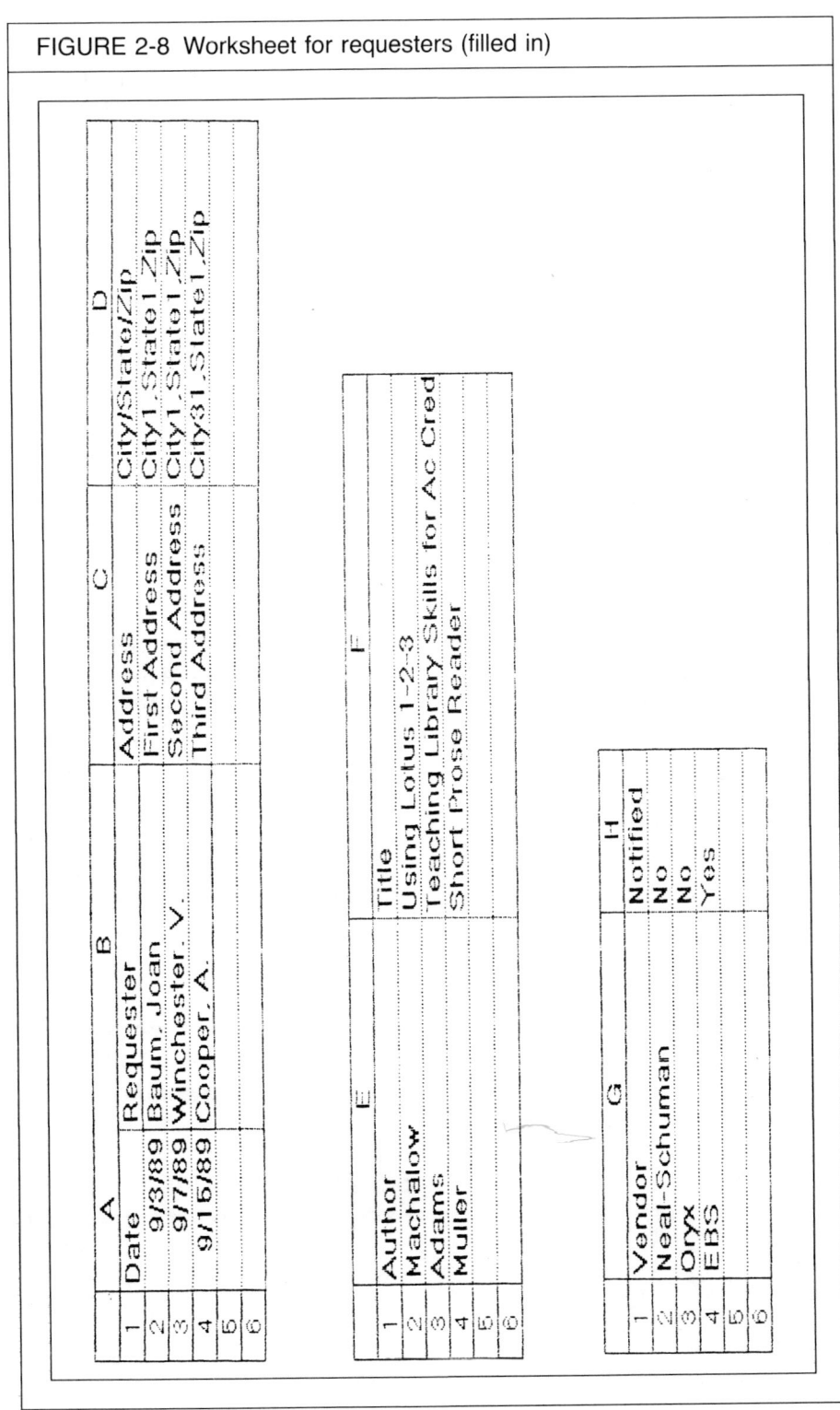

FIGURE 2-8 Worksheet for requesters (filled in)

3 CUSTOMIZING THE DISPLAY

Excel offers the user many ways to customize the display. To practice some of these customizing features, first open the department budget worksheet named circbud. To open an existing worksheet, depress the ALT or / key, select the file pull-down menu and choose open. Excel displays a dialog box which asks for the name of the file that you want to open. Type circbud if you saved the worksheet in the same directory as Excel. Otherwise, type the drive letter followed by a COLON. Then type circbud and depress the ENTER key. Alternatively, when you first saw the dialog box, you could have depressed the ALT and d keys simultaneously and then used the ARROW keys to highlight the letter of the drive you saved the file on. With the mouse, simply double click on the letter of the drive you want to be active. After depressing the ENTER key, you will see a list of files in the box on the left. Using the ARROW keys highlight circbud. When you depress the ENTER key, the file will be opened. With the mouse, double click your choice.

ADDING A TITLE

First, a title for the worksheet might help. To place a title on the first line, you have to insert a line. First select the first line. To select the entire first line place the highlighter in the cell on the left or right border of the first row. Then depress the SHIFT key and the SPACEBAR simultaneously. Alternatively, use the EXTEND key, the function key F8. The entire row will be highlighted. With the mouse, click on the row heading.

Depress the ALT or / key to gain access to the menu bar. Select edit; from the edit pull-down menu choose insert; from the insert dialog box select shift cells down. If you only selected one cell, only that column would be shifted down.

Type the title for the worksheet in cell A1: Circulation Department. Notice that the text overlaps into the adjacent cell. This is okay unless you plan to type something in cell B1. Since nothing will be typed in the adjacent cell, Excel will display the entire text for cell A1.

SELECTING AVAILABLE FONTS

Excel permits up to four different fonts to be displayed on a given worksheet. The four available fonts are displayed on the initial fonts dialog box which is displayed from the format pull-down menu. To select one of the available fonts for the title that was just typed, do the following: select the cell containing the title, gain access to the menu bar by depressing the ALT or / key, and select the format pull-down menu. Choose a font from the font dialog box; you can use the ARROW keys to select different fonts. The first font listed is the default font: everything on the worksheet will be displayed in the first font until you make changes. The available fonts on the initial fonts list may vary, depending on the equipment that you are using. On the sample worksheet, Helv 14 bold italic was chosen for the title of the worksheet. The process was repeated after selecting the second row, which was changed to Helv 10 italic. In addition, column B was selected and given Helv 10 bold. The worksheet now looks like Figure 3.1.

GRIDLINES

If you find the gridlines annoying, Excel can display the information without them. To eliminate the gridlines, depress the ALT or / key, select the options pull-down menu, and select display. From the display dialog box, select gridlines. The display will now look like Figure 3.2. To redisplay the gridlines, repeat the process.

Instead of hiding the gridlines, you could change their color on the display. To do this, gain access to the menu bar by depressing the ALT or / key, select the options pull-down menu, and choose the display dialog box. In the selection box choose the color you want. The gridline colors will be changed on the display.

FIGURE 3-1 Worksheet with different typefaces

	A	B	C	D	E	F	G
1	*Circulation Budget*						
2	Ordered	Vendor	Amount	Total	Received	Invoice	
3	9 9 89	Longman	$125.50	$125.50	10 10 89	$132.80	
4	9 10 89	EBS	$245.00	$370.50	9 30 89	$200.10	
5	9 21 89	Holt	$588.75	$900.25	11 1 89	$478.90	
6	10 2 89	Viking	$333.65	$1,293.90	11 1 89	$345.98	
7	10 3 89	Que	$32.95	$1,326.85	11 3 89	$32.95	
8	10 5 89	Microsoft	$32.00	$1,358.85	10 20 89	$32.00	
9	10 12 89	Microsoft	$22.95	$1,381.80	10 20 89	$22.95	
10	10 22 89	Neal-Schuman	$310.50	$1,692.30	11 5 89	$309.15	
11							
12							
13							

FIGURE 3-2 Worksheet without gridlines

	A	B	C	D	E	F
1	Circulation Budget					
2	Ordered	Vendor	Amount	Total	Received	Invoice
3	9/9/89	Longman	$125.50	$125.50	10/10/89	$132.80
4	9/10/89	EBS	$245.00	$370.50	9/30/89	$200.10
5	9/21/89	Holt	$589.75	$960.25	11/1/89	$478.90
6	10/2/89	Viking	$333.65	$1,293.90	11/1/89	$345.98
7	10/3/89	Que	$32.95	$1,326.85	11/3/89	$32.95
8	10/5/89	Microsoft	$32.00	$1,358.85	10/20/89	$32.00
9	10/12/89	Microsoft	$22.95	$1,381.80	10/20/89	$22.95
10	10/22/89	Neal-Schuman	$310.50	$1,692.30	11/5/89	$300.55

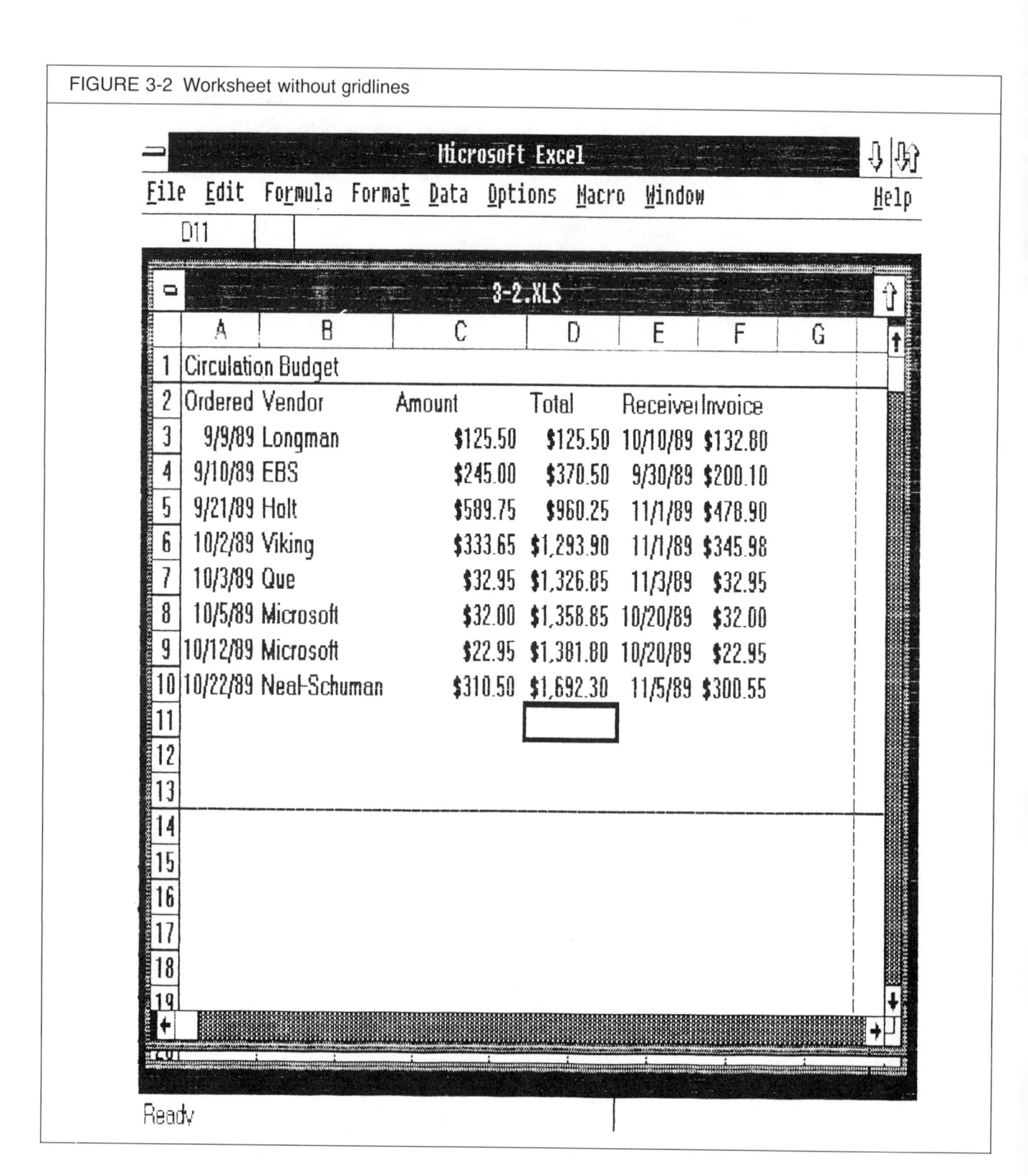

ROW AND COLUMN HEADINGS

In a similar manner to hiding the gridlines, you can hide the row numbers and column letters from the display in Excel. Gain access to the menu bar (depress the ALT or / key), select the options pull-down menu, choose the display dialog box, and turn off the row and column heading box. When the ENTER key is depressed, the row numbers and column letters will not be visible. Repeat the process to redisplay these headings.

The display of a worksheet can be modified in many other ways. The fonts dialog box has the option of another dialog box: when in the initial fonts dialog box, depress the ALT and O keys simultaneously to see the dialog box in Figure 3.3.

CHANGING FONTS

This dialog box offers a great number of other customizing possibilities. The fonts list box enumerates the available fonts and is dependent on whether or not the printer fonts box has been checked. If the printer fonts box has been checked, only fonts that can be printed by your printer will be listed; if the printer fonts box has not been checked, only the fonts which can be displayed by your system's configuration will be listed. To substitute one of the fonts listed on the font list for one of the four available fonts, do the following: select the font you want to redefine from the fonts list which is displayed before the second part of the dialog box is selected, display the second part of the font dialog box, select the options you want to substitute, and then choose the replace button. Every cell that has previously been defined with the replaced font will automatically be changed to the new font. If you change the default font (the first listed font on the fonts list), every cell on the worksheet that is not otherwise defined with a specific font will use this new default font.

SIZE AND STYLE

Also in this dialog box are the options of size and style. The size option lists the available sizes for the selected font. You can choose one of the available sizes or enter any other size. The available sizes depend on whether or not the printer fonts box has been checked. If you choose a size that is not listed, Excel attempts to produce that size. Some equipment may produce results that are not exactly as desired; if the results are not what you want, you can repeat the process until the results are acceptable.

The styles available for the selected fonts include bold, italic, underline and strikeout. These options can be combined as desired.

30 USING MICROSOFT EXCEL

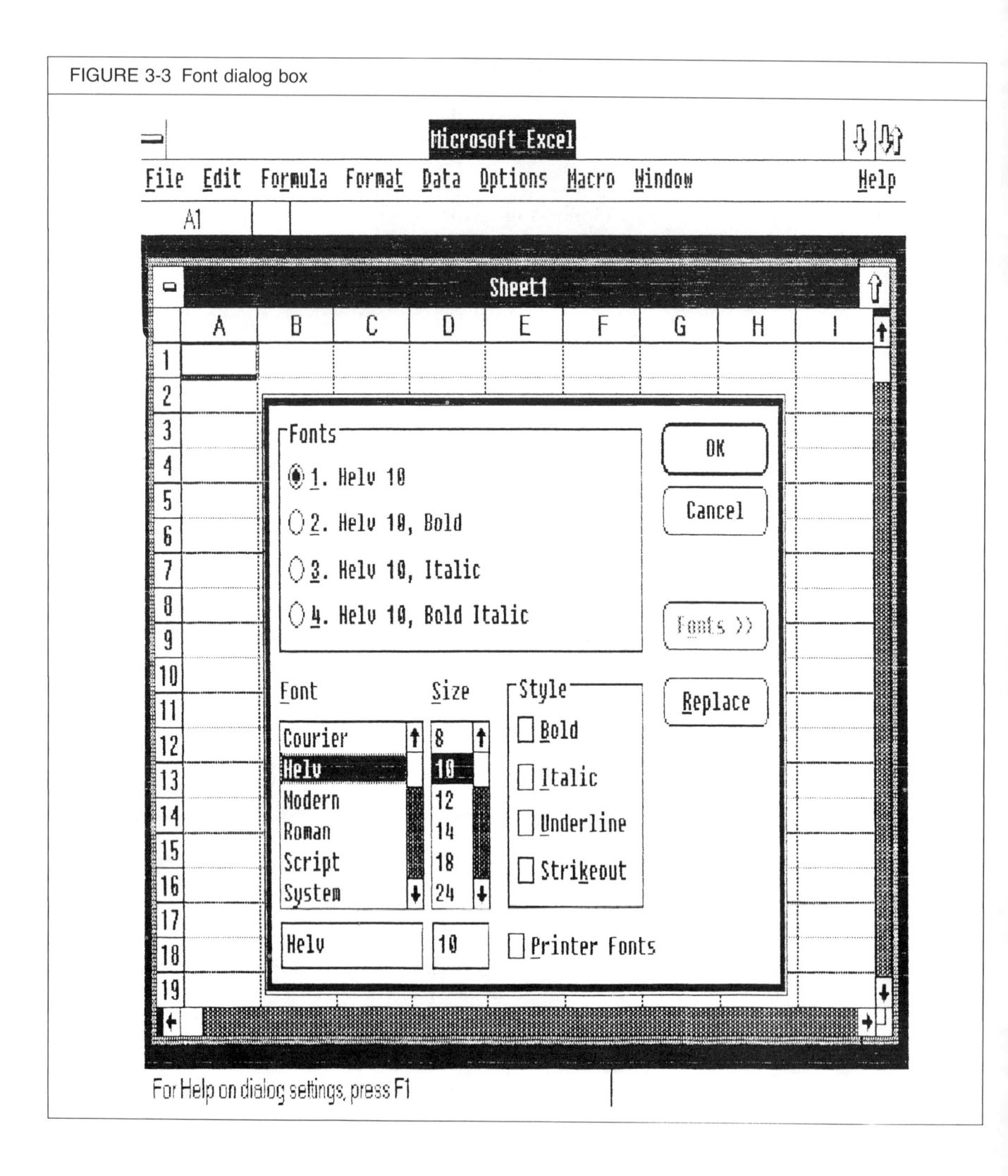

FIGURE 3-3 Font dialog box

The final option, strikeout, places a horizontal line through the contents of the selected cell(s).

When the font, size, and style have been chosen, select the replace button. Excel will modify the initial portion of the dialog box to reflect the changes you have indicated.

ALIGNMENT

On the sample worksheet in Figures 3.1 and 3.2, you will notice that text is aligned to the left, numbers to the right. This is the general alignment in Excel. You can modify this alignment by choosing the format alignment dialog box. Selections from this dialog box include left, right and center; thus, you can choose to have your cell entries displayed anywhere in a given cell.

BORDERS AND SHADING

Excel permits you to add borders and shading to enhance the appearance of a worksheet. To add either a border or shading to a cell or range of cells, first select the cell or range of cells (if you are selecting only one cell, simply place the highlighting on that cell; if you are selecting multiple cells, either use the SHIFT key with the direction keys or use the EXTEND key, the function key F8. Then gain access to the menu bar by depressing the ALT or / key, selecting the format pull-down menu, and choosing the options you desire from the options dialog box. Choose the OK button or depress the ENTER key. The sample worksheet could look like Figure 3.4 after using these options. The second row has had borders added to it as has the column used for totals. In addition, column C has been shaded, since this column records approximate amounts.

Before continuing with this chapter, save your worksheet. To save a worksheet, gain access to the menu bar by depressing either the ALT or / key. Then select the file pull-down menu and choose either save or save as. If you want to retain your first copy of the worksheet, choose save as and use the name circbud2 for it, since it is the second worksheet related to the circulation department budget. If you choose the save command, the original worksheet will be replaced with the updated one, using the same name.

Excel offers many other ways to customize the display. These other techniques will be discussed later in this book.

FIGURE 3-4 Worksheet with borders and shading

	A	B	C	D	E	F
1	*Circulation Budget*					
2	Ordered	Vendor	Amount	Total	Received	Invoice
3	9/9/89	Longman	$125.50	$125.50	10/10/89	$132.80
4	9/10/89	EBS	$245.00	$370.50	9/30/89	$200.10
5	9/21/89	Holt	$589.75	$960.25	11/1/89	$478.90
6	10/2/89	Viking	$333.65	$1,293.90	11/1/89	$345.98
7	10/3/89	Que	$32.95	$1,326.85	11/3/89	$32.95
8	10/5/89	Microsoft	$32.00	$1,358.85	10/20/89	$32.00
9	10/12/89	Microsoft	$22.95	$1,381.80	10/20/89	$22.95
10	10/22/89	Neal-Schuman	$310.50	$1,692.30	11/5/89	$300.55
11						
12						

REVIEW

To review what has been learned in this chapter, we will use the worksheets created in the review section of the previous chapter. First one worksheet will be modified and saved, and then the other worksheet will be manipulated. Prior to opening the first worksheet, be sure that there are no other active documents; if you have just saved the circbud2 worksheet, close the file by depressing the ALT or / key to gain access to the menu bar. Then select the file pull-down menu and choose close. If you have not saved any changes made since the last saving of this document, Excel will ask if you want to save changes.

Open the books worksheet which contains the library's book budget. To open a worksheet, depress the ALT or / key, select the file pull-down menu and choose open. If you want to change the default directory, depress the ALT and d keys simultaneously. Select the desired directory. From the list on the left side of the dialog box, use the ARROW keys to select the worksheet named books. Then depress the ENTER key and the books worksheet will be displayed. Alternatively, you could have typed the name books, specifying the directory if necessary (i.e. a:books or b:books) and depressed the ENTER key.

On this worksheet we also need a title. Insert a row on top by

SUMMARY

In this chapter, you have:

1. inserted a line;
2. selected fonts;
3. manipulated gridlines;
4. hidden row and column headings;
5. changed fonts;
6. changed the size and style of fonts;
7. learned to change alignment;
8. learned to add borders and shading.

shifting the entire worksheet down one row. Remember to select the entire used portion of the row or the entire row. Once the row has been inserted, type the title of the worksheet in cell A1: Library Book Budget.

Now, select the title and change the font used. Something bold would stand out best. To change the font, use the format fonts command and choose one of the available four fonts. At this point, you may want to customize column B, which contains the department names and row 2, which contains the column headings date, department, etc. To do this, use the format fonts command. You can also add borders and shading. You can even eliminate the gridlines and hide the row numbers and column letters. If you did all this, your worksheet might look like Figure 3.5.

The customizing on the sample includes the elimination of gridlines and row and column headings. The type fonts were changed for the title, second row, and second column. Remember that depending on your system's configuration, you may not be able to duplicate the exact fonts. Underlining was chosen as a style for the entries in the second column. Finally, outlines were drawn around the totals on the last line.

Save this worksheet. Use the name books2 if you want to keep a copy of your initial worksheet, since it is the second worksheet being saved for the library book budget. To save a worksheet, depress the ALT or / key, select the file pull-down menu, and choose the save as dialog box. Type the name books2 preceded by a drive specification if necessary (i.e. a:books2 or b:books2).

Close the worksheet to get it out of Excel's memory. To close the worksheet, choose file close (ALT or /, file, close). Then open the second review worksheet, which has the information on which

FIGURE 3-5 Books with customizing

Library Book Budget

Date	Department	Budgeted	Encumbered	Invoiced
Nov-89	Serials	$30,000	$950.00	$800.75
Nov-89	Reference	$10,000	$2,000.45	$1,999.75
Nov-89	Circulation	$35,000	$13,555.75	$15,750.95
Nov-90	Sp. Collection 1	$15,000	$750.95	$888.90
Nov-89	Sp. Collection 2	$10,000	$889.45	$917.75
	Totals	100000	18146.6	20358.1

patrons have requested the purchase of which specific books. To open the worksheet, choose file open (ALT or /, file, open). The name of this file is request.

This worksheet also needs a title. Select the first row and insert a line at the top by shifting the entire worksheet down. Use the edit insert command. Then type the title in cell A1: Requests. Change the font on column E (author) to make it stand out more clearly: a bold font would help. Also change the font of column F (title) to either script or italics. Finally change the font of the final column (notified). Hide the row and column headings, but retain the gridlines. Since the gridlines are being retained, adding a border would not be appropriate since the border would not be seen. The date and requester's name are very close together; you can change this by changing the alignment to left instead of general on column A. With all these modifications, the worksheet might look like Figure 3.6. This worksheet might be a bit easier to use; other customizing may make it even easier for a given individual.

Prior to proceeding to the next chapter, save this worksheet. Then either close this worksheet (ALT or /, file, close) or exit from Excel (ALT or /, file, exit).

FIGURE 3-6 Request worksheet with customizing

	A	B	C	D
1	*Requests*			
2	Date	Requester	Address	City/State/Zip
3	9/3/89	Baum, Joan	First Address	City1,State1,Zip
4	9/7/89	Winchester, V.	Second Address	City1,State1,Zip
5	9/15/89	Cooper, A.	Third Address	City31,State1,Zip
6				
7				

	E	F
1		
2	Author	Title
3	**Machalow**	*Using Lotus 1-2-3*
4	**Adams**	*Teaching Library Skills for the Grade School*
5	**Muller**	*Hard Rain Header*
6		
7		

	G	H
1		
2	Vendor	Notified
3	Neal-Schuman	No
4	Oryx	No
5	EBS	Yes
6		
7		

4 LINKING

One of the advanced features of Excel is that the user can open more than one file at a time and link those files together. This chapter will explore this application.

First open circbud2, the modified circulation budget worksheet. To open this file, depress the ALT or / key, select the file pull-down menu, and choose open. If the circbud2 worksheet is not in the current directory, you can change the default directory by depressing the ALT and d keys simultaneously and then choosing the correct directory. With the mouse, simply double click on the desired drive letter. Then either type the file name (circbud2) or use the ARROW keys to highlight this file. Finally press ENTER. Alternatively, you could type the letter of the drive containing the file (if not the current directory) followed by a COLON (i.e. a:) and then the name of the file. The latter technique is faster but if your files are all in a directory that is not the default directory, it will be easier to change the default directory at this point. Also, if you do not change the default directory, the files will not automatically be saved to the desired drive.

With the circbud2 worksheet displayed, open the books2 worksheet using the same technique as above (Alt or /, file, open). You now can see the books2 worksheet on top of the circbud2 worksheet. Both worksheets are currently in memory and both can be used. As they presently are, you can only view one of these worksheets.

WINDOWS

Each worksheet is in a separate window. You can switch from one window to the other by depressing the ALT or / key, selecting window, and choosing the window that you want to view from the list at the bottom of the pull-down menu. At this point, change from one window to the next; the active window refers to the one that you are currently in.

Though it may be fun and interesting to jump from one window to the other in this way, Excel has techniques to permit you to display several windows at the same time.

WINDOW ARRANGE ALL
To see all the worksheets currently in memory at the same time, you can use the window arrange all command. Depress the ALT or / key, select the window pull-down menu, and choose arrange all.

FIGURE 4-1 Window arrange all with two worksheets and sheet1

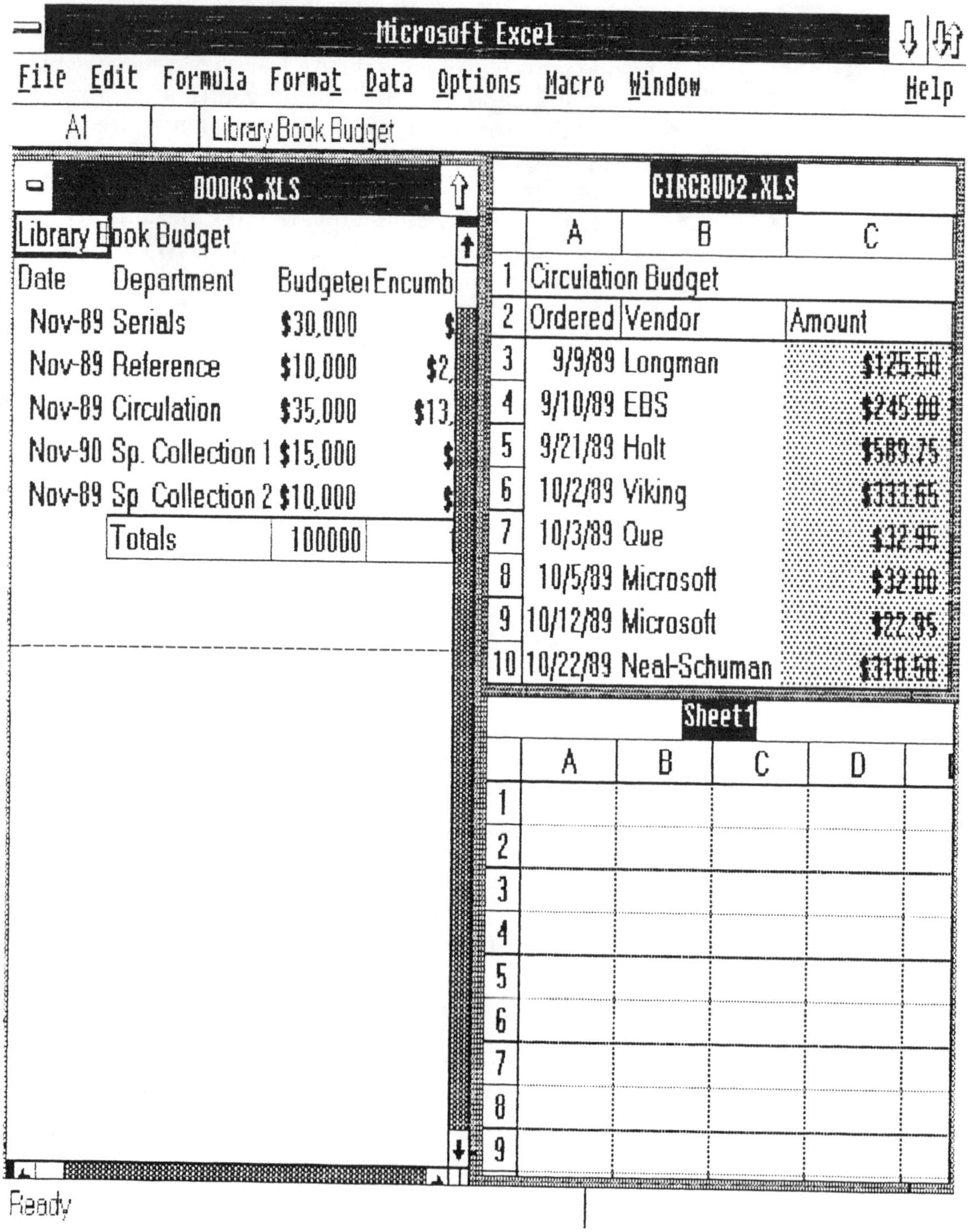

Your display will now look like Figure 4.1. All the worksheets in memory are displayed, though only a portion of each is visible at a time. You can jump from one window to the next using the window command and choosing the desired window and you can scroll through an entire worksheet, each of which scrolls separately. To change the active worksheet with the mouse, point to a cell in it and click. The active worksheet will be changed. You will notice that there are three worksheets displayed; the third is the blank worksheet that was displayed when you began working with Excel.

You can close the blank worksheet to see more of the other worksheets and eliminate possible distractions. To close that worksheet, make it active by jumping to that window (use ALT or / window, and choose the blank worksheet). Then close that file by depressing the ALT or / key, selecting the file pull-down menu, and choosing close. Your display will now look like Figure 4.2. Still only a portion of each worksheet can be seen at a time. You could use window arrange all (ALT or /, window, arrange all) at this point. Alternatively, Excel offers a way to size and move the worksheets so that you can customize the display.

SIZING WINDOWS

To display more than one window at a time, you could size the windows. To size the currently active window, depress the ALT or / key and then the HYPHEN. From this pull-down menu, choose size. Then use the ARROW keys to change the size of the window. At this point, a little experimenting helps.

A mouse can also be used to size a window. To size the active window, drag its gray window border.

MOVING WINDOWS

You can move the entire window. To move a window, depress the ALT or / key and then the HYPHEN. Choose move from the pull-down menu. Use the ARROW keys to move the currently active window to the top of the display. Once again, a little experimenting helps.

A mouse can also be used to move a window. To move the active window, drag its title bar.

Now size and move the other window. First change the currently active window by depressing the ALT or / key; then select the window pull-down menu. Select the other window to make it the active one.

Size this window just as you sized the other: depress the ALT or / key and then the HYPHEN. Choose size and use the ARROW keys

FIGURE 4-2 Window arrange all with two worksheets

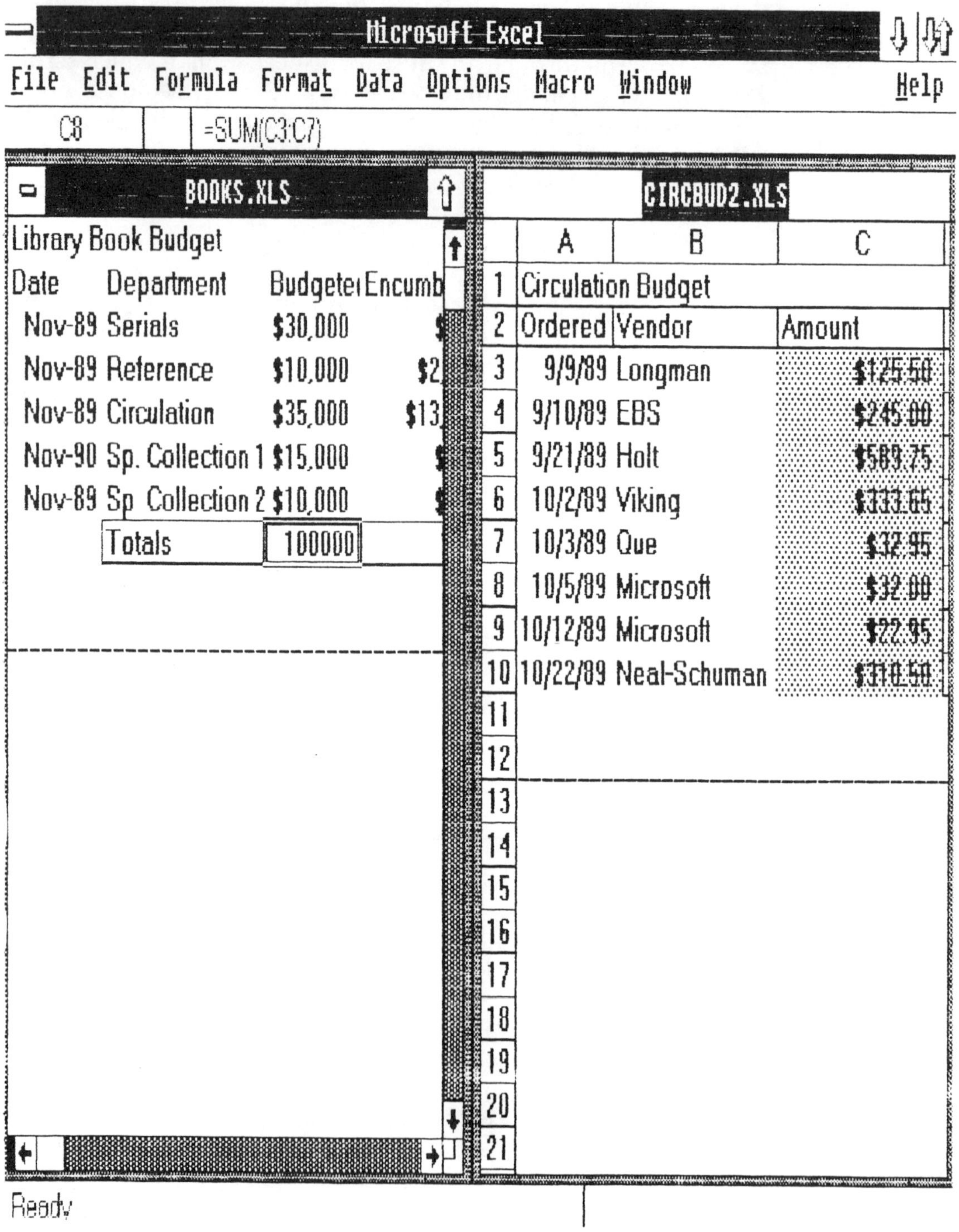
Microsoft Excel
File Edit Formula Format Data Options Macro Window Help
C8
=SUM(C3:C7)
BOOKS.XLS
Library Book Budget
Date Department Budgete Encumb
Nov-89 Serials $30,000
Nov-89 Reference $10,000
Nov-89 Circulation $35,000
Nov-90 Sp. Collection 1 $15,000
Nov-89 Sp Collection 2 $10,000
Totals 100000
CIRCBUD2.XLS
A B C
1 Circulation Budget
2 Ordered Vendor Amount
3 9/9/89 Longman $125.50
4 9/10/89 EBS $245.00
5 9/21/89 Holt $589.75
6 10/2/89 Viking $333.65
7 10/3/89 Que $32.95
8 10/5/89 Microsoft $32.00
9 10/12/89 Microsoft $22.95
10 10/22/89 Neal-Schuman $310.50
Ready

to size the window. When it has been sized to your liking, move it just as you moved the other: ALT or /, HYPHEN, move. Move this window to the bottom of the screen. At his point, your display should look something like Figure 4.3. You can now simultaneously view both worksheets and jump from one to the other by changing the currently active window.

Alternatively, with the two files on screen, you could allow Excel to arrange the panes. To do this, use the window arrange all command (ALT or /, window, arrange all). The display might not be identical to the one you created using the size and move commands.

ADDING RECORDS

Before linking the two worksheets, now is a good time to add information to the circulation budget worksheet. Make that window active; if it is not currently active, depress the ALT or / key to gain access to the menu bar, select the window pull-down menu, and then choose to make the circbud2 worksheet active.

CHANGING RECORDS

This is also a good time to make modifications on the existing records. To modify the contents of a cell, place the highlighting on that cell and type the new information. When you depress the ENTER key or use an ARROW key, the new information will replace the old.

Another way to modify the information in a cell is to use the EDIT key, the function key F2. Highlight the cell and then depress F2. In the formula bar you will be able to make any changes necessary. Once you depress the ENTER key, your changes will be incorporated into the worksheet.

EDIT CLEAR

A final way to change information in a cell is to depress the ALT or / key to gain access to the menu bar, select the edit pull-down menu, and choose clear. A dialog box will appear, asking if you want to clear all, the formats, the formulas, or the notes. You can choose any of these four; when you depress the ENTER key, Excel will clear what you have indicated. At this point you can type in corrections.

The records that you change will only be in columns C and E, the amount encumbered and the amount invoiced. Note that column D, total, will automatically be updated since it uses a formula that is dependent on the amounts in column C.

Add and change the information as shown in Figure 4.4. To

40 USING MICROSOFT EXCEL

FIGURE 4-3 Circbud2 and books2 worksheets together

	A	B	C	D	E	F
1	Circulation Budget					
2	Ordered	Vendor	Amount	Total	Received	Invoice
3	9/9/89	Longman	$125.50	$125.50	10/10/89	$132.80
4	9/10/89	EBS	$245.00	$370.50	9/30/89	$200.10
5	9/21/89	Holt	$589.75	$960.25	11/1/89	$478.90
6	10/2/89	Viking	$333.65	######	11/1/89	$345.98
7	10/3/89	Que	$32.95	######	11/3/89	$32.95
8	10/5/89	Microsoft	$32.00	######	10/20/89	$32.00
9	10/12/89	Microsoft	$22.95	######	10/20/89	$22.95
10	10/22/89	Neal-Schuman	$310.50	######	11/5/89	$300.55

	Library Book Budget			
	Date	Department	Budgeted	Encumbered	Invoiced
15	Nov-89	Serials	$30,000	$950.00	$800.75
16	Nov-89	Reference	$10,000	$2,000.45	$1,999.75
17	Nov-89	Circulation	$35,000	$13,555.75	$15,750.95
18	Nov-90	Sp. Collection 1	$15,000	$750.95	$888.90
19	Nov-89	Sp. Collection 2	$10,000	$889.45	$917.75
20		Totals	100000	18146.6	20358.1

Ready

FIGURE 4-4 Circbud2 worksheet with added entries

	A	B	C	D	E	F
1	*Circulation Budget*					
2	*Ordered*	*Vendor*	*Amount*	*Total*	*Received*	*Invoice*
3	9/9/89	Longman	$725.50	$725.50	10/10/89	$700.90
4	9/10/89	EBS	$1,200.50	$1,926.00	9/30/89	$1,150.97
5	9/21/89	Holt	$589.75	$2,515.75	11/1/89	$478.90
6	10/2/89	Viking	$333.65	$2,849.40	11/1/89	$345.98
7	10/3/89	Que	$135.90	$2,985.30	11/3/89	$132.90
8	10/5/89	Microsoft	$132.50	$3,117.80	10/20/89	$132.00
9	10/12/89	Microsoft	$22.95	$3,140.75	10/20/89	$22.95
10	10/22/89	Neal-Schuman	$310.50	$3,451.25	11/5/89	$300.55
11	10/30/89	Baker & Taylor	$1,999.95	$5,451.20	11/15/89	975.5
12	11/3/89	Yankee Book	$2,175.50	$7,626.70	12/3/89	$2,175.45
13	11/4/89	Random House	$345.00	$7,971.70	12/1/89	$300.15
14	11/5/89	Neal-Schuman	$1,450.50	$9,422.20	12/1/89	$1,450.00
15	11/7/88	Meckler	$150.75	$9,572.95	12/2/89	$150.75
16	11/8/89	Bowker	$200.15	$9,773.10	12/25/89	$200.97
17	11/24/89	Yankee Book	$1,775.00	$11,548.10	12/20/89	$1,770.98
18	11/25/89	Macmillan	$125.75	$11,673.85	12/24/89	$125.70
19	12/1/89	Microsoft	$500.50	$12,174.35	12/20/89	$499.99
20	12/10/89	Que	$750.00	$12,924.35	12/30/89	$700.90
21	12/15/89	Harcourt Brace	$990.00	$13,914.35	1/15/90	$903.50

continue the running total, either copy the formula (edit copy and edit paste) or use edit fill down as previously described. As you continue adding amounts, you will notice that the column width for the totals needs to be increased; widen the column using ALT or /, format, column width.

To beautify the worksheet, add shading to the newly added cells in column C. Also, duplicate the font that you used in column B to the newly added records.

You will notice that the column headings scroll off-screen as you add more information. You can prevent this by dividing the active worksheet into panes and then freezing the panes.

PANES

To divide a window into panes, first depress the ALT or / key to gain access to the menu bar. Then depress the HYPHEN. Finally, choose split from the pull-down menu. Using the ARROW keys, place the split lines under the second row to keep the information on the top two rows visible. Since you are only interested, at this point, in keeping the column headings on screen, do not split the window vertically. When you are satisfied with the split, depress the ENTER key.

You can move from one pane to the other quickly by depressing the function key F6. You can also use the mouse to quickly change panes by moving the mouse pointer to the desired pane and clicking the mouse button.

One use of dividing the worksheet into panes is to be able to display the same worksheet twice, side-by-side, having one pane display the values and the other the formulas. A change in one pane will instantly change the other. To do this, you would have to size and move the panes to be side-by-side and then select display options.

Freezing Panes: So far you have split the window into two panes, but the two panes scroll together as you move in them. In this case you will want to freeze the panes to keep the column headings on screen.

To freeze the panes, first depress the ALT or / key to gain access to the menu bar. Then select the options pull-down menu. Finally choose freeze pane. When you depress the ENTER key, the column headings will remain on screen as you scroll through the entries in this window.

LINKING

Having the two worksheets displayed simultaneously is useful, but Excel offers a feature that may be even more useful: linking. You can link the worksheets so that the total spent on circulating books is automatically displayed in the library budget worksheet. To do this, you will have to write a formula in the books2 worksheet.

A formula that links worksheets is similar to other formulas, but it has an additional part. The formula starts, as all Excel formulas start, with an equal sign (=). This is followed by the name of the worksheet from which the information is to be obtained; in this case, the worksheet is circbud2. This is followed by an exclamation point (!) and then the cell reference in the circbud2 worksheet. Notice that the cell reference is an absolute reference. The formula in this case would be:

=circbud2.xls!d21

If you change the value in cell D21 of the circbud2.xls worksheet the value in the books2 worksheet is automatically updated. If you do not save the changes, including those changes which were made automatically by Excel because of the linking formulas, when you try to close the worksheets Excel will ask if you want to update the files.

EDIT PASTE LINK

Excel also permits you to copy information from one worksheet and paste it into another. To do this, you will use the edit paste link command.

First select the cell(s) to be copied on the source work-sheet. Then depress the ALT or / key, select the edit pull-down menu, and choose copy. Then select the cell(s) into which the copied information is to be pasted on the other worksheet. Finally depress the ALT or / key, select the edit pull-down menu, and choose paste link. Excel will paste the link indicated. When the source worksheet changes, so will the other worksheet.

If you are copying non-formula information from one worksheet to another, you can use edit paste, edit paste link, or edit paste special after edit copy has been executed. Edit paste link is very useful for copying formulas; edit paste special permits the user to copy formulas, values, formats, notes, or all from one worksheet to another. Edit paste special also permits the user to perform arithmetic operations if values are being combined from the two worksheets.

NAMING CELLS

This formula works well for the worksheets as they currently stand, but there is a problem: when more information is added to the circbud2 worksheet, the cell reference for the total will be different. As the formula is written, when the cell containing the total changes, Excel will not know where to find the information it needs. To avoid this problem, Excel offers the ability to name cells.

You can use the cell under the last running total cell for a grand total, and then name the cell total. First, select this cell by highlighting it. Then depress the ALT or / key, select the formula pull-down menu, and choose define name. Type the name total; when naming cells, it is always advisable to use an easy to remember name. Then either accept or type a different refers to. Finally choose OK or depress ENTER. At this point, you can use the name of the cell instead of the cell address in formulas. The linking formula would then be written as:

=circbud2.xls!total

The elements of the linking formula are the same: the formula begins with an equal sign (=), followed by the name of the worksheet on which the information is to be found, then an exclamation point (!) followed by the cell reference, in this case a name.

Once the cell total has been named, you will insert rows into the worksheet when you add more information. As you shift the named cell down, the running total will be maintained because a relative address was used in the formula. To insert rows, select the rows to be inserted, depress the ALT or / key, select the edit pull-down menu, choose the insert dialog box, and choose row.

There are several other ways to name cells. To use these other ways, you have to be sure that you are operating in the full menu mode of Excel. To change from the short menus to full menus, depress the ALT or / key, select the options pull-down menu, and choose full menus. The full menus permit the user to use all the Excel commands; the short menus permit access to Excel's most commonly used commands.

NAMING SEVERAL CELLS

You can name several cells simultaneously if the names are already on the worksheet when operating under Excel's full menus. First select the range that includes the column or row containing the names you want to use. Depress the ALT or / key to gain access to the menu bar, select the formula pull-down menu, and choose the create names dialog box. Once in this dialog box, turn on the appropriate check box, which will tell Excel where the names are: top or bottom row, left or right column. Then choose OK or depress the ENTER key. Excel will automatically name the cells for you.

FORMULA PASTE NAME

You can paste the names created into the formula bar to make cell references simpler. To accomplish this, once in the formula bar, select an insertion point. Then depress the ALT or / key, select the formula pull-down menu, and select paste name. From the paste name dialog box, select the name and paste it. When you choose

SUMMARY

In this chapter, you have:

1. opened windows;
2. used window arrange all;
3. sized windows;
4. moved windows;
5. added and modified records;
6. learned about edit clear;
7. divided a window into panes;
8. frozen panes;
9. linked worksheets with a formula;
10. learned about edit paste link;
11. learned about naming single and multiple cells;
12. learned about formula paste name;
13. applied names;
14. saved a workspace.

OK or depress the ENTER key, the selected name will be pasted into the formula bar at the point indicated.

APPLYING NAMES

When you choose to apply names, Excel will replace cell references with the appropriate names in a selected range. First select the range in which to apply names. Then depress the ALT or / key to gain access to the menu bar. Select the formula pull-down menu and choose apply names. From the dialog box, select one or more of the names to apply from the list box. At this point, you can adjust options if necessary. Finally choose OK or depress the ENTER key. The names chosen will be substituted for their cell references in the range that you selected.

Save Workspace

At this point, you should save the workspace as well as the individual files. When you open a workspace that was previously saved, Excel automatically opens all the files, in the positions and sizes they were in when the workspace was saved. Saving a workspace does not save the files themselves. These must be saved separately.

First save the files: depress the ALT or / key, select the file pull-down menu, and save each of the open files separately. If you want to replace the files on your disk with the new ones, use file save. Otherwise, use file save as and select a separate name for the files: the names circbud3 and books3 have been used here. Then, to save the workspace, depress either the ALT or / key, select the file pull-down menu, and choose save workspace. The workspace was saved under the name work. For saved workspaces, Excel automatically supplies the .xlw extension.

REVIEW

Start Excel as you usually do; if you have been working on Excel, be sure that all files have been saved and closed. To save a file, depress ALT or /, select the file pull-down menu, and choose save or save as. To close a currently active file, depress ALT or /, select the file pull-down menu, and choose close. Then open a new worksheet by depressing ALT or /, selecting the file pull-down menu, and choosing open. A dialog box will ask if you want to open a new worksheet, chart or macro sheet. Choose worksheet, depress ENTER or choose OK, and you will be ready to begin the review of this chapter.

In this review you will be using the blank worksheet to create a short letter telling a patron that the book he or she requested has been received and processed. Since you will be using Excel to type a letter, it will be best to eliminate the gridlines and row and column headings. To do this, depress the ALT or / key, select the options pull-down menu, and choose the display dialog box. In this dialog box, change the markings for gridlines and headings. When ENTER is depressed or OK chosen, the gridlines and headings will no longer be displayed.

Now type the letter as you would type it on a typewriter. Do not worry, at this point, that your text will overlap into adjacent cells: as long as you do not specify something for the adjacent cell, the text will be visible. Your letter may look like the one in Figure 4.5. Now you will have to erase the word 'by' from the cell by using the

FIGURE 4-5 Blank letter

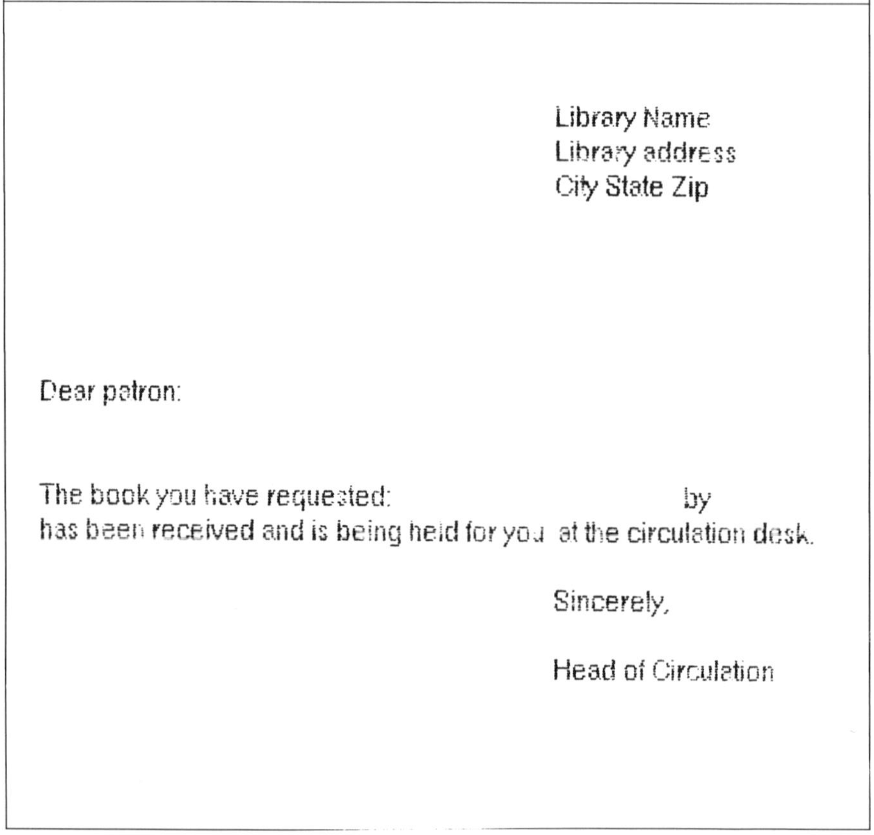

```
                                                    Library Name
                                                    Library address
                                                    City State Zip




Dear patron:


The book you have requested:                        by
has been received and is being held for you  at the circulation desk.

                                                    Sincerely,

                                                    Head of Circulation
```

EDIT key, the function key F2: you will want to have the title of the book requested in one cell to the left of the word 'by' and the author in the cell to the right of this word. By narrowing the column width of the cell containing the word 'by' the letter will look better. To narrow the width of a column, depress the ALT or / key, select the edit pull-down menu, and choose the column width dialog box. In the sample, the width was changed to three.

If you were simply typing a letter, you could use the format justify command to have the letter with all the cells displayed at approximately the same width. Since you are not just typing a letter, the format justify command will not be useful.

Save this worksheet, using file save as letter. Do not close it. Open the worksheet having the names of the requesters. At this point the two worksheets cannot be seen at the same time; instead, you can jump from one worksheet to the other using the window command (ALT or /, window, and then choose one of the windows to be active).

At this point, let Excel arrange the windows: depress the ALT or / key, select the window pull-down menu, and choose arrange all. Now the two worksheets should be displayed side-by-side. Not all of the worksheets can be seen, but you can jump from one to the other easily. You can also scroll through the requests worksheet to find information, such as the name and address of the patron, to plug into the letter.

If this is not convenient, size and move the worksheets. Placing them one on the top half of the display and the other on the bottom might be convenient. To size a worksheet, depress the ALT or / key, depress the HYPHEN, and then choose size. Manipulate the ARROW keys until the size is suitable, and then depress ENTER. Moving a worksheet is accomplished in a similar way: ALT or /, HYPHEN, and move. Use the ARROW keys to move the worksheet. Repeat the process if necessary.

Making the request worksheet active, divide it into panes and then freeze the pane so that the name of the requester will be on screen at all times. To divide a window into panes, depress the ALT or / key, depress the HYPHEN, and choose split. Use the ARROW keys to define the split and then depress ENTER. To freeze the pane, depress the ALT or / key, select the options pull-down menu, and choose freeze pane. At this point, no matter how far to the right you scroll on the worksheet the patron's name will be visible.

Save the workspace by depressing the ALT or / key, selecting the file pull-down menu, and choosing to save workspace as reqlet. If you reopen this workspace, both files will be opened and displayed.

With both worksheets visible, it is easier to copy the information into the letter. Instead of actually retyping, you can copy the information from one worksheet and paste it into the other.

Make the request worksheet the active worksheet. Select the patron's name, cell B3. Then depress the ALT or / key, select the edit pull-down menu, and choose copy. Then make the letter worksheet the active worksheet. Select the location for the patron's name. Depress the ALT or / key, select the edit pull-down menu and choose paste. The patron's name will be pasted into the letter in the spot you choose. This process can be repeated until all the information has been pasted into the letter.

Instead of repeating this process several times, you can write formulas to copy the patron's information into the letter. These formulas will link the two worksheets. The formulas will be similar to the linking formulas described in this chapter: they will each begin with an equal sign (=), followed by the name of the

```
FIGURE 4-6  Letter filled in


                                            Library Name
                                            Library address
                                            City State Zip

Baum, Joan
First Address
City1, State1, Zip


Dear patron:



The book you have requested:   Using Lotus 1-2-3    by  Machalow
has been received and is being held for you  at the circulation desk.

                                            Sincerely,

                                            Head of Circulation
```

worksheet on which to find the information, followed by an exclamation point (!), and then the cell location of the information. For example where the name of the patron will be placed on the letter worksheet the following linking formula could be written:

=request.xls!b3

When the ENTER key is depressed, the patron's name from cell B3 of the request worksheet is on the letter. Similar formulas are used throughout the letter; the result can be seen in Figure 4.6.

This process is quicker than using edit copy and edit paste; it is much quicker and more accurate than copying the information manually.

5 PRINTING

So far, we have created several worksheets and manipulated their displays. Now we will want to obtain a printed record of a worksheet. Excel offers several ways to modify printouts of an active document or window; only the active document can be printed.

Make the active document the worksheet books3. To open that worksheet, depress the ALT or / key, select the file pull-down menu, and choose the open dialog box. As always, if your file is in a directory which is not the current default directory, depress ALT and d simultaneously, select the directory that contains this file and depress ENTER. Using the mouse, simply double click on the desired drive letter. Then select the file by depressing the ALT and f keys simultaneously and then highlight the file books3 and depress the ENTER key. Using the mouse, double click on the file name. Alternatively, you could have typed the directory followed by a COLON and then the name books3 and depressed the ENTER key. Either way, books3 should now be the active file.

PRINTING ENTIRE FILE

If you want to print the entire file, depress the ALT or / key, select the file pull-down menu, and choose the print dialog box. The file print dialog box looks like Figure 5.1.

You can print multiple copies of an active document, print all or selected pages of a document that is on several pages, and even preview the printed page. Previewing the document to be printed can help you to decide if any modifications need to be made prior to printing. If preview is selected, you will be shown a miniature of the printed pages, one at a time; you can zoom in and see individual portions of the miniature pages if desired. You can even choose to print in draft quality: the printing will be faster, but the quality will be somewhat less.

Choose OK or depress the ENTER key to start printing the entire document. After a few seconds, Excel will send this worksheet to the printer and you will have a printed copy.

PRINTING PART OF A WORKSHEET

If you decide to print only part of an active worksheet, you have to do several things before choosing file print. First you would have to select the portion of the worksheet to be printed and set the print area.

Set Print Area: Select the portion of the worksheet you want to print. Select this area just as you would select any other area in Excel: while depressing the SHIFT key, use the ARROW keys or

FIGURE 5-1 File print dialog box

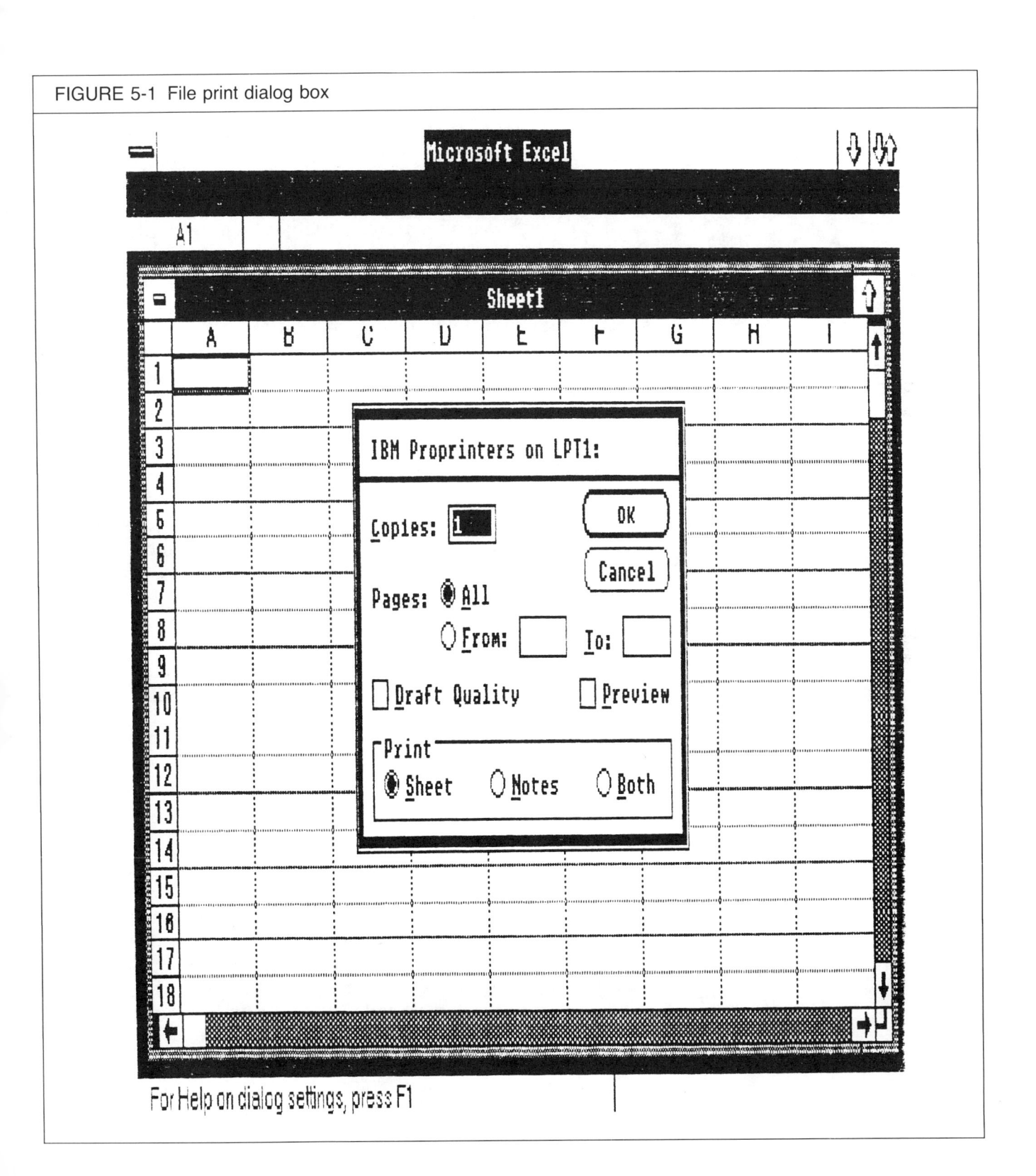

FIGURE 5-2 Books3 worksheet without amount encumbered

	A	B	C
1	Library Book Budget		
2	Date	Department	Budgeted
3	Nov-89	Serials	$30,000
4	Nov-89	Reference	$10,000
5	Nov-89	Circulation	$35,000
6	Nov-89	Sp. Collection 1	$15,000
7	Nov-89	Sp. Collection 2	$10,000
8		Totals	100000

	E
1	
2	Invoiced
3	$800.75
4	$1,999.75
5	$15,750.95
6	$888.90
7	$917.75
8	20358.1

use the EXTEND key, the function key F8. In either case, after selecting the area to be printed, depress the ALT or / key, select the options pull-down menu, and choose set print area. The default for Excel is to print the entire worksheet, but you can use options set print area to indicate a portion or the entire worksheet.

You can select nonadjacent ranges using the EXTEND key, the function key F8. If you select nonadjacent ranges, they will be printed by Excel in the order that you have selected them.

After setting the print area, you print the worksheet just as you printed the entire worksheet before: depress the ALT or / key, select the file pull-down menu, and choose print.

Select the entire worksheet other than the column containing the amount encumbered by each of the departments. Then print this worksheet (see Figure 5.2).

Deleting Print Area: If you later decide that you want to change the print area, you can go through the same procedure and set another print area; only one print area can be active on a given document. If you decide to print the entire worksheet, you can select the entire worksheet and then set the print area. Alternatively, you can delete the range named print area, restoring the default, which is to print the entire document.

To delete the range named print area, depress the ALT or / key, select the formula pull-down menu, and choose the define name dialog box. Once there, choose to delete the name Print_Area.

Delete the print area setting.

PAGE SETUP

Excel allows the user to customize the printed worksheet in several ways. The first is to use the file page setup dialog box (see Figure 5.3). This dialog box permits you to modify the left, right, top, and bottom margins of the printout. Headers and footers can be designated; the default header is the name of the worksheet; the default footer is the word page and the page number. Refer to the Microsoft Excel manual to learn the codes available; these codes include permitting you to left or right align either the header or footer, select to print the header or footer in bold or italics, and print the current date and/or time.

In addition, this dialog box permits you to choose whether or not gridlines and row and column headings are to be printed. Remember, in this case what you see on the screen is not necessarily what will be printed.

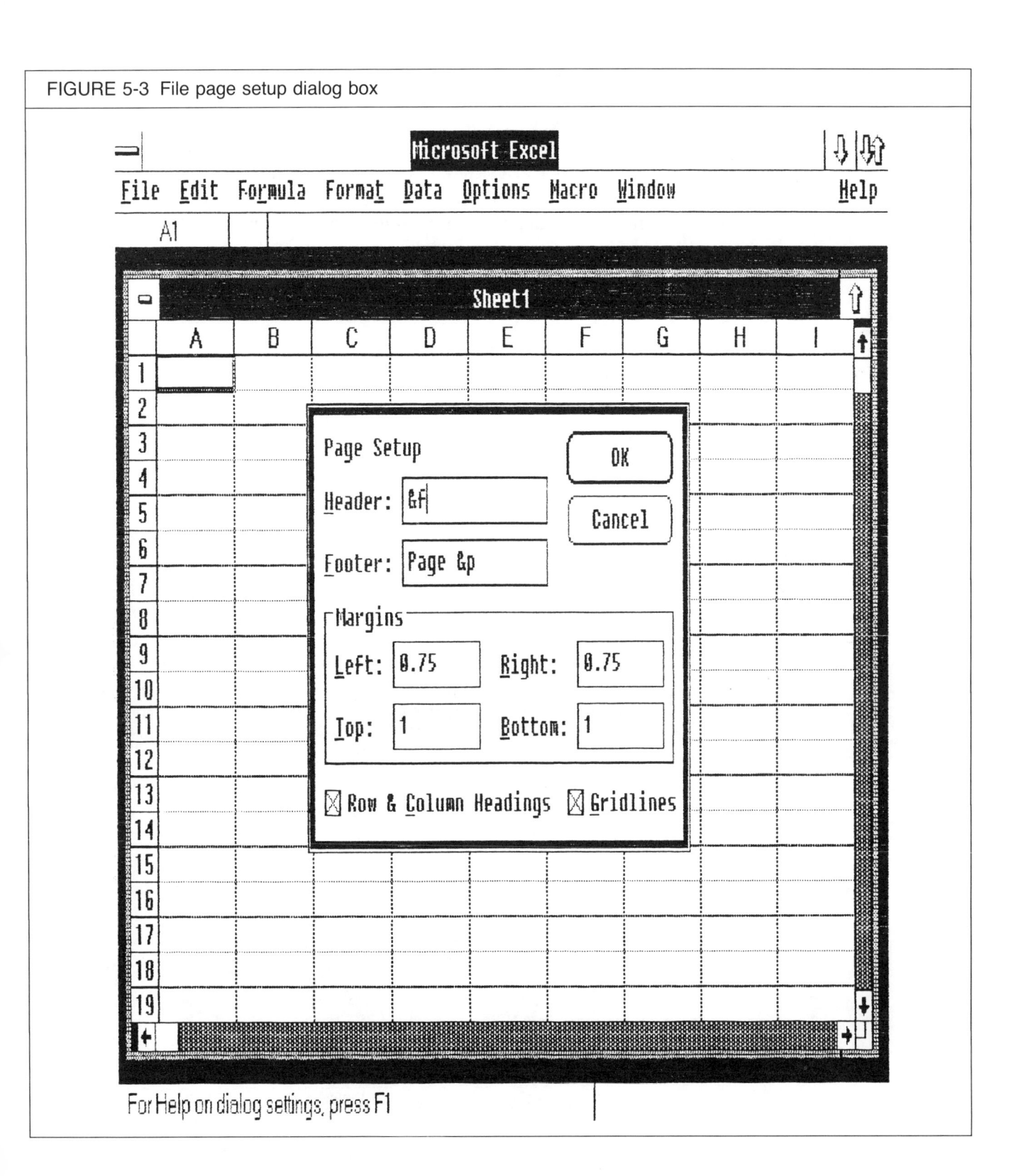

FIGURE 5-3 File page setup dialog box

Remove the row and column headings but retain the gridlines. In addition, remove the header and footer. Choose OK or depress the ENTER key. Then depress the ALT or / key, select the file pull-down menu, and choose the print dialog box. Print the document. Figure 5.4 shows what the document would look like if you also aligned the headings in columns D and E (select the column headings, depress ALT, select format, choose alignment). Excel will print the document as you have indicated.

Depending on the printer you are using, Excel may offer other customizations in the printer setup command.

FILE PRINTER SETUP

The file printer setup dialog box displays the name of the printer you have installed. By depressing the ALT and s keys simultaneously, other options may be shown depending on the printer you have installed. Some of the options may include telling Excel to print landscape (horizontally) or portrait (vertically).

PRINT TITLES

On multiple page worksheets, you may want to have one or more lines or columns of text printed on each page; these are considered print titles. These should not be confused with the header or footer. To indicate to Excel which portion of the text is to be considered a print title, first select the entire row(s) and/or column(s); only entire row(s) or column(s) can be selected as print titles.

Then depress the ALT or / key, select the options pull-down menu, and choose set print titles. When you print the worksheet, the selected area will print on each page of the printout. When using the set print titles command, you should also set the print

FIGURE 5-4 Books3 worksheet without column or row heads; with grids

Library Book Budget				
Date	Department	Budgeted	Encumbered	Invoiced
Nov-89	Serials	$30,000	$950.00	$800.75
Nov-89	Reference	$10,000	$2,000.45	$1,999.75
Nov-89	Circulation	$35,000	$13,555.75	$15,750.95
Nov-90	Sp. Collection 1	$15,000	$750.95	$886.90
Nov-89	Sp. Collection 2	$10,000	$889.45	$917.75
	Totals	100000	18146.6	20353.1

SUMMARY

In this chapter, you have:

1. printed an entire worksheet;
2. printed a portion of a worksheet;
3. set a print area;
4. deleted a print area;
5. used file page setup to customize a printout;
6. learned about file printer setup;
7. learned about setting print titles;
8. learned to delete print titles;
9. learned about setting page breaks.

area. Do not include the cells that have been selected for print titles in the print area; otherwise, these cells will be printed twice on the first page of the printout.

DELETING PRINT TITLES

Delete print titles the same way you previously deleted the print area. Depress the ALT or / key to gain access to the menu bar, select the formula pull-down menu, and choose the define name dialog box. In this case, delete the name Print_Titles.

PAGE BREAKS

Excel automatically breaks a worksheet into pages depending on the options specified (such as margins) and the size of your worksheet. You can manually set page breaks in your worksheet by using the options set page breaks command. When you choose this command, the page break will appear one cell above and to the left of the active cell in the worksheet. If you use this command, be sure to preview your printout prior to printing: in this way, you will be certain that the page break has been placed correctly.

REVIEW

To review printing, close the active worksheet and open the workspace reqlet, which contains both the list of patrons who requested the purchase of specific books and the blank letter. Make the letter the active window, and fill in the patron's name, address, the name of the book, and the author's name as described in the previous chapter. You can use either edit copy and edit paste several times or formulas to link the two worksheets.

Now remove the row and column headings and gridlines from the printed worksheet by using file page setup (depress the ALT or / key, select the file pull-down menu, and choose the page setup dialog box). While in this dialog box, also remove the header and footer.

Now print the worksheet by depressing the ALT or / key, selecting the file pull-down menu, and choosing the print dialog box. Depress ENTER or choose OK. The letter will be printed in a few seconds.

Now make the list of requesters the active window. Select the portion of the worksheet containing the dates, the names of the books requested, and their author's names. Depress the ALT or /

FIGURE 5-5 Requesters: date, title, author; no columns or row heads

Date	Author	Title
9/3/89	Machalow	*Using Lotus 1-2-3*
9/7/89	Adams	*Teaching Library Skills for the Credit*
9/15/89	Muller	*Short Run Books*

key to gain access to the menu bar, select the options pull-down menu, and choose to set the print area.

Once again depress the ALT or / key, choose the file pull-down menu, and choose the page setup dialog box. Change the header to Books Requested and delete the footer. Also delete the row and column headings. Choose OK or depress the ENTER key.

Finally depress the ALT or / key, select the file pull-down menu, and choose print. When you depress the ENTER key or choose OK, Excel will print the worksheet (see Figure 5.5).

6 DATABASES

A database is a collection of information organized in a logical, consistent order, which permits simple and flexible retrieval and updating. Though you may not have realized it, you have been working with several databases in the first chapters of this book. Excel offers many techniques to manipulate information in databases.

Before actually manipulating, it will be useful to learn a bit of vocabulary specific to databases. These terms include database range, field, record, and criteria.

Database Range: A database range is a rectangular area on a worksheet that contains the information of the database. The database range should contain several blank rows (records) at the bottom. The database range includes the column headings, called field headings or names.

Field: A field is a category of information in a database. In Excel, each field occupies one column. The field can be textual or computed (the result of a formula). Field names must be text; they cannot be anything else. Field names must appear in the first row of the database.

Record: A record is all the information about one item in a database. All the information will be on one row of the database.

Criteria: The criteria tells Excel what information in the database is being looked for. This information is usually specified in a criteria range. When Excel uses the criteria, capitalization is ignored.

CREATING A DATABASE

To create a database, it is usually advisable to plan what information will be needed for all the records in the database. Then decide how the information should be arranged. Finally decide on field names that will be clear. Place the field names in the first row of the database. You can type information for each of the records and then define the database or you can define the database first. In either case, select the cells that constitute the database using the EXTEND key, the function key F8. Then depress the ALT or / key to gain access to the menu bar. Select the data pull-down menu. Choose set database.

USING A DATABASE

At this point, open the file that has the names of the requesters of library materials. This will be the database we will begin using. To open the worksheet, depress the ALT or / key, select the file pull-down menu, and choose the open dialog box. Change the default directory if necessary, and either type in the name of the file or scroll through the list box to highlight the file name. Then depress ENTER and the file will be opened.

You can add records to this database by positioning the highlighting in a blank cell, typing in the information, and then moving the highlighting to the next cell. Since this worksheet is too wide to fit on one screen, this might get a little confusing. As the worksheet gets longer, the column headings will have to be frozen to make data entry less confusing. Excel offers an easier way: the data form.

SET DATABASE

In order to use an Excel data form, you must first define the database. Select the cells that constitute the database, including several blank rows at the bottom. Be sure to include the column headings (field names) as the first line of the database. Do not include the title of the worksheet. When the database has been selected (using the EXTEND key, the function key F8 is the easiest method), depress the ALT or / key, select the data pull-down menu, and choose set database. The database has now been defined. Excel has named the selected range database.

DATA FORM

Once the database has been named, depress the ALT or / key, select the data pull-down menu, and choose form. This selection will create a dialog box like Figure 6.1. Notice that the field names (the column headings on the first row of the selected database) are listed in the left column of the form. Next to each field name there is a text box; collectively these fields make up an entire database record. In the upper right hand corner of the dialog box you see a position indicator, telling you which record in the database is being displayed.

The right-hand column of the dialog box has several buttons that can be used to control the manipulation of the database. Choose the new button by either tabbing to highlight this selection, depressing the ALT and w keys simultaneously, or positioning and clicking the mouse. A new, blank record is displayed on the data form; the position indicator changes to new record. Use the blank data form to add several new records to the database. When you are finished, the database will look like Figure 6.2.

FIGURE 6-1 Data form dialog box

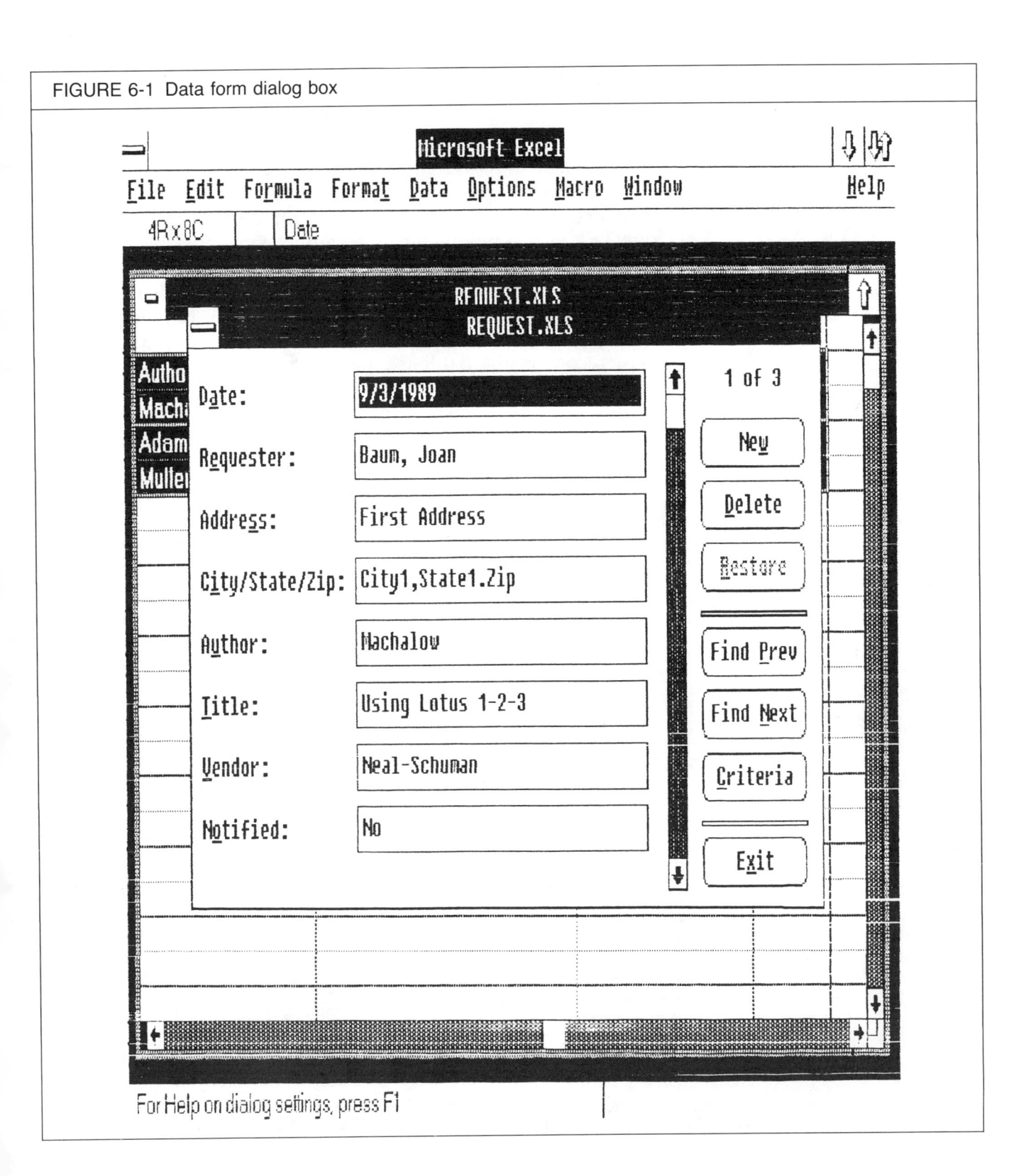

Adding Records: To move to a new field in a data form, you can depress the TAB key; to move to a previous field, depress the SHIFT and TAB keys simultaneously. Alternatively, you can depress the ALT key and the underlined letter of the field name simultaneously to move to a new field in the data form. To move to the first field in a new record, depress the ENTER key; to move to the first field in the previous record, depress the SHIFT and ENTER keys simultaneously. To move to the same field in the next record in the data form, you can depress the DOWN ARROW key; to move to the same field in the previous record, depress the UP ARROW key. To move to the first record in the database, depress the CONTROL and PAGE UP keys simultaneously; to move to the last record in the database, depress the CONTROL and PAGE DOWN keys simultaneously.

When you are finished adding information, you can exit from the data form by tabbing to the exit button and depressing the

FIGURE 6-2 Request2 database with new records

Requests

Date	Requester	Address	City/State/Zip
9/3/89	Baum, Joan	First Address	City1, State1, Zip
9/7/89	Winchester, V.	Second Address	City1, State1, Zip
9/15/89	Cooper, A	Third Address	City31, State1, Zip
9/25/89	Baum, Joan	First address	City1, State1, Zip
9/25/89	Cooper, A	Second Address	City1, State1, Zip
9/25/89	Cooper, A	Second Address	City1, State1, Zip
10/1/89	Goetz, David	Address four	City1, State1, Zip
10/3/89	Pederson Goetz, Cindy	Address Five	City1, State1, Zip
10/3/89	Kalaydjian, E	Address Six	City1, State1, Zip
10/4/89	Kalaydjian, E	Address Six	City1, State1, Zip

Author	Title	Vendor	Notified
Machalow		Neal-Schuman	
Adams		Oryx	
Muller		EBS	No
Irving		Yankee	Yes
Fitzpatrick		Yankee	No
Fitzpatrick		Yankee	No
Evans		Tab	No
Krumm		EBS	No
Stark		EBS	Yes
Ridington and Tucker		EBS	Yes
			Yes

ENTER key or by depressing the ALT and x keys simultaneously. As you move from one record to the next, the information that was entered on the data form is placed into the database.

Deleting Records: The data form can also be used to delete records. To do this, find the record to be deleted. Then either TAB to highlight the delete button and depress the ENTER key or depress the ALT and d keys simultaneously. If you are using a mouse, you can position the pointer on the delete button and click. If you decide to delete a record, Excel will shift the remaining records up one row.

Restoring Records: The restore button in the data form dialog box will restore the currently displayed record to its unedited state. This button cannot be used to restore previously deleted records.

Criteria: You can use the data form to find records. Choose the criteria button and then define what you want to find by filling in selected fields in the form. Excel will then find the records that match the criteria stated. If more than one record matches the stated criteria, you can use the find previous and find next buttons to scroll through all the entries that match the stated criteria.

For example, using the data form (see Figure 6.2) find all the books requested by Joan Baum. To do this, set the criteria. First, choose the criteria button on the data form (TAB to criteria and depress ENTER, depress the ALT and c keys simultaneously, or position the mouse pointer on criteria and click). Excel will present you with a blank form. The position indicator will indicate criteria.

You can fill in as many fields as you want, but Excel will only display exact matches. In this case, you will simply type Baum, Joan in the requester field. When you depress the ENTER key, a matching record is displayed. You can then use the find previous and find next buttons to display all the matching records. You can return to the data form by selecting the form button; this button replaced the criteria button in the data form dialog box.

Exit: To leave the data form at any time, you can choose the exit button. You will be returned to the active worksheet; in this case you will be returned to the requests worksheet, with all the added information. Before going any further, save this worksheet using file save or save as. If using file save as, name the worksheet request2.

The data menu permits you to manipulate the records in a database in several ways other than using a data form. For example, you can easily sort a database using the data sort command.

DATA SORT
If you want to sort the entire database by a particular row or column, depress the ALT or / key, select the data pull-down menu, and choose the sort dialog box. This dialog box will ask if you want to sort the database by rows or columns; you will also be asked to specify up to three sort keys. To sort, choose OK or depress the ENTER key.

For example, you could sort the database by the names of the people who have requested the purchase of specific books. First select the range to be sorted. To select the range, it is easiest to use the EXTEND key, the function key F8. When selecting the range, do not include the field names because if you were to include them, they would be sorted also. On the other hand, do include all the columns for each record; you want all the information about each item to stay together during the sort.

Then depress the ALT or / key, select the data pull-down menu, and choose the sort dialog box. Choose to sort by rows, and make the first sort key B3, which is the column with the names of the requesters. Excel permits up to three sort keys, but in a database of this size, only one is necessary. Then choose the OK button or depress the ENTER key. The sort will be carried out.

EDIT UNDO
If you see that the sort was not performed as you desired, you can undo the sort. Depress the ALT or / key, select the edit pull-down menu, and choose undo. The database will be restored.

Edit undo can be used to immediately undo some Excel commands. Remember that edit undo can only work on some of the commands, and that it can only undo the most recently issued command. Before performing a sort, or for that matter many of the more complex commands that change the database significantly, it is wise to save a copy of the worksheet; in this way, if a mistake is made, you can always go back to the worksheet prior to the modification.

SET CRITERIA
Excel permits the user of a database to find and delete specific records from a database. Before performing either of these manipulations, Excel requires that a criteria range be set.

The criteria range must contain at least two rows. On the first row are listed the criteria to be found; these must be exactly the same as the field names used on the database. Not all the field names need to be placed in the criteria range, but it might be easiest to simply copy the field names for all the fields into a blank area of the worksheet. To copy the field names, first select them using the SHIFT and ARROW keys or the EXTEND key, the function key F8. If you are skipping some of the field names, the use of the EXTEND key is necessary. Then depress the ALT or / key to gain access to the menu bar, select the edit pull-down menu, and choose copy. Then move to a blank area of the worksheet which will be used for the criteria range and paste the field names (ALT or /, edit, paste).

The rows under the copied field names are then used to specify criteria. Only records that match the stated criteria will be found or deleted. If the criteria range contains a blank row, all the database records will be considered as matching it.

USING WILDCARDS

The criteria can use wildcards. A question mark (?) can be used to replace any one character in a specified criteria. An asterisk (*) can be used to represent any number of characters. Thus Jo?n will retrieve Joan and John; Micro* will retrieve Microsoft and Microscope.

You can use specific numbers, logical values, or text as criteria. If you are using text, be aware that the criteria ma will retrieve all entries in the specified field that begin with ma. To match only specific text, use the following format for criteria: ="=ma". In this case, only entries with ma in the specified field will be matched.

DATA FIND

Once the database and the criteria have been selected, Excel can be used to find matching records. Simply depress the ALT or / key to gain access to the menu bar, select the data pull-down menu, and choose find. You can then scroll through matching records selected by Excel.

When executing a data find, the data pull-down menu changes slightly: the find choice is replaced by exit find. Choose this command to exit data find.

DATA DELETE

You can set criteria and then delete all the records that match the stated criteria. Instead of choosing data find, in this case you would choose data delete. Be very careful: a deletion cannot be undone using edit undo. Some precautions that you could take are: save the database before performing a data delete; this way you can always open the file that has the undeleted records. Also, you could preview the records to be deleted using data find or data extract.

DATA EXTRACT

To perform a data extract, you must select the database range, the criteria range, and an extract range. The extract range is a blank area in the worksheet onto which Excel will copy all the records that match the stated criteria. The extract range must contain a row that has the field names (these can be copied just as the headings for the criteria range were; they must be exact matches for the field names in the database). If only this row is specified as the extract range, any information below this to the bottom of the worksheet will be erased. On the other hand, you could specify a set number of rows for the extract range.

When you have selected the database and specified the criteria to be matched, select the extract range (either the single row or the range). Select this range as you would any other: hold down the SHIFT key while using the ARROW keys or use the EXTEND key, the function key F8. Then depress the ALT or / key, select the data pull-down menu, and choose extract. Excel will copy all the records from the database that match the specified criteria. Be sure not to include any blank lines in the criteria; otherwise, Excel will copy the entire database to the extract range since a blank line is interpreted by Excel as matching all the records.

For example, copy the field names from the database for the criteria and extract ranges. Use a blank portion of the worksheet, placing the extract range under the criteria range. Type the name Baum under requester in the criteria range. Then set the criteria range.

Now select the extract range; in this case only select the row containing the column headings. When you select data extract, the two records matching the criteria will be copied to the extract range. Notice that Excel matches the records for Baum, Joan since an exact text matching was not requested. If you typed ="=Baum" in the criteria range, no records would have been extracted.

DATA SERIES

The data series command is also useful when working with a database. The data series command fills a selected range with a series of numbers or dates. In the data series dialog box, you can specify that the series is in rows or columns, and specify a step value (linear adds the step value; growth multiples by the step value; date

SUMMARY

In this chapter you have:

1. learned the vocabulary of databases;
2. set a database;
3. used a data form to add records;
4. learned how to delete records using a data form;
5. learned to restore records using a data form;
6. specified criteria on a data form;
7. sorted data;
8. learned about edit undo;
9. set criteria;
10. learned about wildcards in criteria;
11. learned about data find;
12. learned about data delete;
13. extracted data;
14. used data series;
15. learned about data tables.

calculates a series of dates which can be limited to weekdays if desired).

Use the data series command to number the entries on the book budget worksheet. Use the right hand column for the data series.

To use the data series command, type 1 in the first cell. Depress the ALT or / key, select the data pull-down menu, and choose the data series dialog box. Select columns (which fills the series down), linear, a step value of 1, and a stop value which is larger than the number of entries in the database. Then depress the ENTER key or choose OK. The column will be filled with the series specified.

DATA TABLE

A data table can be used to compute what if situations in a database. The data table actually shows the results of substituting different values in one or two cells in a worksheet. Excel offers both a one-input data table and a two-input data table.

REVIEW

To review this chapter, we will manipulate the data in the circulation department budget. Open this database by depressing the ALT or / key. Then select file and choose open. Change the default directory if necessary (depress ALT and d simultaneously, and choose the directory) and then specify the file name by either typing it in the box or choosing it from the list.

First we will be using a data form to add records. Select the database, with the first row of the selected area being the field names. Do not include the worksheet title in your selection. Then depress the ALT or / key, select the data pull-down menu, and choose form. Depress ALT and w simultaneously to see a blank form. Add the records shown below to the bottom of the database and then exit the data form.

Remember that you move in the data form by using the TAB key or by depressing the ALT and underlined key simultaneously. To go to a new form, depress the ALT and w keys simultaneously; to exit the data form depress the ALT and x keys simultaneously.

At this point, your database should look like Figure 6.3.

Now sort this database by vendor using data sort. First select the portion of the database to be sorted. Do not include the field names

FIGURE 6-3 Circulation budget plus two records

	A	B	C	D	E	F
1	*Circulation Budget*					
2	*Ordered*	*Vendor*	*Amount*	*Total*	*Received*	*Invoice*
3	9/9/89	Longman	$725.50	$725.50	10/10/89	$700.90
4	9/10/89	EBS	$1,200.50	$1,926.00	9/30/89	$1,150.97
5	9/21/89	Holt	$589.75	$2,515.75	11/1/89	$478.90
6	10/2/89	Viking	$333.65	$2,849.40	11/1/89	$345.98
7	10/3/89	Que	$135.90	$2,985.30	11/3/89	$132.90
8	10/5/89	Microsoft	$132.50	$3,117.80	10/20/89	$132.00
9	10/12/89	Microsoft	$22.95	$3,140.75	10/20/89	$22.95
10	10/22/89	Neal-Schuman	$310.50	$3,451.25	11/5/89	$300.55
11	10/30/89	Baker & Taylor	$1,999.95	$5,451.20	11/15/89	975.5
12	11/3/89	Yankee Book	$2,175.50	$7,626.70	12/3/89	$2,175.45
13	11/4/89	Random House	$345.00	$7,971.70	12/1/89	$300.15
14	11/5/89	Neal-Schuman	$1,450.50	$9,422.20	12/1/89	$1,450.00
15	11/7/88	Meckler	$150.75	$9,572.95	12/2/89	$150.75
16	11/8/89	Bowker	$200.15	$9,773.10	12/25/89	$200.97
17	11/24/89	Yankee Book	$1,775.00	$11,548.10	12/20/89	$1,770.98
18	11/25/89	Macmillan	$125.75	$11,673.85	12/24/89	$125.70
19	12/1/89	Microsoft	$500.50	$12,174.35	12/20/89	$499.99
20	12/10/89	Que	$750.00	$12,924.35	12/30/89	$700.90
21	12/15/89	Harcourt Brace	$990.00	$13,914.35	1/15/90	$903.50
22	12/17/89	Tab	$350.00	$14,264.35	2/1/89	$315.75
23	12/23/89	Neal-Schuman	$225.00	$14,489.35	2/1/89	$225.00

FIGURE 6-4 Sorted database: problem on totals column

	A	B	C	D	E	F
1	*Circulation Budget*					
2	*Ordered*	*Vendor*	*Amount*	*Total*	*Received*	*Invoice*
3	10/30/89	Baker & Taylor	$1,999.95	$1,999.95	11/15/89	975.5
4	11/8/89	Bowker	$200.15	$2,200.10	12/25/89	$200.97
5	9/10/89	EBS	$1,200.50	$3,400.60	9/30/89	$1,150.97
6	12/15/89	Harcourt Brace	$990.00	$4,390.60	1/15/90	$903.50
7	9/21/89	Holt	$589.75	$4,980.35	11/1/89	$478.90
8	9/9/89	Longman	$725.50	$725.50	10/10/89	$700.90
9	11/25/89	Macmillan	$125.75	$5,831.60	12/24/89	$125.70
10	11/7/88	Meckler	$150.75	$5,982.35	12/2/89	$150.75
11	10/5/89	Microsoft	$132.50	$6,114.85	10/20/89	$132.00
12	10/12/89	Microsoft	$22.95	$6,137.80	10/20/89	$22.95
13	12/1/89	Microsoft	$500.50	$6,638.30	12/20/89	$499.99
14	10/22/89	Neal-Schuman	$310.50	$6,948.80	11/5/89	$300.55
15	11/5/89	Neal-Schuman	$1,450.50	$8,399.30	12/1/89	$1,450.00
16	12/23/89	Neal-Schuman	$225.00	$8,624.30	2/1/89	$225.00
17	10/3/89	Que	$135.90	$8,760.20	11/3/89	$132.90
18	12/10/89	Que	$750.00	$9,510.20	12/30/89	$700.90
19	11/4/89	Random House	$345.00	$9,855.20	12/1/89	$300.15
20	12/17/89	Tab	$350.00	$10,205.20	2/1/89	$315.75
21	10/2/89	Viking	$333.65	$10,538.85	11/1/89	$345.98
22	11/24/89	Yankee Book	$1,775.00	$12,313.85	12/20/89	$1,770.98
23	11/3/89	Yankee Book	$2,175.50	$14,489.35	12/3/89	$2,175.45
24						

in your selection: you want the field names to remain at the top of the sorted entries. Remember to include all the columns in your selection so that all the information about one order will remain together.

Depress the ALT or / key, select data, and choose sort. Indicate that you want to sort by rows, and that the first sort key is B3 (the first vendor's name). When you choose OK or depress the ENTER key, the database will be sorted (see Figure 6.4).

Examine the results of the sort: the totals column is completely confused. Before doing anything else, undo the sort. Depress the ALT or / key, select the edit pull-down menu, and choose undo sort. The database will be restored.

You cannot change your selection to exclude the column with the totals from the sort: Excel will tell you that sorting a multiple selection cannot be accomplished. The other possibility is to move the column with the totals out of the sort range and then perform the sort once again.

To move the totals column, select it and then depress the ALT or / key, select edit, and choose cut. Move your highlighting to a column to the right of the database and once again depress the ALT or / key, select edit, and choose paste. The column with the totals, due to the absolute references, remains valid.

Now select the range to be sorted once again. Then invoke the data sort command, indicate that the primary sort will be the vendor (B3) and depress ENTER or choose OK. The database will be sorted by vendor, and the totals column will remain valid (see Figure 6.5).

Now sort the database again, this time by invoiced amount. Select the range and invoke data sort using cell F3 as the primary sort key. Choose ascending order. Your sorted database will look like Figure 6.6. Excel permits you to sort not only by textual entries, but by amounts.

Now you can move the totals column back to its proper place. Select the range to be moved and use edit cut; select the range to which it will be moved and use edit paste (see Figure 6.7).

Now we will use the same database to practice data find and data extract. To do both, you need a criteria range. Copy the field headings from the database to a blank portion of the worksheet. Use edit copy and then edit paste. Type the name Neal-Schuman under vendor and then select the criteria range. With the criteria range highlighted, depress ALT or /, select data, and choose set criteria. Be sure that the database has been set (if not, Excel will display an error message when you attempt data find).

Depress the ALT or / key, select data, and choose find. The first

FIGURE 6-5 Sorted database by vendor with totals out

	A	B	C	D	E
1	*Circulation Budget*				
2	*Ordered*	*Vendor*	*Amount*		*Received*
3	9/9/89	Baker & Taylor	$1,999.95		11/15/89
4	9/10/89	Bowker	$200.15		12/25/89
5	9/21/89	EBS	$1,200.50		9/30/89
6	10/2/89	Harcourt Brace	$990.00		1/15/90
7	10/3/89	Holt	$669.75		11/1/89
8	10/5/89	Longman	$725.50		10/10/89
9	10/12/89	Macmillan	$126.75		12/24/89
10	10/22/89	Meckler	$150.75		12/2/89
11	10/30/89	Microsoft	$132.50		10/20/89
12	11/3/89	Microsoft	$22.95		10/20/89
13	11/4/89	Microsoft	$500.50		12/20/89
14	11/5/89	Neal-Schuman	$310.50		11/5/89
15	11/7/88	Neal-Schuman	$1,450.50		12/1/89
16	11/8/89	Neal-Schuman	$225.00		2/1/89
17	11/24/89	Que	$135.90		11/3/89
18	11/25/89	Que	$750.00		12/30/89
19	12/1/89	Random House	$345.00		12/1/89
20	12/10/89	Tab	$350.00		2/1/89
21	12/15/89	Viking	$333.65		11/1/89
22	12/17/89	Yankee Book	$1,775.00		12/20/89
23	12/23/89	Yankee Book	$2,175.50		12/3/89

	F	G	H
1			
2	*Invoice*		*Total*
3	975.5		$1,999.95
4	$200.97		$2,200.10
5	$1,150.97		$3,400.60
6	$903.50		$4,390.60
7	$478.90		$4,980.35
8	$700.90		$5,705.85
9	$125.70		$5,831.60
10	$150.75		$5,982.35
11	$132.00		$6,114.85
12	$22.95		$6,137.80
13	$499.99		$6,638.30
14	$300.55		$6,948.80
15	$1,450.00		$8,399.30
16	$225.00		$8,624.30
17	$132.90		$8,760.20
18	$700.90		$9,510.20
19	$300.15		$9,855.20
20	$315.75		$10,205.20
21	$345.98		$10,538.85
22	$1,770.98		$12,313.85
23	$2,175.45		$14,489.35

FIGURE 6-6 Sorted database by invoiced amount

	A	B	C	D	E	F
1	*Circulation Budget*					
2	Ordered	Vendor	Amount	Total	Received	Invoice
3	10/12/89	Microsoft	$22.95	$22.95	10/20/89	$22.95
4	11/25/89	Macmillan	$125.75	$148.70	12/24/89	$125.70
5	10/5/89	Microsoft	$132.50	$281.20	10/20/89	$132.00
6	10/3/89	Que	$135.90	$417.10	11/3/89	$132.90
7	11/7/88	Meckler	$150.75	$567.85	12/2/89	$150.75
8	11/8/89	Bowker	$200.15	$768.00	12/25/89	$200.97
9	12/23/89	Neal-Schuman	$225.00	$993.00	2/1/89	$225.00
10	11/4/89	Random House	$345.00	$1,338.00	12/1/89	$300.15
11	10/22/89	Neal-Schuman	$310.50	$1,648.50	11/5/89	$300.55
12	12/17/89	Tab	$350.00	$1,998.50	2/1/89	$315.75
13	10/2/89	Viking	$333.65	$2,332.15	11/1/89	$345.98
14	9/21/89	Holt	$589.75	$2,921.90	11/1/89	$478.90
15	12/1/89	Microsoft	$500.50	$3,422.40	12/20/89	$499.99
16	9/9/89	Longman	$725.50	$725.50	10/10/89	$700.90
17	12/10/89	Que	$750.00	$4,897.90	12/30/89	$700.90
18	12/15/89	Harcourt Brace	$990.00	$5,887.90	1/15/90	$903.50
19	10/30/89	Baker & Taylor	$1,999.95	$7,887.85	11/15/89	$975.50
20	9/10/89	EBS	$1,200.50	$9,088.35	9/30/89	$1,150.97
21	11/5/89	Neal-Schuman	$1,450.50	$10,538.85	12/1/89	$1,450.00
22	11/24/89	Yankee Book	$1,775.00	$12,313.85	12/20/89	$1,770.98
23	11/3/89	Yankee Book	$2,175.50	$14,489.35	12/3/89	$2,175.45
24						

record that matches the stated criteria will be highlighted. Use the ARROW keys to highlight all the matching records. To exit from data find, depress the ALT or / key, select data, and choose exit find.

Now copy the headings from the criteria range to a blank portion of the worksheet; this will be the extract range. To copy these headings, use the same technique as used before: edit copy and edit paste. Be sure that there is no information below the extract range headings: since only one row will be specified for the extract range, all information below it will be erased when data extract is invoked. Alternatively, you could specify a certain number of rows for the extract range; if there aren't enough rows Excel will post a message.

While the extract headings are highlighted, depress the ALT or / key, select data, and then choose extract. All the records that match the stated criteria will be copied to the extract range.

FIGURE 6-7 Sorted by invoiced amount with totals

	A	B	C	D	E	F
1	*Circulation Budget*					
2	Ordered	Vendor	Amount	Total	Received	Invoice
3	9/9/89	Baker & Taylor	$1,999.95	$1,999.95	11/15/89	975.5
4	9/10/89	Bowker	$200.15	$2,200.10	12/25/89	$200.97
5	9/21/89	EBS	$1,200.50	$3,400.60	9/30/89	$1,150.97
6	10/2/89	Harcourt Brace	$990.00	$4,390.60	1/15/90	$903.50
7	10/3/89	Holt	$589.75	$4,980.35	11/1/89	$478.90
8	10/5/89	Longman	$725.50	$5,705.85	10/10/89	$700.90
9	10/12/89	Macmillan	$125.75	$5,831.60	12/24/89	$125.70
10	10/22/89	Meckler	$150.75	$5,982.35	12/2/89	$150.75
11	10/30/89	Microsoft	$132.50	$6,114.85	10/20/89	$132.00
12	11/3/89	Microsoft	$22.95	$6,137.80	10/20/89	$22.95
13	11/4/89	Microsoft	$500.50	$6,638.30	12/20/89	$499.99
14	11/5/89	Neal-Schuman	$310.50	$6,948.80	11/5/89	$300.55
15	11/7/88	Neal-Schuman	$1,450.50	$8,399.30	12/1/89	$1,450.00
16	11/8/89	Neal-Schuman	$225.00	$8,624.30	2/1/89	$225.00
17	11/24/89	Que	$135.90	$8,760.20	11/3/89	$132.90
18	11/25/89	Que	$750.00	$9,510.20	12/30/89	$700.90
19	12/1/89	Random House	$345.00	$9,855.20	12/1/89	$300.15
20	12/10/89	Tab	$350.00	$10,205.20	2/1/89	$315.75
21	12/15/89	Viking	$333.65	$10,538.85	11/1/89	$345.98
22	12/17/89	Yankee Book	$1,775.00	$12,313.85	12/20/89	$1,770.98
23	12/23/89	Yankee Book	$2,175.50	$14,489.35	12/3/89	$2,175.45

7 FORMULAS AND FUNCTIONS

Excel permits the use of a worksheet to manipulate information using formulas and functions. A formula is used to calculate a new value from existing values. A function is actually a prewritten formula.

FORMULAS

Operator Types: A formula can be used to compute arithmetic expressions. Excel permits the following arithmetic operators: + (addition), - (subtraction), * (multiplication), / (division), % (percentage) and ^ (exponential). Values can be compared using = (equal to), > (greater than), < (less than), > = (greater than or equal to), < = (less than or equal to) and < > (not equal to). Text can be joined using & (the ampersand). Reference operators combine cell references and produce a new reference. The reference operators of Excel are : (the colon, indicating range), space (indicating intersection) and , (the comma, indicating union).

Formulas: To use a formula, select a cell or range of cells. Type an equal sign (=): all formulas in Excel begin with an equal sign. Then you can use any one or a combination of the following methods:

   a. type the formula in the formula bar;
   b. select worksheet cells while in the formula bar;
   c. paste a function using formula paste function; remember that a function is actually a prewritten formula;
   d. paste a name using formula paste name;
   e. paste a link to another worksheet.

When the formula is complete, depress the ENTER key to leave the formula bar. Using the mouse, click on the enter box on the formula bar. The function will be placed in the cell(s) selected.

Formula Examples: If you wanted to add the values in cells A1, B1, and C1 you could write the formula =A1+B1+C1. Similarly, if you wanted to multiply the value in cell D2 by the value in cell E2, you could write the formula =D2*E2.

You could also combine text using a formula. if cell A1 contained the text "Joan " and cell B1 contained the text "Baum", writing the formula =A1&B1 in cell D1 will produce Joan Baum. The space after "Joan " is needed to assure that the names will be separated by a space. Other techniques will be discussed later.

Using formulas is useful, but combining formulas with functions makes Excel a very powerful tool.

FUNCTIONS

A function is actually a prewritten formula; a user can certainly get along without functions, but they shorten a lot of the work of using a worksheet. Excel has a great number of functions, including database functions, date and time functions, financial functions, information functions, logical functions, lookup functions, mathematical functions, matrix functions, statistical functions, text functions, and trigonometric functions.

Function Format: All functions in Excel have the same format:

= function name(arguments)

Since a function is actually a prewritten formula, it begins with an equal sign (=) if it is the first element of a cell; remember that functions can be a part of a formula.

Following the equal sign is the function's name. The function's name can be typed in upper or lowercase, or a combination. When you complete typing the function, Excel changes the function name to all uppercase letters. You can make a habit of typing the function name in lowercase letters and having Excel check your spelling for you: if the name is transformed into caps, you know that you typed it correctly.

Following the function's name are the arguments associated with the particular function. Arguments are always enclosed in parentheses. Arguments can be of different types, depending on the function. Some arguments are values, such as 37 or 38. Some arguments are cell references, such as A1. Some arguments are ranges, such as A1:A10. Arguments can also be named ranges, such as inflation. Some functions even have optional arguments. It is very difficult to remember which or how many arguments a function takes; Excel offers help.

Pasting a Function: Excel permits you to paste a function into the formula bar. When pasting the function, you can indicate that you want Excel to include place holders indicating the arguments for the function selected.

To paste a function, first select the cell or range of cells into which the function will be placed. Then depress the ALT or / key to gain access to the menu bar. Select the formula pull-down menu. Choose the paste function dialog box. All the built-in functions of Excel will be listed. Select the function desired. If you want place holders, turn on the paste arguments box. These place holders must be replaced, but they are very useful. Depress the ENTER key or choose OK. This will permit you to leave the formula paste function dialog box. Then edit the function as it appears in the formula bar. When you depress the ENTER key, you leave the formula bar, and the function is placed in the cell(s) you selected.

Function Examples: You have already used one function: the SUM() function. To obtain a total of the values in a range, the SUM() function can be used:

=SUM(A1:A10)

This function will produce the sum of the values in cells A1 through A10 on a worksheet. Similarly,

=SUM(A1:D10)

will produce the sum of the values in the cells A1 through D10.
 Excel also offers a function that will compute the average of the values in a range.

=AVERAGE(A1:A3)

This function computes the average of the values in cells A1 through A3 in a worksheet. Similarly,

=AVERAGE(A1:D10)

will produce the average of the values in the cells A1 through D10.
 Excel has a function that counts the number of entries in a range:

=COUNT(A1:A3)

will count the number of entries in the range from A1 to A3. Similarly,

=COUNT(A!:D10)

will count the number of entries in the range A1 to D10.
 Excel even has a function that will indicate the number of the day of the week for a given date:

=WEEKDAY("1/1/91")

will indicate the number of the day of the week for the first day of January of 1991.

Excel's functions are varied. Some of them will be used in this chapter; many others will be used in the library applications section of this book.

COMBINING FORMULAS AND FUNCTIONS

Formulas can contain functions. For example, if you wanted to add the contents of cell A1 to the sum of the values in cells B1 through B7, you could write:

=A1+SUM(B1:B7)

Notice that the entire formula begins with the equal sign (=); since the function is not the first element of the formula, the equal sign is not included directly prior to the SUM() function.

COMBINING FUNCTIONS

Functions can be combined in Excel. For example, the function:

=NOW()

will enter the serial number of the current date and time if your computer has a built-in clock or you correctly responded to the DOS prompts for date and time when you started using the computer at the beginning of the day. This function can be combined to display the year, number of the month, number of the weekday, hour, minute or second.

To display the year, use the function:

=YEAR(NOW())

Similarly, you can display the month, using

=MONTH(NOW())

the weekday using

= WEEKDAY(NOW())

the hour using

= HOUR(NOW())

the minute using

= MINUTE(NOW())

and the second using

= SECOND(NOW())

Excel will calculate the time and date functions only when the worksheet is recalculated; they are not continually recalculated. Notice that the NOW() function does not take any arguments; the empty parentheses are required; without them, Excel will not recognize it as a function.

USING FORMULAS AND FUNCTIONS

In order to practice using formulas and functions, we will use the worksheet containing the circulation department budget. Open that worksheet. To open a worksheet, depress the ALT or / key to gain access to the menu bar, select the file pull-down menu, and choose the open dialog box. Change the default directory if necessary, and choose the file from the list. When you depress the ENTER key or choose OK, the file will be opened.

First, we will obtain a sum of the invoice column (we have already obtained a running total on the amount encumbered). To obtain a sum, we can use the function:

= SUM(F3:F23)

On the other hand, since we are using a database, we can use a database function.

DATABASE FUNCTIONS

Database functions may seem to be more complicated, but in fact they have several advantages. They take several arguments: the database, the field to be used, and the criteria to use. Since we are working with a named database (we have used the data set database command and Excel has named the database database), we can use that name as the first argument. The field name to be totaled is easier to write than trying to remember the cell locations. The criteria are like all other criteria: you can use the criteria range already set, which Excel has named criteria.

In this case, we want to obtain a sum of the entire field in the database, and to do that we simply leave the second line of the criteria range blank. Excel interprets this to mean all the records on the database are to be used. If we wanted to limit the database operation to those records meeting certain criteria, we could specify them in the criteria range. For example, we could easily obtain a total for the invoice field for those orders placed to Neal-Schuman.

Database Sum: To obtain the sum of the invoices, we could use the database sum function as follows:

=DSUM(database,"Invoice",criteria)

The function begins with the equal sign (=) and is followed by the name of the function, (DSUM()). The arguments follow: the named database (database), the field name in quotes ("Invoice"), and the named criteria (criteria). In the cell that this is typed, the total of the invoice column is revealed.

Database Average: To obtain the average invoiced amount, you could use the Excel AVERAGE() function, but you would have to specify the cell references. Instead, you could use a database average function:

=DAVERAGE(database,"Invoice",criteria)

Once again, the database was named, the field name is in quotation marks, and the criteria contains a blank line so that all records are used.

Database Count: To count the number of records in a database, Excel offers several functions: COUNT(), COUNTA(), DCOUNT(), and DCOUNTA(). The first two are Excel functions where you would have to supply the range; the second two are database functions. COUNT() and DCOUNT() count the number of records; COUNTA() and DCOUNTA() count the number of values in the range.

Using the database functions to count is simple, once the database and criteria are named:

=DCOUNT(database,"Invoice",criteria)
=DCOUNTA(database,"Invoice",criteria)

In the circulation department budget, these two functions will reveal the identical number since all the records have invoice amounts.

TEXT FUNCTIONS

The second column (column B) has the names of the venders. Excel offers several text functions which can be used to manipulate textual information. Three of these are LOWER(), UPPER() and PROPER(). When using these functions, only text is modified; numbers are unchanged.

LOWER(): If you wanted to change a textual reference into all lowercase letters, you could use the LOWER() function:

=LOWER(B3)

This function will place a lowercase copy of the entry in cell B3 in the cell in which this function is written.

UPPER(): In a similar manner, Excel permits the user to change a cell entry into all uppercase letters:

=UPPER(B3)

This function will place an uppercase copy of cell B3 in the cell in which this function is written.

PROPER(): Possibly a more useful function is the PROPER() function. It is used to place a capital letter at the beginning of each word in a cell entry. Its form is identical to the LOWER() and UPPER() form:

=PROPER(B3)

This will place a properly capitalized copy of the entry in cell B3 in the cell in which this function is written.

SUMMARY

In this chapter, you have:

1. learned about formula operators;
2. learned about formulas;
3. learned about functions;
4. learned to paste functions and their arguments;
5. learned to combine formulas and functions;
6. learned to combine functions;
7. used functions: SUM(), AVERAGE(), COUNT(), and COUNTA();
8. used database functions: DSUM(). DAVERAGE(), DCOUNT(), and DCOUNTA();
9. learned about text functions: LOWER(), UPPER(), and PROPER().

REVIEW

To review formulas and functions, open the worksheet that contains the library's book budget. To open a file, depress the ALT or / key, select the file pull-down menu, and choose the open dialog box. Change the default directory if necessary and then open the file.

First, use this file as a database. Select the worksheet, beginning with the second row that contains the field names, continuing for the entire used portion of the worksheet. Then depress the ALT or / key, select the data pull-down menu, and choose set database. Excel will name the selected portion with the name database; this name will be used in the database functions.

Next copy the field names to a blank portion of the worksheet: this will be the criteria range. To copy the field names, select them and then depress the ALT or / key, select the edit pull-down menu, and choose copy. Select a blank portion of the worksheet, depress ALT or /, select edit, and choose paste. Select the field names and a row beneath them: this will be the criteria range. With them selected, depress the ALT or / key, select the data pull-down menu, and choose set criteria; Excel will name the selected range criteria; this name will also be used in the database functions.

Using the column for the amounts invoiced, obtain a sum, an average, a maximum, and a minimum. To find the maximum amount, use this database function:

=DMAX(database,field,criteria)

To find the minimum amount, use this database function:

=DMIN(database,field,criteria)

Be sure to enclose the field name in quotation marks. In a database this small, locating the maximum and minimum amounts may not be significant, but in larger databases it will be. Remember to leave the criteria's second line blank so that Excel will examine the entire database.

Then place the date on the line above the database functions. This will be the date of the last update. You can type in today's date and try to remember to change it each time the worksheet is updated, or you could use Excel functions. To obtain the month, use:

$$= \text{MONTH(NOW())}$$

To obtain the day of the month, use:

$$= \text{DAY(NOW())}$$

Connect these functions as you would other text:
&"/"& (you will want the slash between the month and the date: the quotation marks insure that exactly what you type will be placed between the functions).

Excel also offers a shortcut to place the date in a selected cell. Simply depress the CONTROL and SEMICOLON keys simultaneously. The date will be placed in the selected cell. Though not being used in this chapter, you can place the time in a cell by depressing the CONTROL and COLON keys simultaneously.

The result of the database functions and the date functions will look like Figure 7.1. Note that the illustration has two copies of the worksheet visible: separate windows were used for each. One window shows the results of the functions; the other shows the functions themselves. Your worksheet will only have the one column with the results. If you want to examine the functions, you can examine them one at a time in the formula bar when the highlighting is on the individual cell. On the other hand, you could change the display to show formulas rather than values. To do this, depress the ALT or / key, select the options pull-down menu, and choose display. Here you can choose to display the formulas.

Now add a final column to the worksheet to obtain the amount remaining in each of the budgeted lines. To do this, you will have to subtract the invoiced amount from the budgeted amount. A formula in cell F3 will accomplish this:

$$= \text{C3-E3}$$

This formula is then copied down the column, and the relative cell references are adjusted by Excel. To copy the formula, select the cell containing it, depress the ALT or / key, select the edit pull-down menu, and choose copy. Then select the cells into which you want to paste the formula. Then depress the ALT or / key, select the edit pull-down menu, and choose paste. After right aligning columns D, E, and F (select the columns, then depress ALT, select format, choose alighment right), the results will look like Figure 7.2.

Save the worksheet. Use ALT or /, file, save as. Then specify a name to save it under. You can exit from Excel now (depress ALT

80 USING MICROSOFT EXCEL

FIGURE 7-1 Dfunctions and date; 2 windows: a. values   b. formulas

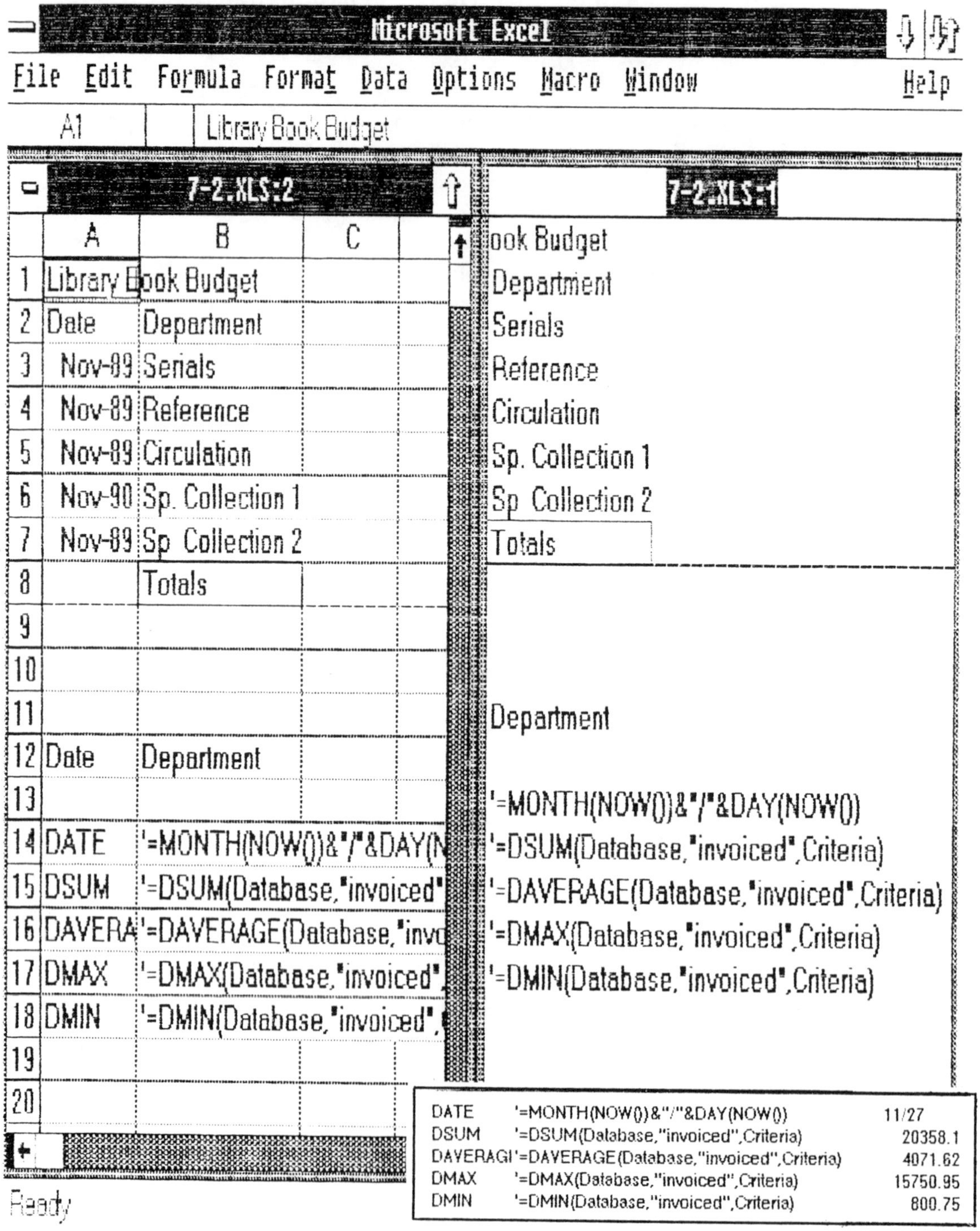

FIGURE 7-2 Book budget with remaining column

Library Book Budget

Date	Department	Budgeted	Encumbered	Invoiced	Remaining
Nov-89	Serials	$30,000	$950.00	$800.75	29199.25
Nov-89	Reference	$10,000	$2,000.45	$1,999.75	8000.25
Nov-89	Circulation	$35,000	$13,555.75	$15,750.95	19249.05
Nov-90	Sp. Collection 1	$15,000	$750.95	$688.90	14111.1
Nov-89	Sp. Collection 2	$10,000	$889.45	$917.75	9082.25
	Totals	100000	18146.6	20358.1	79641.9

or /, select file, and choose exit) or you can go on to the next chapter. If you try to exit from Excel prior to saving the file, Excel will post a warning.

8 EXCEL FEATURES I

We will now explore some of Excel's features by using the budget worksheet for the circulation department. If you have any other Excel files open, close them now by depressing the ALT or / key to gain access to the menu bar, selecting the file pull-down menu, and choosing close. Then open the circulation department's worksheet by depressing the ALT or / key, selecting the file pull-down menu, and choosing the open dialog box. Change the default directory if necessary and choose the file.

FORMULA NOTE

Select the cell with the heading total. It might be nice to be able to write a note describing how the column was computed. Excel permits you to do just that. Depress the ALT or / key and select the formula pull-down menu. Then choose the note dialog box. In this dialog box you can type a note to go along with the cell. This note will not be displayed on the worksheet but it can be viewed.

WINDOW SHOW INFO

After the ENTER key is depressed, the note disappears. To display the note, depress the ALT or / key, select the window pull-down menu, and choose show info. The information, including notes, for the selected cell will be displayed (see Figure 8.1).

WINDOW SHOW DOCUMENT

At this point you cannot scroll through the circulation department budget worksheet. You will have to depress the ALT or / key to gain access to the menu bar, select the window pull-down menu, and choose show document or select the document that you want to display. This will hide the window with the cell's information.

WINDOW ARRANGE ALL

You can display the information in the window while working on a worksheet. Depress the ALT or / key, select the window pull-down menu, and choose arrange all. This will permit you to see the information window about individual cells while scrolling through the worksheet.

Depress the ALT or / key to gain access to the menu bar. Then select the window pull-down menu and choose show info to make the information window the active document. At this point, you will notice that the menu bar has been modified: there are only four menu choices here: file, info, macro, window. Select the info pull-down menu.

FIGURE 8-1 Circbud total with note displayed

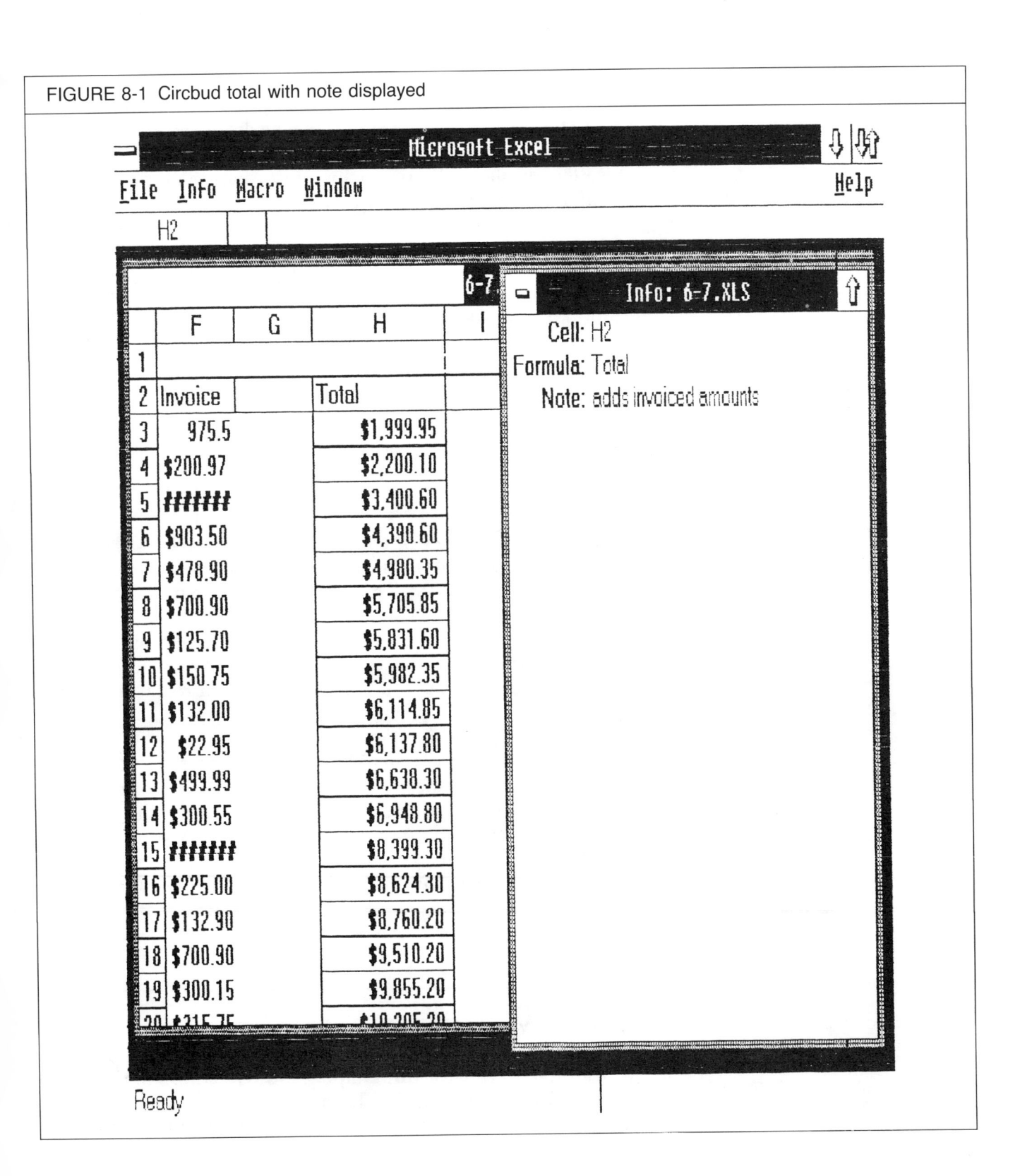

WINDOW INFO

This pull-down menu has a number of pieces of information that can be checked; the checked items will be displayed in the information window. Scroll down to highlight format and depress ENTER. The display will now include information on the format of the highlighted cell (see Figure 8.2).

FORMULA SELECT SPECIAL

Instead of scrolling through the worksheet, looking for cells that contain a note, you can use formula select special. Using this command, you can have Excel select cells having specified characteristics. To get to the dialog box in which you specify these characteristics, depress the ALT or / key, select the formula pull-down menu, and choose the select special dialog box (see Figure 8.3). First simply select the box for notes and depress the ENTER key or choose OK. Excel will highlight cell H2, the cell in which we placed a note.

Now, depress the ALT or / key, pull down the formula menu, and choose select special again. This time, select formulas and depress the ENTER key or choose OK. Excel will highlight all the cells that have formulas: the entire totals column, excluding the heading will be displayed. To go from one cell to the next, depress the TAB or ENTER key; to go back, depress the SHIFT and TAB or SHIFT and ENTER keys simultaneously. If you decided, on looking at the formulas, that there was something that needed to be replaced in all of them, you could use formula replace.

FORMULA REPLACE

The formula replace command can be used to find and replace characters in a worksheet. It can replace part or all of a cell as desired. The formula replace dialog box looks like Figure 8.4.

Specify the text that you want to replace, such as a name of a vendor if it was mistyped or if it has changed. Then specify what it is to be replaced with. When ENTER is depressed or OK chosen, Excel will automatically make the replacements.

SUMMARY

In this chapter, you have:

1. made a note;
2. displayed a note;
3. hidden a note;
4. made a note visible;
5. arranged an information window and worksheet to display simultaneously;
6. used formula select special;
7. learned about formula replace.

REVIEW

To begin our review of this chapter, we will continue to use the circulation budget worksheet. If it is not presently on screen, open the file. In addition, open the file with the names of the requesters:

FIGURE 8-2 Window show info including format

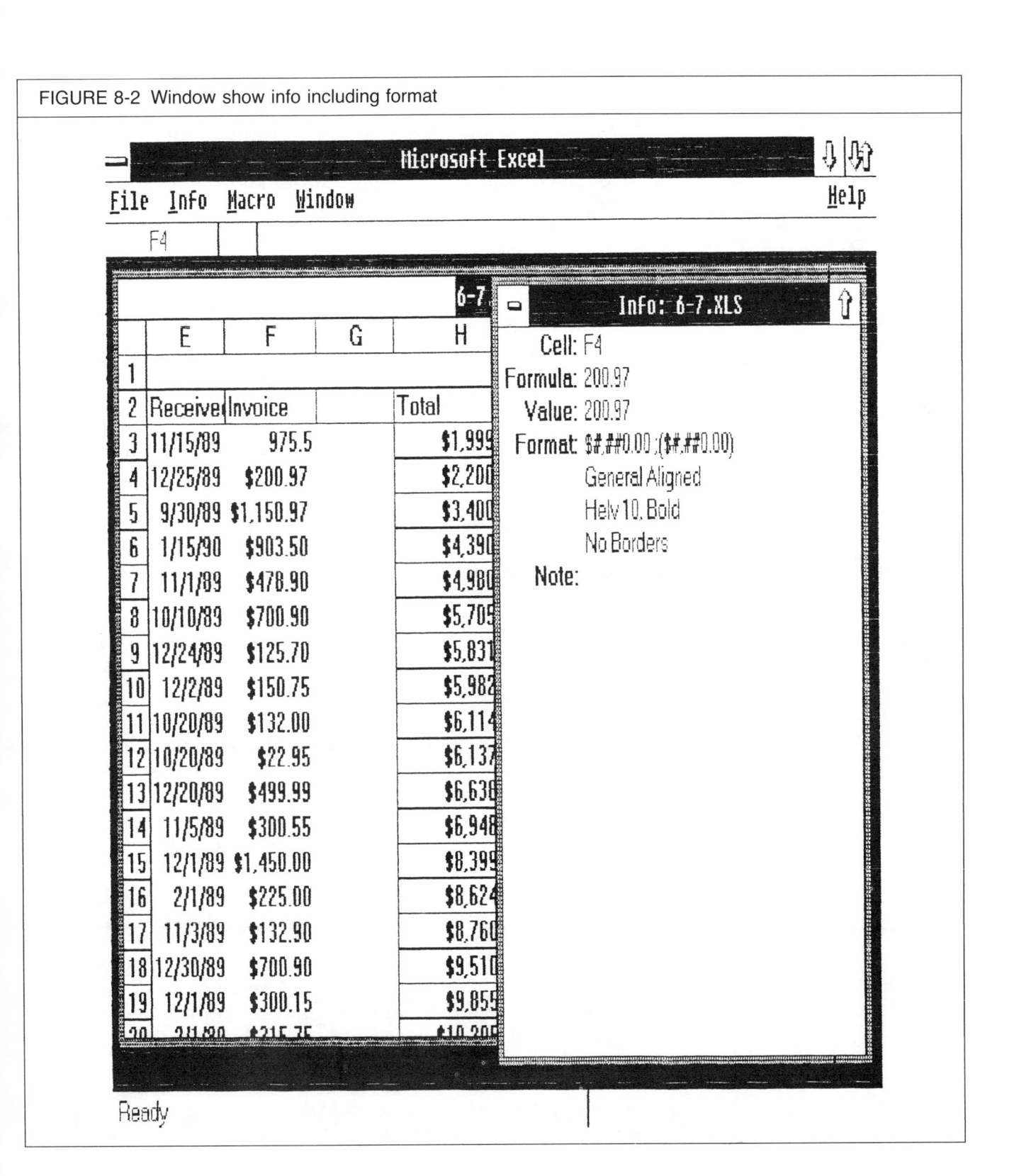

	E	F	G	H
1				
2	Received	Invoice		Total
3	11/15/89	975.5		$1,999
4	12/25/89	$200.97		$2,200
5	9/30/89	$1,150.97		$3,400
6	1/15/90	$903.50		$4,390
7	11/1/89	$478.90		$4,980
8	10/10/89	$700.90		$5,705
9	12/24/89	$125.70		$5,831
10	12/2/89	$150.75		$5,982
11	10/20/89	$132.00		$6,114
12	10/20/89	$22.95		$6,137
13	12/20/89	$499.99		$6,638
14	11/5/89	$300.55		$6,948
15	12/1/89	$1,450.00		$8,399
16	2/1/89	$225.00		$8,624
17	11/3/89	$132.90		$8,760
18	12/30/89	$700.90		$9,510
19	12/1/89	$300.15		$9,855
20	2/1/90	$215.75		$10,205

Info: 6-7.XLS

Cell: F4
Formula: 200.97
Value: 200.97
Format: $#,##0.00_);($#,##0.00)
    General Aligned
    Helv 10, Bold
    No Borders
Note:

we will be using both files. To open the files, use ALT or /, file, open; change the default directory if necessary. Then arrange to have both files displayed simultaneously (use window arrange all).

We will use the file of requesters to add notes to the circulation budget worksheet: you might want to know when to consult the requester worksheet when an order comes in. Thus, you will add a note to each vendor's name if a request has been made. To add a note, select the cell, depress the ALT or / key to gain access to the menu bar, select the formula pull-down menu, and choose note. Then type the appropriate notes for the vendors.

Now you can use formula select special to discover which cells have notes. To do this, depress the ALT or / key, pull-down the formula menu, and choose the select special dialog box. Indicate notes and then depress the ENTER key or choose OK. The cells with notes will be selected by Excel.

If you were using this worksheet, you could have the notes displayed as you scrolled through the worksheet. To do this, use window show info and window arrange all. The information, including the notes, associated with each selected cell will be shown.

Save the workspace; when you open the workspace, both worksheets will be opened for you and you will be able to use them together. To save a workspace, depress the ALT or / key, select the file pull-down menu, and choose the save workspace dialog box. Name the workspace; then depress the ENTER key or choose OK. Then close both files.

To continue the review, open the worksheet with the library's book budget. Select the cell with the heading remaining and add a note to it detailing where the remaining number came from (budget minus invoice might be sufficient). To add a note, depress the ALT or / key, select formula, and choose note. Then type the note. When ENTER is depressed or OK chosen, the note will be added.

Now add notes to the totals at the bottom of the used portion of the worksheet. For each one, add a note detailing how the figure was obtained. After the notes have been added, you can use formula select special to select those cells which have notes.

At this point you will not be able to read the notes. To read them depress the ALT or / key, select window, and choose show info. Then repeat the process of selecting window and choose arrange all. This will permit you to view the worksheet and the information about the highlighted cell simultaneously.

Now use formula select special again to select the cells containing notes. As you highlight each of the selected cells (using the TAB or ENTER key to move forward through the selections or the

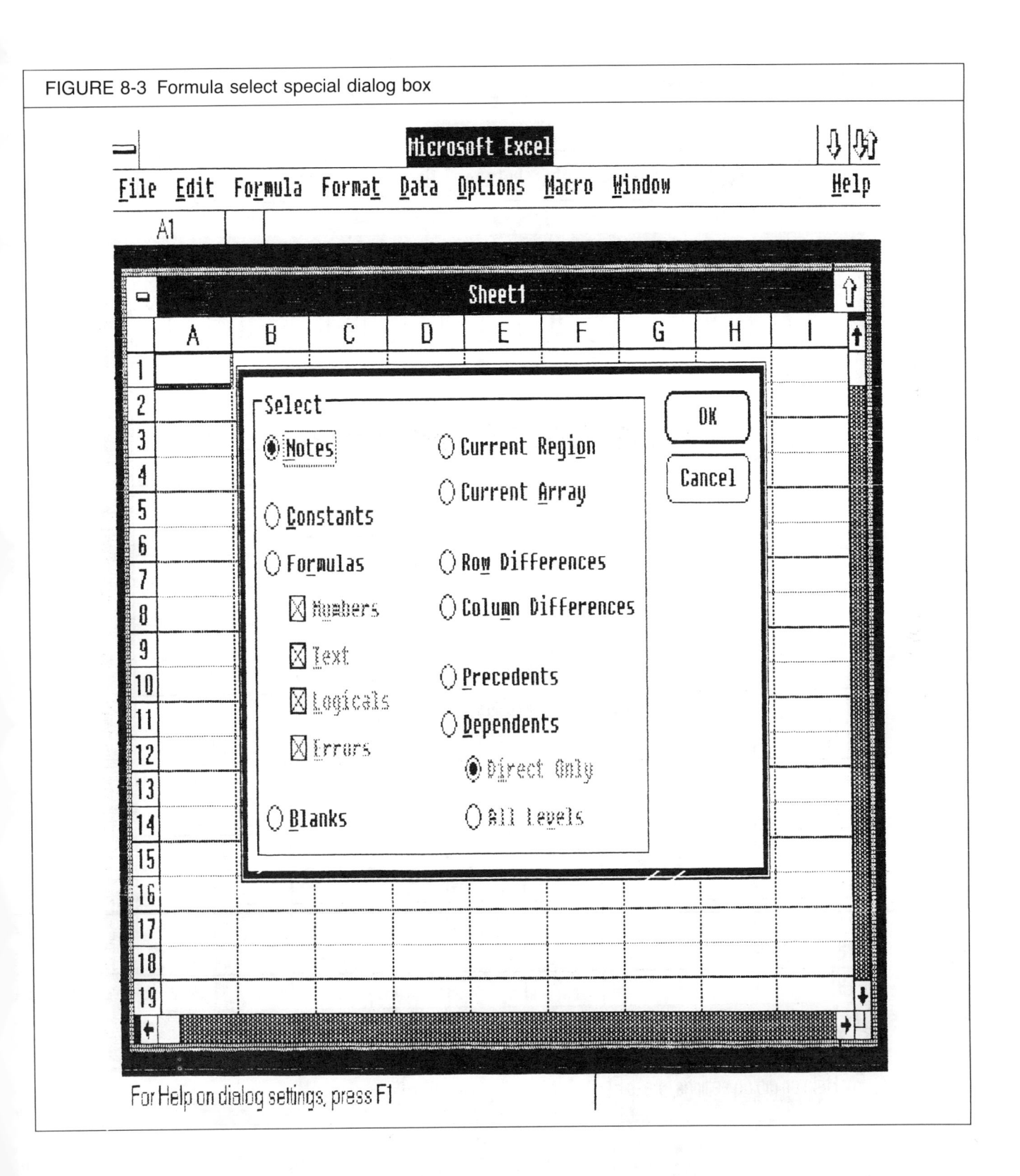

EXCEL FEATURES I **87**

FIGURE 8-3 Formula select special dialog box

Select
- ◉ Notes
- ○ Constants
- ○ Formulas
  - ☒ Numbers
  - ☒ Text
  - ☒ Logicals
  - ☒ Errors
- ○ Blanks
- ○ Current Region
- ○ Current Array
- ○ Row Differences
- ○ Column Differences
- ○ Precedents
- ○ Dependents
  - ◉ Direct Only
  - ○ All Levels

[OK] [Cancel]

For Help on dialog settings, press F1

FIGURE 8-4 Formula replace dialog box

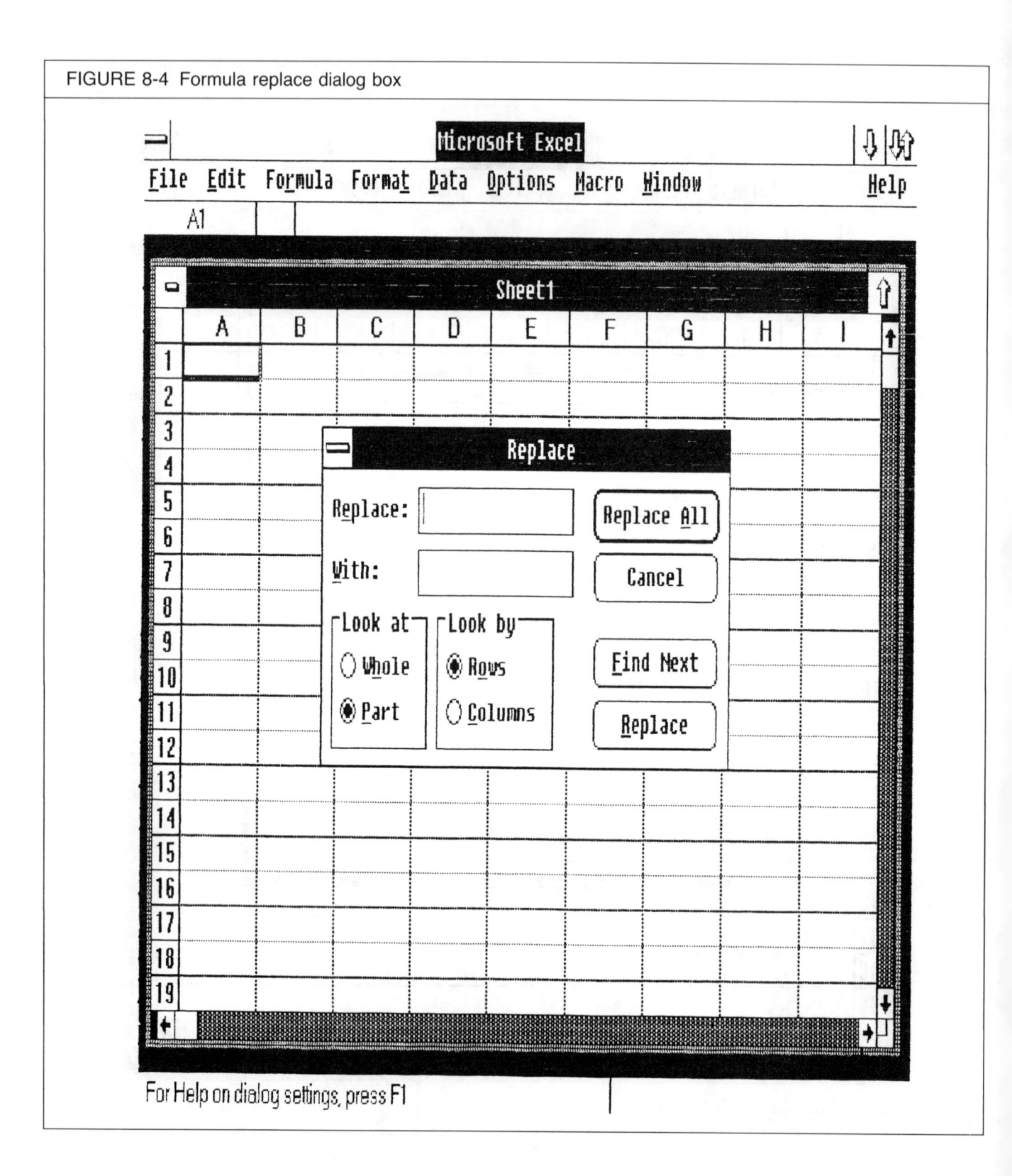

SHIFT and TAB or SHIFT and ENTER keys to move backwards through the selections) the information about the highlighted cell, including the note, is visible.

Save the worksheet, giving it a new name if you want to keep this file as a separate file. Use file save as to give it a new name; if you use file save you will replace the old file with the new. Then you can save the workspace; when the workspace is opened, the information window will also be opened. To save a workspace, use file save workspace.

9 EXCEL FEATURES II

To continue our tour through Excel we will use the circulation department's budget worksheet. Before opening that file, close all other open files. To close a file, depress the ALT or / key to gain access to the menu bar, select the file pull-down menu, and choose close. To open a file, repeat the process except choose open from the file pull-down menu. Change the default directory if necessary.

With the circulation department budget worksheet on screen, depress the ALT or / key, select the window pull-down menu, and choose show info. Then repeat the process of selecting the window pull-down menu and choose arrange all: you will now have the circulation department budget and the information about the highlighted cell displayed simultaneously.

You may have a problem at this point: the window arrange all command may have included a blank worksheet which may have been displayed at the beginning of your Excel session. If this is the case, depress the ALT or / key, select the window pull-down menu, and make the blank worksheet the active worksheet. Then depress the ALT or / key, select the file pull-down menu, and choose close. This will close the blank worksheet. Then depress the ALT or / key, select the window pull-down menu, and choose arrange all. Now only the circulation department budget sheet and its information window will be displayed.

Make the information window the active document. To do this, depress the ALT or / key, select window, and choose show info. Using a mouse, move the pointer to the information window and click. Then depress the ALT or / key, select the info pull-down menu (this pull-down menu is only available when the window is the active document), and you will see a list of the items of information that can be shown in the window information display. Choose format and depress the ENTER key (see Figure 9.1).

Now the window display shows the cell location, the formula (if any), the format (including the alignment, font, and borders if any), and the note (if any). Make the circulation budget the active document (ALT or /, window, and choose the worksheet). Scroll through the document. Notice that the formats are different for many of the cells.

FORMATS

Though you have not yet specified any formats, Excel automatically recognizes some formats. The formats automatically recognized

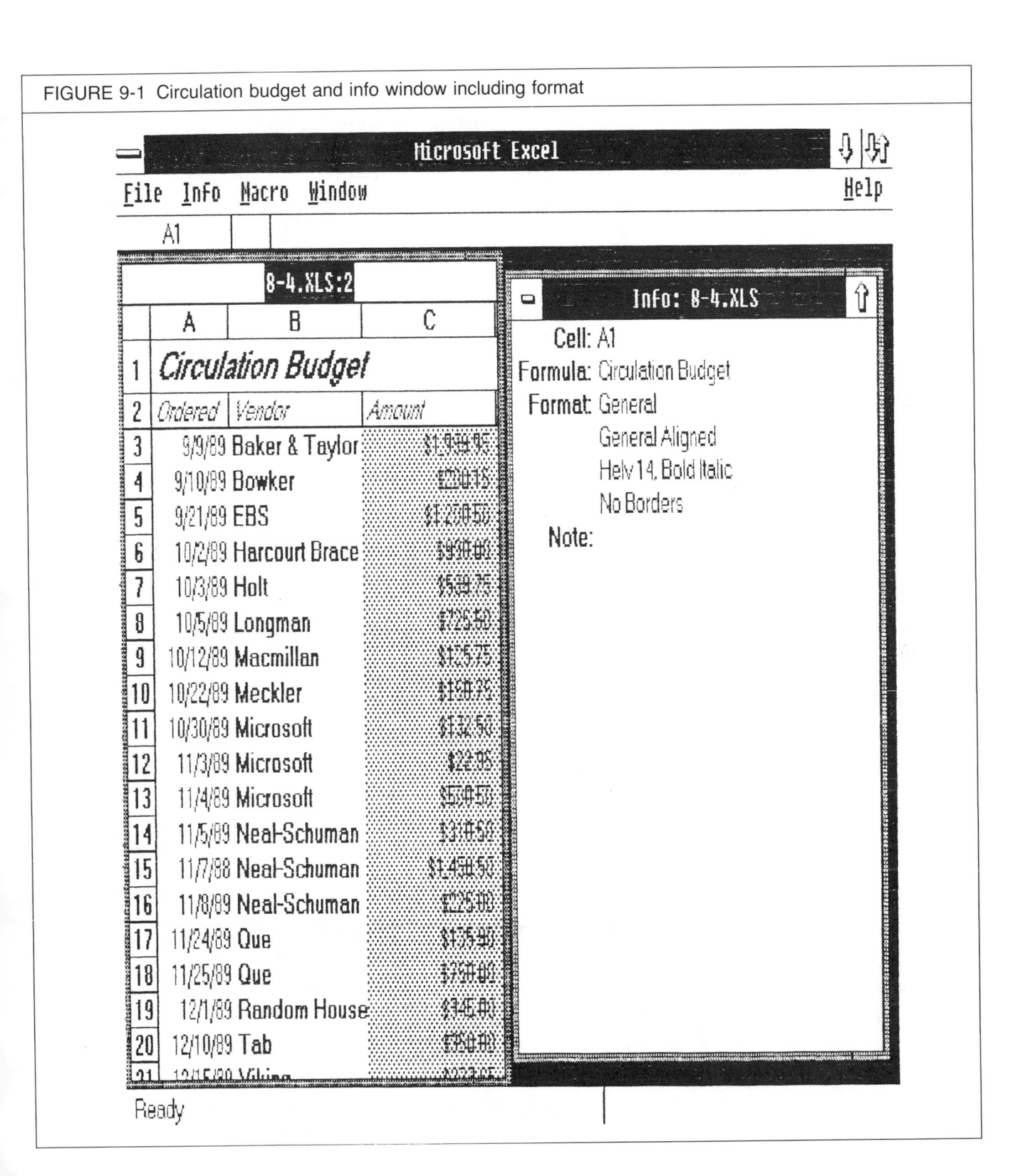

FIGURE 9-1 Circulation budget and info window including format

by Excel are: dollar, percent, negative number, date, and text. In other words, when you typed a dollar amount such as $45.05 in a cell, Excel converted the format of the cell to dollar format. Likewise, when you typed a date such as 11/23/90, Excel converted that cell to a date format.

The format chosen for a particular cell or range of cells determines how the entry will be displayed. Excel has 21 built-in formats, and you can design your own if you need one that is not listed. To discover what formats are available, depress the ALT or / key to gain access to the menu bar, select the format pull-down menu, and choose the number dialog box. You can examine all the available formats in the list box; if you add custom formats to the list, they will be placed at the end. If you add a custom format, you can delete it; only custom formats can be deleted.

It must be stressed that formatting does not change the number that was entered. Formatting only changes the manner in which the number is displayed and printed.

USING FORMATS

To format a cell or range of cells, select it. Then depress the ALT or / key to gain access to the menu bar. Select the format pull-down menu. Then choose the number dialog box. From the list of available formats, choose one. Depress the ENTER key or choose the OK button. Excel will format the cell or range of cells as you indicated.

To see the way that Excel uses the different formats, you can select a blank range of the worksheet and use different formats for different cells; use three adjacent cells for each format. Then type a number in each of the top three cells. Let the first number be a positive number (23), the second a negative number (-23), and the third a decimal number (.23). Then copy the contents of the three cells down to the rest of the formatted cells using edit copy and edit paste. Notice how the display changes depending on the format chosen for the individual cells.

Edit Clear: When you are finished examining this portion of your worksheet, select all the cells you used to examine formatting and then depress the ALT or / key to gain access to the menu bar. Then select edit and choose clear. Clear all. Edit clear can be used to clear formulas, values, and/or formats.

Number Formats: The number formats are composed of a maximum of four parts separated by semicolons. The final section is the text section, and it is optional. If the format has fewer than four sections, the text section must be preceded by the @ symbol: this indicates to Excel that the following is a text format.

If there are three other sections, the first section determines how positive numbers are formatted. The second section determines how negative numbers are formatted. The third section determines the formatting for zeros.

If there are only two sections in the number portion of a format, the first determines the format for positive numbers and zeros. The second section determines the format for negative numbers.

If the format has only one section in the number portion of the format, that formatting applies to all numbers.

Format Symbols: Excel uses symbols in the format number list box to indicate the formats available. The Excel manual lists all of these symbols and explains what each accomplishes. You can use these symbols to create your own number formats.

For example, both 0 and # are digit place holders. Text placed between quotation marks (such as "Text") will be displayed. You can also indicate colors for the display of particular portions of the cell format (for example, negative numbers can be displayed in red while positive numbers can be displayed in black).

CUSTOM FORMATS

To create a custom format, select the cell or cells that you want to format. Then depress the ALT or / key, select the format pull-down menu, and choose number. In the format box either edit an existing format or type a new one. Finally depress the ENTER key or choose the OK button. The selection will be formatted as desired.

For example, though Excel does not offer it as a standard format, you could design a format that hides entries from view. By designing a format that has just three semicolons (;;;), and choosing a cell or range of cells to format using this custom format, you will hide the information from view. This happens because there is no indication of how Excel should display positive numbers, negative numbers, zeros, or text. Therefore, the cells would be hidden.

You could also have a custom format for social security numbers. In the format box you could type

000-00-0000

When a cell is formatted using this custom format, the person entering the information could type

123456789

Excel would display

123-45-6789

You could even add to this custom format to make it a bit more specific:

"SS#" 000-00-0000

Because the "SS#" is in quotation marks, it will be used as text in all the entries placed in cells formatted with this custom format, followed by the entered number:

SS# 123-45-6789

Thus the formatting can eliminate the need for repetitive typing.

EDIT PASTE SPECIAL

Excel offers a command that allows you to copy a cell's format to another cell or range of cells. You can use this command to copy the format, formula, value, and/or note.

Select the cell to be copied first. Depress the ALT or / key, select the edit pull-down menu, and choose copy. Then choose the cell or range of cells to which you want to copy. Depress the ALT or / key, select the edit pull-down menu, and choose the paste special dialog box (see Figure 9.2). From this dialog box choose the information that you want copied. In addition, you can choose to add, subtract, multiply or divide the values in the cells with those being pasted. Otherwise you can replace the present cell contents with those being pasted using the edit paste special command. Complete the command by depressing the ENTER key or choosing the OK button.

FORMAT CELL PROTECTION

Once your worksheet has formulas, you may be concerned that someone might change one of them. Excel offers a way to prevent a formula from being edited: format cell protection. Select the cell or range of cells that you want to protect. Depress the ALT or / key to gain access to the menu bar. Select the format pull-down menu. Choose the cell protection dialog box. This dialog box has only two choices: locked and hidden. For either of the choices to be in effect, the user must also use the options protect document command.

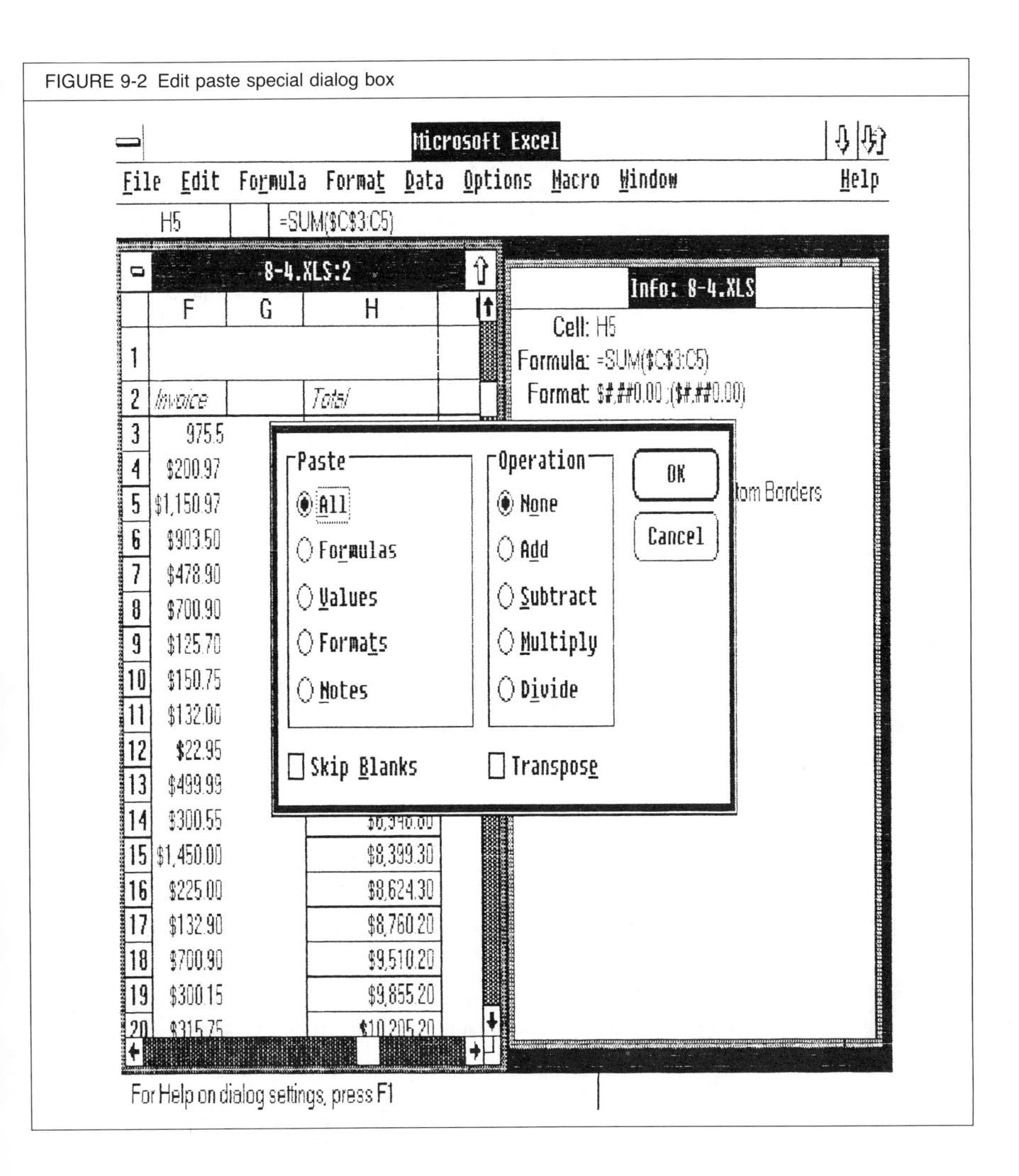

FIGURE 9-2 Edit paste special dialog box

Options Protect Document: This command controls whether the format cell protection is in effect or not. This command effects the entire worksheet. The dialog box revealed by depressing the ALT or / key, selecting the options pull-down menu, and choosing protect document offers the choice of protecting the contents and/or the windows. By protecting the contents, the user will not be able to change the contents or formats of the protected cells. By protecting the windows, the user cannot move, size, or hide a window.

This dialog box also offers the user a chance to include a password. If a password is specified, protection can only be taken off with the password. If the password is lost or forgotten, the worksheet's protection cannot be reversed.

Format cell protection is only in effect if the options protect document command is used. If it is not used, Excel will ignore format cell protection commands.

Locked and Hidden Cell Protection: Choosing locked in the format cell protection dialog box indicates that the specified cells cannot be edited. When you begin an Excel session, all cells in a worksheet are locked. The locking is only in effect if you invoke the options protect document command.

Choosing hidden and invoking the options protect document command will prevent the selected cells from having their formulas displayed in the formula bar. At the beginning of an Excel session, no cells are hidden.

Remember that the format cell protection command only works in conjunction with the options protect document command. Used independently, the format cell protection command is ignored by Excel.

LARGE WORKSHEETS

When working with a large worksheet, it may be difficult to go to a particular cell, find information in a cell, or allow Excel to calculate the worksheet. Excel offers a number of handy commands that can save time. Among these commands are: formula goto, formula find, options calculation, and options calculate now.

Formula Goto: If you want to quickly go to a named reference on a worksheet, use formula goto. For example, if you wanted to move the cellpointer to cell A10 quickly without having to use the direction keys, you could simply depress the ALT or / key to gain access to the menu bar, select the formula pull-down menu, and choose goto. A shortcut key to obtain the formula goto dialog box is the function key F5. The formula goto dialog box will look like Figure 9.3.

The dialog box lists the named references on the current worksheet. To go to one of these named references, choose it from the list box. On the other hand, to go to a specific cell, type that cell's address in the reference box. When you depress the ENTER key or choose OK, the cellpointer will be moved. Obtain the formula goto dialog box and move the cellpointer to cell A10.

Now that you are in cell A10, move the cellpointer to cell C12 using the formula goto command. You can use the shortcut key, the function key F5.

If you again depress the shortcut key, the function key F5, you will notice that Excel has proposed a reference for you: your previous location, cell A10. Using the formula goto command allows you to toggle back and forth between two locations.

You can also use the formula goto command to go to a cell on a different worksheet. In the reference box type the name of the worksheet followed by an exclamation point (!). Then type the named reference or the cell location. When you depress the ENTER key or choose OK, the cellpointer will be moved.

Formula Find: Excel offers a command that allows the user to locate text or numbers in cells in a worksheet. This is the formula find command. To use it, depress the ALT or / key to gain access to the menu bar, select the formula pull-down menu, and choose the formula find dialog box (see Figure 9.4).

The formula find dialog box asks what you want to find. In this box type =SUM. Then choose to look in formulas. Choose to look at part rather than the whole; if you look in part, Excel will match what you have typed to a part of the cell; if you look in whole, the entire cell must match what you have typed. Depress the ENTER key or choose OK and Excel will highlight a cell that contains the characters =SUM. To go to the next occurrence, depress the function key F7; to go to the previous occurrence, depress the SHIFT and F7 keys simultaneously.

Formula find is used to find specific text or numbers in a cell. You can have Excel look in formulas, values, or notes. To find specific records in a database, you should use the data find command.

When using formula find, if you select a range of cells, Excel will only look in the selected range. If you select only one cell, Excel will search the entire worksheet.

When typing what to find, Excel permits you to use wildcards.

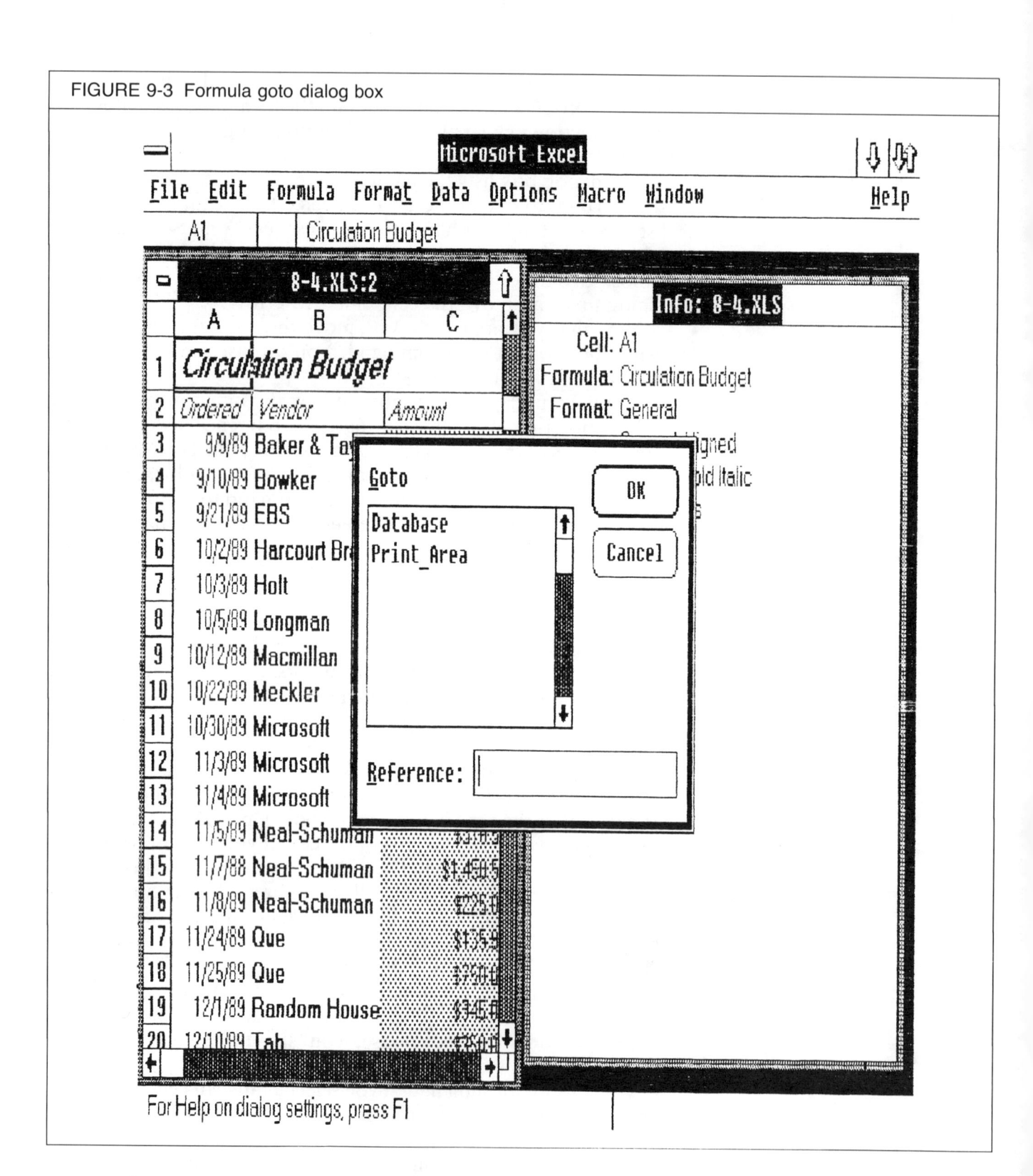

FIGURE 9-3 Formula goto dialog box

EXCEL FEATURES II **99**

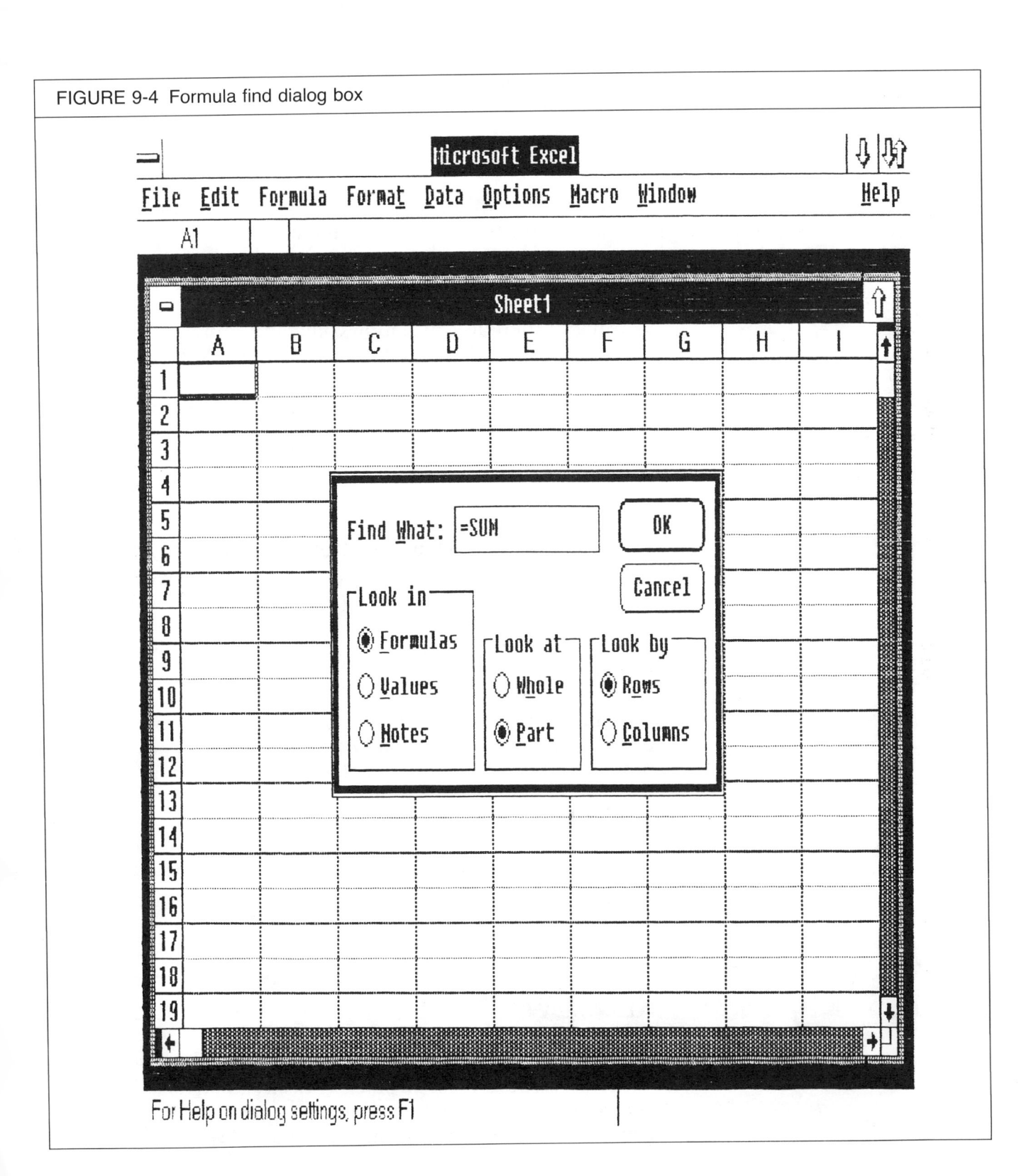

FIGURE 9-4 Formula find dialog box

SUMMARY

In this chapter, you have:

1. learned about formats;
2. used edit clear;
3. learned about number formats;
4. created custom formats;
5. used edit paste special;
6. learned about cell protection;
7. learned about options protect document;
8. learned about locked and hidden cells;
9. used formula goto;
10. used formula find;
11. learned about options calculation;
12. learned about options calculate now;
13. learned about options calculate document.

The question mark (?) can stand for any one character. The asterisk (*) can stand for any number of characters.

The shortcut key for the formula find command is the function key F7.

Options Calculation: In a large and complex worksheet, Excel may take some time to calculate the worksheet. Excel only calculates those formulas that need to be calculated, but in a large worksheet you may not want to spend that much time. Excel offers a solution: the options calculation command.

Using the options calculation command, you can tell Excel not to calculate the worksheet automatically. To do this, depress the ALT or / key to gain access to the menu bar, select the options pull-down menu, and choose the calculation dialog box. In it you can change the default calculation method from automatic to manual. If you do this, Excel will not calculate the worksheet until you tell it to by using the options calculate now or options calculate document command.

Options Calculate Now and Options Calculate Document: Once the calculation of a document has been changed from automatic, you must invoke the options calculate now or options calculate document command to calculate the worksheet. The options calculate now command calculates worksheets, charts, etc; the options calculate document only calculates the active worksheet, chart, etc.

To invoke the options calculate now command, depress the ALT or / key, select the options pull-down menu, and choose calculate now. The shortcut key for this command is the function key F9. To invoke the options calculate document command, depress the ALT or / key, hold down the SHIFT key while selecting the options pull-down menu, and choose calculate document. This option only appears when you hold down the SHIFT key while selecting the options menu.

REVIEW

To review what was learned in this chapter we will use the library budget worksheet. Close all other worksheets and then retrieve the library budget. To close worksheets, depress the ALT or / key, select the file pull-down menu, and choose close. If you have not previously saved any changes on the open worksheet, Excel will ask if you want to save these changes. To open a worksheet, depress the ALT or / key, select the file pull-down menu, and choose open. Change the default directory if necessary. Then choose the file containing the library's budget.

First show the information about each highlighted cell in an information window. To do this, depress the ALT or / key, select window, and choose show info. The information about the highlighted cell will be shown, but you will not be able to see the worksheet.

Choose to show both the worksheet and the cell information. To do this, depress the ALT or / key, select the window pull-down menu, and choose arrange all.

If you began working with the blank worksheet displayed before retrieving the library budget worksheet, you will have three panes on screen. If this is the case, close the blank worksheet window. To close this window, make it the active window by depressing ALT or /, selecting window, and choosing the blank window. Then depress ALT or /, select file, and choose close. Now you will have to arrange all again by depressing the ALT or / key, selecting window, and choosing arrange all.

If the information window does not include information about the highlighted cell's format, make that visible also. To do this, make the info window active (depress ALT or /, select window, and choose show info). Then depress ALT or /, select info, and choose format. The format of the highlighted cell will be included in the info window.

Scroll through the document noting the different formats for the different cells. On this worksheet, Excel has automatically formatted some cells because of the types of information that were entered.

Now format cells G3 through G8 for percent. To format a range of cells, select the cells using the SHIFT and ARROW keys or the EXTEND key, the function key F8. Then depress the ALT or / key, select the format pull-down menu, and choose the number dialog box. Select the percent format. When you depress the ENTER key or choose OK, the selected cells will be formatted for percent.

Use the G column to compute the percent of the budget for each department that was already spent. To do this, type the formula

$$=E3/C3$$

in the cell G3. When you depress the ENTER key, the percent already spent will be displayed.

102 USING MICROSOFT EXCEL

Now copy this formula down the column. Use edit copy and edit paste to copy the formula to cells G4 through G8. Excel automatically adjusts the relative cell references and the percents are displayed.

Use the next column (column H) to compute the percent remaining. You could subtract the percent spent from 100, but another way of doing it is to use a formula:

= F3/C3

Copy this formula down the column as you copied the formula above. The relative cell addresses are adjusted automatically by Excel.

Look at your worksheet: the final column has not been formatted for percents. You can format the cells now in one of two ways.

First, you could select the cells and then depress the ALT or / key, select the format pull-down menu, and choose number. Then choose the percent format.

Alternatively, you could use edit paste special to copy the format from the G column to the H column. First select the used portion of the G column. Then depress the ALT or / key, select the edit pull-down menu, and choose copy. Then select the used portion of the H column, depress the ALT or / key, select the edit pull-down menu, and choose the paste special dialog box. From this dialog box choose format. The format will be copied to the indicated cells. After adjusting the columns alignments (select the columns and then depress ALT, select format, choose alignment), the result will be like Figure 9.5.

Now practice using the formula goto command (see Figure 9.6). You can depress the ALT or / key, select the formula pull-down menu, and choose the goto dialog box. Or you could use the Excel

---

FIGURE 9-5 Book budget with percents

Library Book Budget

Date	Department	Budgeted	Encumbered	Invoiced	Remaining	Percent Spent	Percent Remaining
Nov-89	Serials	$30,000	$950.00	$800.75	29199.25	3%	97%
Nov-89	Reference	$10,000	$2,000.45	$1,999.75	8000.25	20%	80%
Nov-89	Circulation	$35,000	$13,555.75	$15,750.95	19249.05	45%	55%
Nov-90	Sp. Collection 1	$15,000	$750.95	$888.90	14111.1	6%	94%
Nov-89	Sp. Collection 2	$10,000	$889.45	$917.75	9082.25	9%	91%
	Totals	100000	18146.6	20358.1	79641.9	20%	80%

shortcut key, the function key F5. In either case, indicate that you want to go to cell A10. When you depress the ENTER key, cell A10 will be highlighted.

Now use the formula goto command again. Notice that the reference box lists your former cell location. You can now toggle back and forth between cell A10 and your previous location.

Use formula find to discover which cells have a division in them. To do this, you will have to use wildcards in the box asking what is to be found as follows:

=*/*

In other words, you are trying to find which cells contain a formula with anything divided by anything.

Excel highlights the first cell that meets this criteria. To scroll through the entire worksheet for cells that match this criteria, use

---

FIGURE 9-6 Books with formulas

Library Book Budget

Date	Department	Budgeted
32813	Serials	30000
32813	Reference	10000
32813	Circulation	35000
33178	Sp. Collection 1	15000
32813	Sp. Collection 2	10000
	Totals	=SUM(C3:C7)

Encumbered	Invoiced
950	800.75
2000.45	1999.75
13555.75	15750.95
750.95	888.9
889.45	917.75
=SUM(D3:D7)	=SUM(E3:E7)

Remaining	Percent Spent	Percent Remaining
=+C3-E3	=E3/C3	=F3/C3
=+C4-E4	=E4/C4	=F4/C4
=+C5-E5	=E5/C5	=F5/C5
=+C6-E6	=E6/C6	=F6/C6
=+C7-E7	=E7/C7	=F7/C7
=+C8-E8	=E8/C8	=F8/C8

the function key F7 to go forward and the combination of the SHIFT key and function key F7 to go backwards.

Save the worksheet with the new columns. To save the worksheet, depress the ALT or / key, select the file pull-down menu, and choose save (if you want to replace the existing library budget worksheet with the new one) or save as (if you want to retain the old and new library budgets).

10 CHARTING

Excel offers 44 predetermined charts, including area, bar. column, line, pie, scatter, and combination charts. These charts can be linked to a worksheet so that changes on the worksheet are automatically reflected on the chart.

To explore the world of Excel charts, we will be using the library book budget worksheet. First close any open worksheets, including the blank worksheet that Excel displays when beginning a session. To close a worksheet, depress the ALT or / key to gain access to the menu bar, select the file pull-down menu, and choose close. Then open the library book budget worksheet. To open the worksheet, depress the ALT or / key, select the file pull-down menu, and choose the open dialog box. Change the default directory if necessary and choose the appropriate file. When you depress the ENTER key or choose OK, the selected worksheet will be displayed.

Select the column containing the budgeted amounts. You can select these cells by holding down the SHIFT key while using the ARROW keys or by depressing the EXTEND key, the function key F8; then use the ARROW keys.

When the used portion of the column has been selected, press the function key F11. This is the chart key. You will see a display that looks like Figure 10.1.

Notice that the menu bar has been modified: this is the chart menu bar. Several of the items on the chart menu bar are the same as on the worksheet menu bar, but some items are different. The pull-down menus on the chart menu bar are: file, edit, gallery, chart, format, macro, and window.

GALLERY

The gallery pull-down menu lists the types of charts that are available. To change the type of chart displayed, depress the ALT or / key to gain access to the menu bar, select the gallery pull-down menu, and choose the chart type you want displayed (see Figure 10.2).

Notice that each of the chart types is followed by ellipses. This indicates that each of these choices will reveal a dialog box. These dialog boxes are actually different charts of each type, based on the selected data. For example, choose pie from the gallery pull-down menu. Then choose the fourth chart from the dialog box. Once one of the dialog box charts is chosen, Excel fills the entire display with that chart (see Figure 10.3). In the dialog box for each of the chart types there are also buttons for next and previous. These relate to the list of chart types from the gallery menu. You can use these choices to scroll through all the available chart types.

FIGURE 10-1 Initial chart

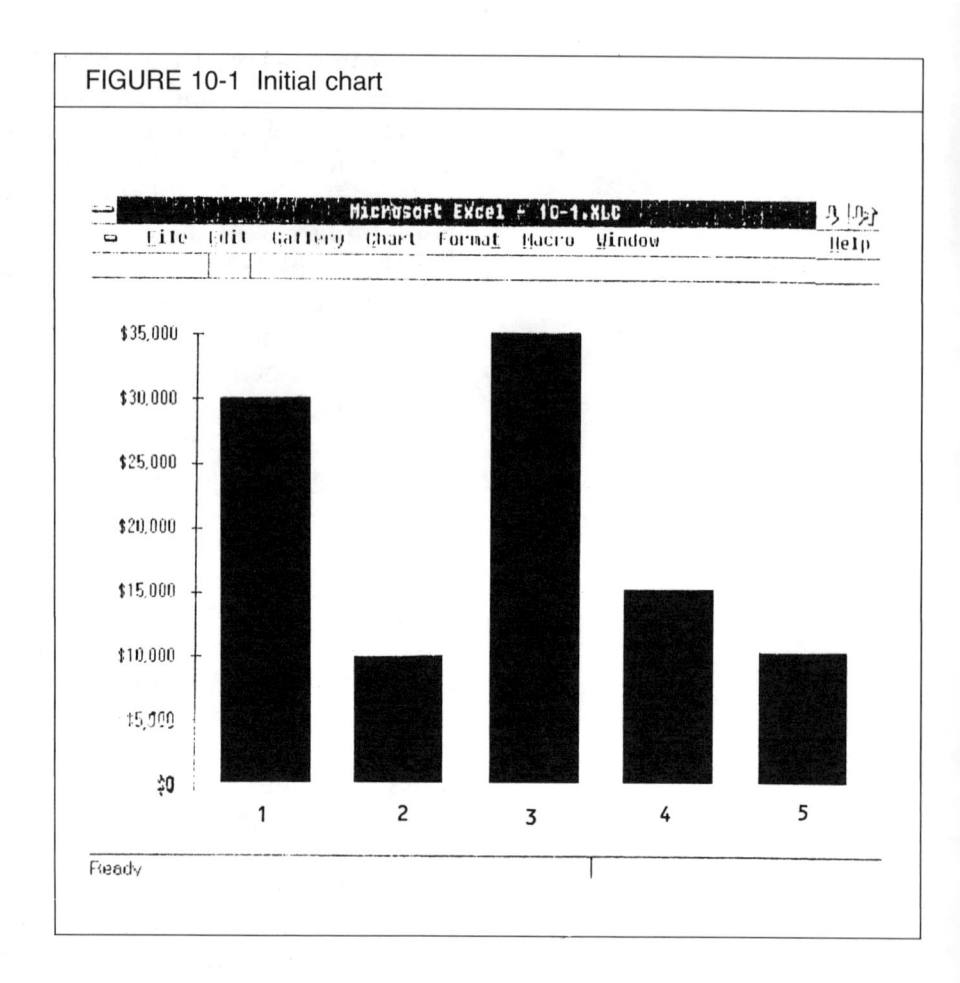

Also on the gallery pull-down menu are set preferred and preferred. You can use these two to set the type of chart that will be displayed when you depress the function key F11. To set a preferred chart, display that chart and then depress the ALT or / key, select the gallery pull-down menu, and then choose set preferred. After that, when you depress F11 or the ALT or / key, select the gallery pull-down menu, and choose preferred, the indicated chart type will be displayed. The initial default preferred chart is the column chart.

WINDOW ARRANGE ALL

As with multiple worksheets, you will probably want to be able to see the worksheet and its chart simultaneously. To do this, depress the ALT or / key, select the window pull-down menu, and choose

FIGURE 10-2 Gallery pull-down menus

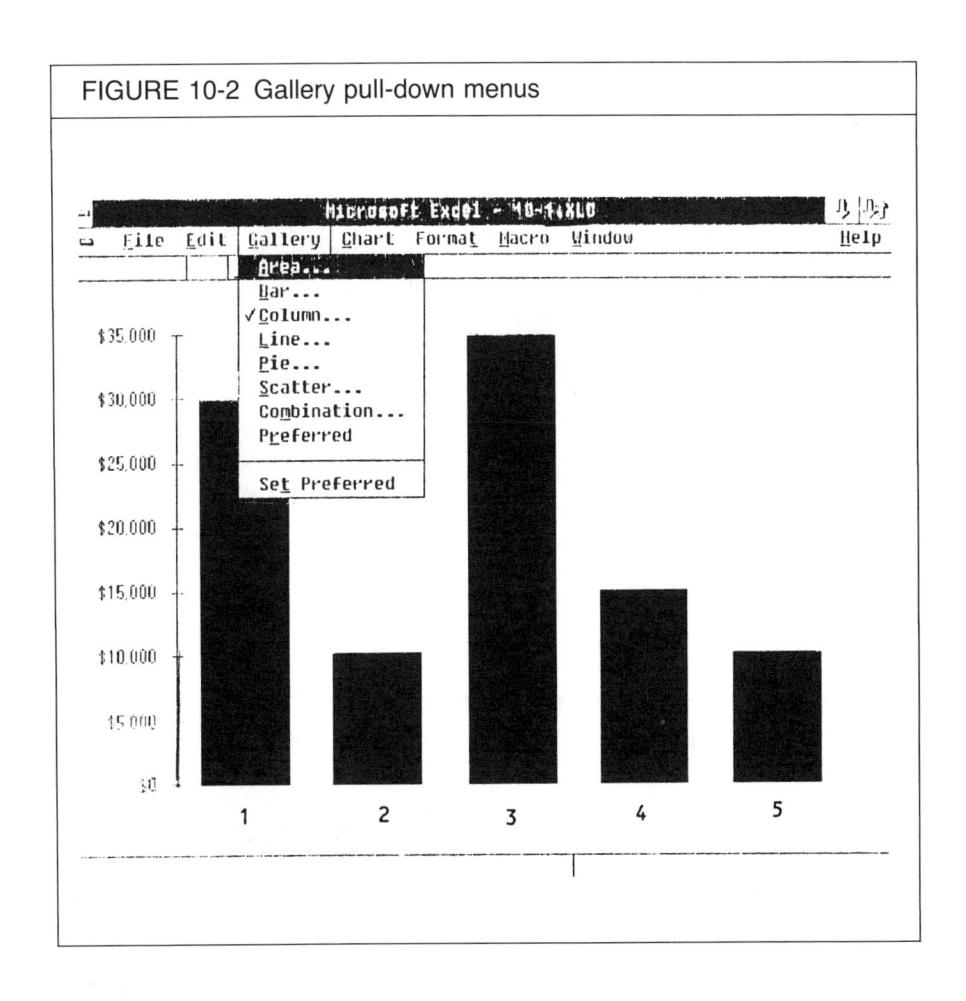

arrange all. The chart and worksheet will now be displayed side-by-side.

If you did not close the blank worksheet before opening the library book budget worksheet, you can now close it. To do this, make it the active window (ALT or /, window, and choose it); then use ALT or /, file, close. Then use ALT or /, window, arrange all again to have the chart and worksheet take the entire display area.

ADDING A TITLE

To add a title to the chart, make the chart the active document. If it is not the active document, depress the ALT or / key, select the window pull-down menu, and choose the chart. With a mouse, point and click on the chart. Then depress the ALT or / key, select the chart pull-down menu, and choose the attach text dialog box.

From this dialog box choose title. The word title will be placed at the top of the chart.

With the word title on the top of the chart, you can edit it by placing the word in the formula bar. Select the word and press the EDIT key, the function key F2. Then replace the word title with Book Budget. When you depress the ENTER key, the word title is replaced with Book Budget.

FORMAT FONT

The title on a chart should stand out, but this one doesn't. You can change the size of the font, make it bold, and underline it using the format font command. Depress the ALT or / key, select the format pull-down menu, and choose the font dialog box. From this dialog box choose to increase the size, make the title bold, and underline it. Then depress the ENTER key or choose OK (see Figure 10.4).

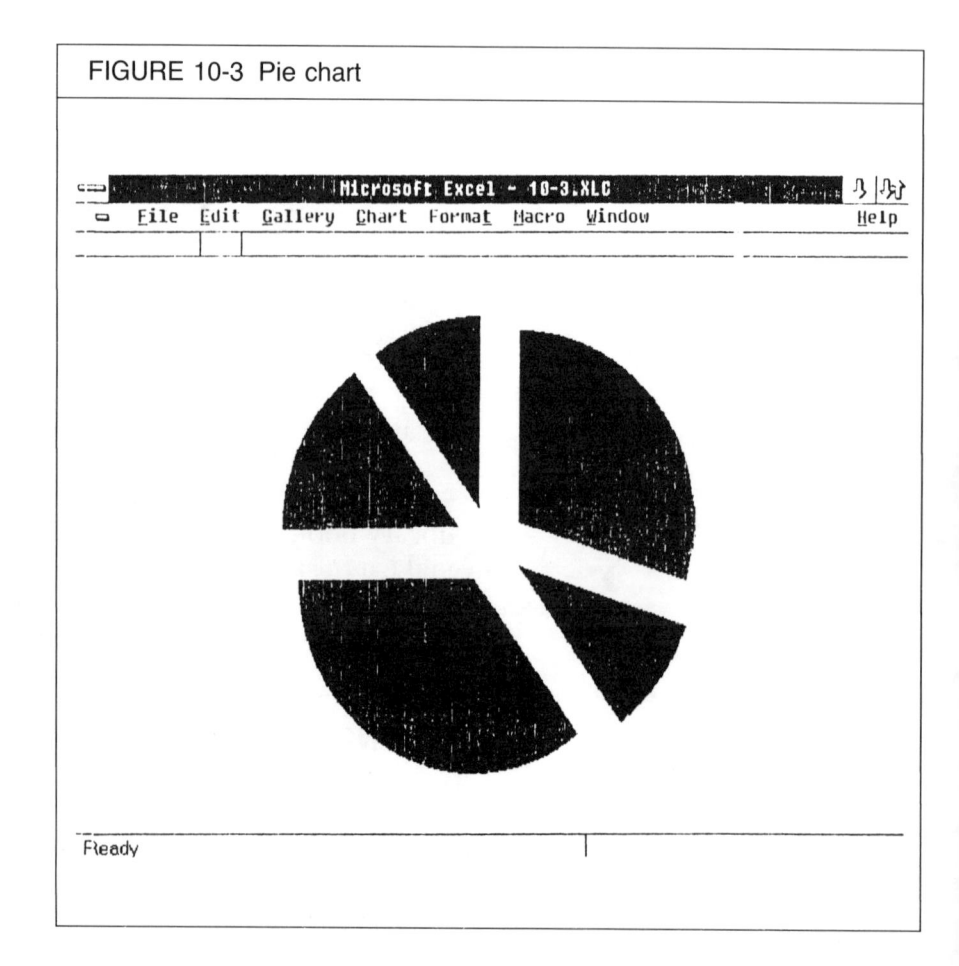

FIGURE 10-3 Pie chart

CATEGORIES LABELED

You can have Excel label the different categories automatically, or you can label them yourself. To have Excel label them, select the columns containing the department names and their budgeted amounts. Then depress the function key F11. The chart will look like Figure 10.5.

Now depress the ALT or / key to gain access to the menu bar. Select the gallery pull-down menu, and select various chart types to see how Excel handles the labels; on some charts the labels are displayed; on others they are not.

If you decide to use this labeling technique, use chart attach text to place a title on the chart. Then remember to use format font to make the text larger, bold, and underlined.

Excel also allows you to label the parts of a chart after it is created.

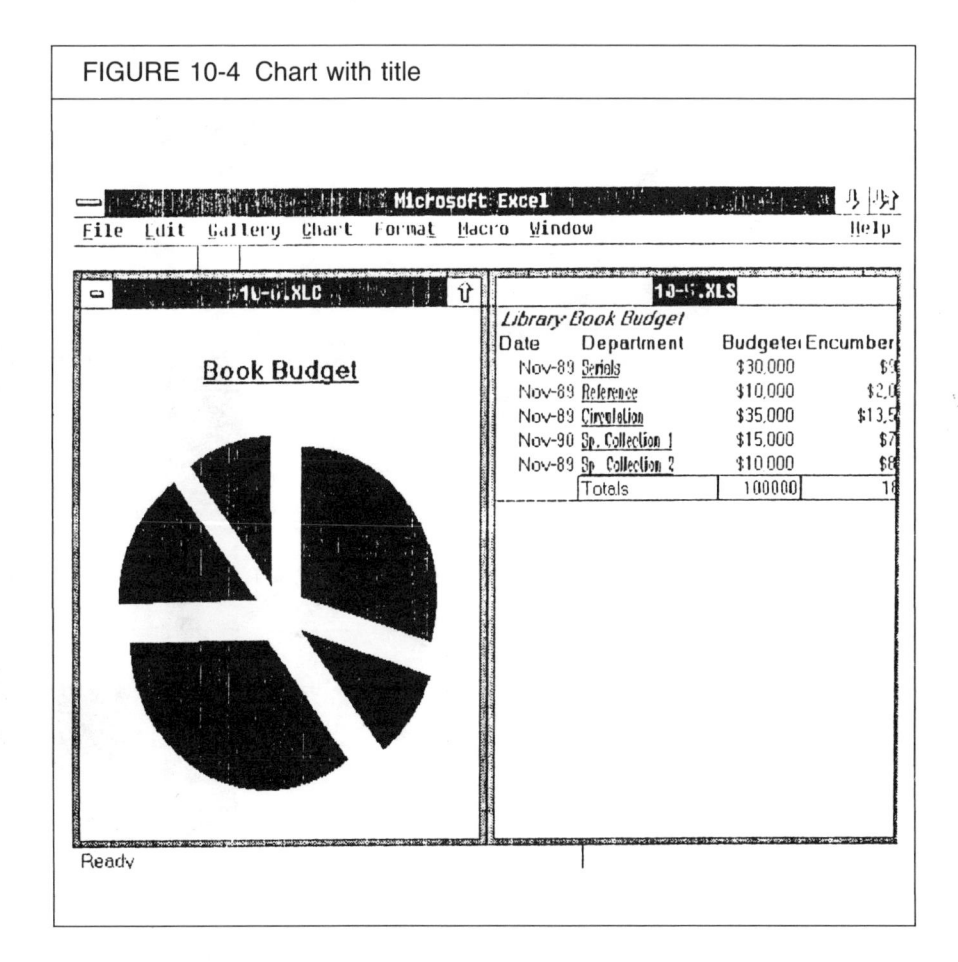

FIGURE 10-4 Chart with title

ATTACHING TEXT

To attach text to a chart, make the chart the active window and type the text. It will appear in the formula bar; when the ENTER key is depressed, it will appear toward the middle of the chart. Of course, you might not want to display the text where Excel has placed it, so you can move it.

MOVING TEXT

To move text on a chart, select the text, then depress the ALT or / key, select the format pull-down menu, and choose move. The text you have typed will be seen in a small box, which can be moved with the ARROW keys or mouse. As you move the box, the text does not follow. It will be placed where the box is once the ENTER key is depressed.

Type the word Serials and then depress the ENTER key. Now

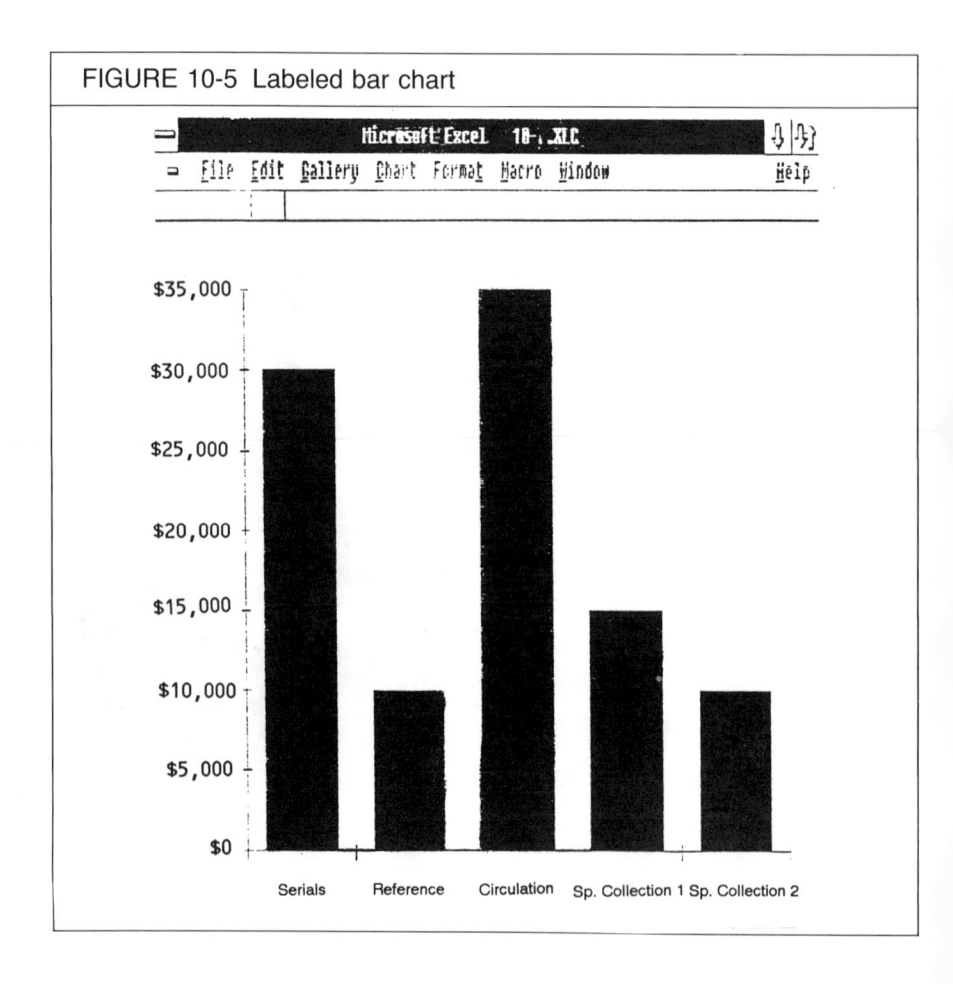

FIGURE 10-5 Labeled bar chart

move it to the appropriate part of the chart. You can place the word outside the piece of pie or you can place it directly on the appropriate slice.

SIZING TEXT

You can make the objects or text on the chart a different size by selecting the text or object and then using the format size command. To select text or an object, use the ARROW keys to enclose it in small boxes; use the ARROW keys repeatedly until the correct object or text is highlighted. Then depress the ALT or / key, select the format pull-down menu, and choose size. Use the ARROW keys to change the outline of the box that appears. When the ENTER key is depressed, the size of the object or text selected will be changed.

Select the word Serials and make it larger. Then use the format size command and make the word larger.

Label each of the sections of the chart in this manner. Type the label into the formula bar, depress ENTER, and then move and size each of them.

ADDING AN ARROW

To call special attention to one portion of a chart, you can add an arrow. To add an arrow, depress the ALT or / key, select the chart pull-down menu, and choose add arrow. The arrow will appear in the top left portion of the chart.

This may not be where you want to have the arrow placed; it can be moved and sized. To move the arrow, select it if it is not already selected, depress the ALT or / key, select the format pull-down menu, and choose size first. The format size command changes the size of the arrow and can also be used to change the direction in which the arrow is pointing. Use the ARROW keys. Depress the ENTER key to make the changes to the arrow.

After sizing the arrow, move it by depressing the ALT or / key, selecting the format pull-down menu, and choosing the move command. Move the arrow using the ARROW keys. When you have placed it where you want it, depress the ENTER key.

Add an arrow to the chart to draw more attention to the reference budget. Depress the ALT or / key, select the chart pull-down menu, and choose add arrow. Now size the arrow and change the direction it is pointing. To size the arrow, depress the ALT or / key, select the format pull-down menu, and choose size. Use the ARROW keys or mouse to adjust the size. Then move the arrow. To move the arrow, depress the ALT or / key, select the format pull-down menu, and choose move. Use the ARROW keys or mouse to move the arrow.

CHANGING THE APPEARANCE OF TEXT

You can now change the appearance of the text by using the format font command. These changes include changing the font, changing its size, and even underlining it. The procedure is identical to that described in modifying the title of the chart: select the text to be modified, depress the ALT or / key, select format, and choose the font dialog box. Make your selections and then depress the ENTER key or choose OK.

Excel allows you to customize charts with many other commands. Many of them are only available when using the full menus associated with the chart menus. To change from short to full menus, depress the ALT or / key to gain access to the menu bar, select the chart pull-down menu, and choose full menus. To return to the short menus, repeat the process and choose short menus. The short menus choice only appears when the full menus are displayed; the full menus choice only appears when the short menus are displayed.

Each of the following commands is invoked by depressing the ALT or / key to gain access to the menu bar, selecting the appropriate pull-down menu, and making the indicated choice. These commands will only be available when the chart is the active document.

Chart Axes: This command determines whether or not the chart's axes will be visible. Excel names the axes value and category axes. The value axis is usually the Y axis; the category axis is usually the X axis. In bar charts, however, these are reversed. This command is not available for charts that do not have axes, such as the pie chart.

Chart Add Overlay: This command can be used to divide the chart series in half, with half the series being placed on the main chart and half on the overlay.

Format Overlay: The format overlay command controls the type and format of the overlay chart.

Format Main Chart: This command controls the main chart's type and format. Some of the options in the dialog box may be grayed; these choices are not available for the chosen chart.

Chart Gridlines: The chart gridlines command determines whether or not major and minor gridlines will be displayed on the chart. This command is only available with certain types of charts.

Chart Delete: You can delete arrows, legends, or overlays by using the chart delete command.

Chart Calculate Now: If you have changed the calculation method from automatic, you can use the chart calculate now command to calculate the chart. The shortcut key for this command is the function key F9.

Chart Protect Document: This command determines whether the series and formats for a chart can be altered. In addition, it determines if a chart window can be sized, moved, or altered. The command is similar to options protect document. Including a password is possible.

Chart Select Chart: The chart select chart command selects the entire chart in the active window. This command can be used before some of the other commands, such as format pattern.

Format Patterns: The format patterns command controls the appearance of a selected object on a chart. If you want to select the entire chart, use the chart select chart. The options available may include invisible, which if chosen means the object will not be displayed, style, shadow, and weight of a line, border, etc.

Format Legend: This command controls the position and orientation of the legend. Format legend options include top, bottom, corner, and vertical. Also included are font and pattern.

Format Scale: The format scale command controls the appearance of the axes and the order of category values.

Format Text: This command controls the alignment of selected chart text.

LINKING TEXT TO CHART
Text can be linked to a chart in a manner similar to linking two worksheets in Excel. Use a formula like this in a chart:

=BOOK2.xls!$A$1

SUMMARY

In this chapter, you have:

1. created a chart;
2. used the chart gallery command;
3. simultaneously displayed a chart and the worksheet on which it was based;
4. added a title;
5. changed fonts;
6. added text;
7. attached text;
8. moved text and objects;
9. sized text and objects;
10. added an arrow;
11. learned other chart related commands;
12. learned to link a worksheet and a chart;
13. saved a chart.

The formula begins with an equal sign as all formulas in Excel do. It is followed by the name of the worksheet to be linked, which is followed by an exclamation point (!). Then the cell location is written.

The source worksheet must be open when the link is created. When used, if the source worksheet is changed, Excel will ask if the chart should also be changed.

SAVING A CHART

Save the chart by making it the active document and saving it as you would any other Excel document. Depress the ALT or / key, select the file pull-down menu, and choose save or save as. Name the chart and depress the ENTER key or choose OK.

REVIEW

To review charting, we will create another chart using the data on the library book budget worksheet. Close all open worksheets (ALT or /, file, close). Then open the library book budget worksheet (ALT or /, file, open). The worksheet should now be displayed.

Select the column having the amount remaining in each of the library departments' budgets. To select, use the ARROW keys while depressing the SHIFT key or use the EXTEND key, the function key F8, and the ARROW keys.

Depress the function key F11. A chart will be created based on the selected cells. The columns will not be labeled in any way. You can change the type of chart if you want by using the chart gallery command. To use the gallery command, make the chart the active document, depress the ALT or / key, select the gallery pull-down menu, and choose the dialog box associated with the type of chart you want displayed. Finally choose the chart from the dialog box. While in the dialog box, you can use the next and previous buttons to scroll through the chart types.

When you have decided on the type of chart you want, display both the chart and its worksheet simultaneously. To do this, use the window arrange all command (ALT or /, window, arrange all). If you failed to close all your worksheets prior to starting this review, you may have to close some of them now (make the extra window the active one by using ALT or /, window, and choosing it). Then close it (ALT or /, file, close). After doing this, use window arrange all again.

Create a title for the chart. To add a title, use the chart attach text command (ALT or /, chart, attach text) and choose title. The word title will appear on the chart. With that word selected, edit the title in the formula bar (use the EDIT key, the function key F2). Change the word title to Budget Remaining. Depress the ENTER key and the title will be as desired.

Now continue working on the title to make it larger, bolder, and underlined. To do these things, use the format font command (ALT or /, format, font). From the dialog box make all the appropriate choices. Then depress the ENTER key or choose OK and the title will be modified.

Now label each of the sections of the chart. To do this, select an area and type the text in the formula bar. When you have finished typing the text, depress the ENTER key and the text will appear on the chart. Now you will probably have to move and/or size the text. To move the text, select it, depress the ALT or / key, select the format pull-down menu, and choose move. Then use the ARROW keys to move the text. When you depress the ENTER key, the text will be placed where you have moved it. Repeat the process to size the text, choosing size instead of move.

Repeat the process for each of the items on the chart. Each item can have text of a different size if you want. In addition, you can use the format font command on each of the text statements.

Add an arrow to the chart. To add an arrow, depress the ALT or / key, select the chart pull-down menu, and choose add arrow. The arrow may have to be sized and moved. Arrows are sized and moved just as text is sized and moved.

Save this chart. To save a chart, depress the ALT or / key, select file, and choose save or save as.

Now close the chart portion of the display. To close a chart, make it the active window, depress the ALT or / key, select file, and choose close. That portion of the display will be closed.

Using the same worksheet, make another chart. This time select both the column with the names of the departments and the column with the amount remaining in each budget. To select the nonadjacent columns, you must use the EXTEND key, the function key F8. Depress F8 and select the column with the department names. Then depress the SHIFT key and the function key F8 simultaneously. Move to the column containing the amounts remaining. Then depress the function key F8 again and continue selecting the cells using the ARROW keys.

With the two columns selected, depress the function key F11. A new chart will be drawn for you, and each of the items will be labeled.

Use the gallery command to choose the type of chart you want. Notice that some of the charts are labeled automatically while some are not. Choose the one similar to the one created before if the labels are shown.

Display both the chart and worksheet simultaneously. To do this, use the window arrange all command.

Add a title to this chart using chart attach text and choosing title. First make the chart the active document using the window pull-down menu and choosing it. Then use the chart attach text command and choose title. Edit the title using the EDIT key, the function key F2.

Change the size and font of the title using the format font command. Increase the size and make it bold. Also underline it.

Now add an arrow to this chart using the chart add arrow command. You will have to size and move the arrow to point to one of the items on the chart.

You can now select the headings for the items and change them to a bold font to make them easier to read. To do this, use the format font command.

Save this chart also. To save the chart, use the file save or save as command.

Now open the first chart that you made for this review. The first chart will be displayed, and you will not be able to see the other chart and worksheet. Use window arrange all to see all three simultaneously.

Compare the chart that was initially made with the one you just created. You can close the worksheet to be able to compare the charts more easily. To close the worksheet, make it the active document using the window command and choosing it. Then use file close to close it. Use window arrange all to arrange the two charts.

If you think that you might want to see the two charts together again, save the workspace. To save a workspace, use file save workspace. Name the workspace file. Then depress the ENTER key. When you open the workspace, the charts will be displayed together.

11 MACROS

A macro is a set of instructions for a program to follow. These instructions are followed in sequence, automatically. In Excel, macros are placed on separate sheets called macro sheets. Excel has two types of macros: command macros and functions macros. A command macro executes a sequence of actions. It is similar to using a set of Excel commands with the keyboard or mouse. A function macro computes a value. It is similar to using an Excel function.

A macro is written and executed when a user frequently does the same set of commands or computes the same values. A macro is actually a shortcut.

A command macro can be recorded or written. A function macro must be written by the user.

OPENING A MACRO SHEET

The first step in using, writing, or recording a macro is to open a macro sheet. You can record several macros on the same sheet if you want. To open a macro sheet, depress the ALT or / key to gain access to the menu bar, select the file pull-down menu, and choose open to open an existing macro sheet or new to open a new macro sheet. If you are opening an existing macro sheet, you will be able to choose the appropriate name from a list box and then depress the ENTER key or choose OK.

RECORDING A COMMAND MACRO

You can record a command macro once a macro sheet is open. Recording a macro means that Excel will record each relevant keystroke you make and place a representation of it on the open macro sheet.

Let's record our first command macro. Open the library book budget worksheet. You may notice that the print of this, as well as almost all other Excel worksheets, is not very large. You can increase the size of each entry using various keystrokes. These keystrokes can be recorded and then used with other worksheets to increase the size of the entries.

With the library book budget worksheet displayed, depress the ALT or / key, select the file pull-down menu, and since we do not have a macro sheet to add to, choose the new dialog box. From this dialog box choose macro sheet. A new macro sheet will be displayed.

Depress the ALT or / key and select the macro pull-down menu.

Choose set recorder. This command tells Excel where to record the macro on the macro sheet. You can either specify a range of cells or simply one cell. If a range is selected before invoking this command, Excel will only record commands up to the end of the range and then warn you that you have run out of room on the macro record range. If you only select one cell, Excel will use as many cells as it needs to record the macro.

Depress the ALT or / key, select the window pull-down menu, and choose the library book budget worksheet to be the active document. At this point you can have both the worksheet and the macro sheet displayed simultaneously by using the window arrange all command.

With the book budget worksheet as the active document, depress the ALT or / key. Select the macro pull-down menu. Choose record. Excel will ask you to name the macro and provide a shortcut key for invoking the macro. The name used in this example is enlarge; the shortcut key is e. The case of the letter used as the shortcut key is significant. Depress the ENTER key or choose OK.

From now on, whatever actions you take on the worksheet will be recorded in the macro named enlarge. Select the entire used portion of the worksheet using the SHIFT key with the ARROW keys or by using the EXTEND key, the function key F8, and the ARROW keys.

With the used portion of the worksheet selected, depress the ALT or / key, select the format pull-down menu, and choose the font dialog box. In the dialog box choose the bold font and then view the rest of the dialog box by depressing the ALT and o keys simultaneously. To change the size, depress the ALT and s keys simultaneously and then scroll down to choose a large size such as 24. Depress the ENTER key or choose OK.

On the display you will notice that the print has been enlarged, but the columns are now too narrow to accommodate the print. With the entire used portion of the worksheet still selected, depress the ALT or / key, select the format pull-down menu, and choose column width. Change the column widths to 40. Depress the ENTER key or choose OK.

Now the display on the worksheet has been made large enough for most people to read without any trouble. Stop the macro recorder at this point by depressing the ALT or / key, selecting the macro pull-down menu, and choosing stop recorder. The macro has been recorded.

Make the macro sheet the active document to see what Excel has recorded. To make the macro sheet the active document, depress the ALT or / key, select the window pull-down menu, and choose the macro sheet (see Figure 11.1).

Save this macro sheet. To save an active macro sheet, depress the ALT or /, select the file pull-down menu, and choose save or save as. Excel will save the macro sheet with an .xlm extension.

UNDERSTANDING MACRO FUNCTION ARGUMENTS

Macro functions are usually followed by information enclosed in parentheses. These are the macro function's arguments. Each macro function requires different arguments. Examining the macro just recorded on the macro sheet shows that we have used REPLACE.FONT() and FORMAT.FONT().

The REPLACE.FONT() macro function is equivalent to choosing the format font command, selecting a font from the four listed fonts, and choosing the replace button. It has seven arguments as follows:

=REPLACE.FONT(font,name_text,size_number, bold,italic,underline,strikeout)

The font refers to one of the four listed fonts and must be a number between one and four. The name_text is the name of the new font as it appears in the format font dialog box. The size_number refers to the size of the new font. The last four arguments are the style of the font. If, for example, the font is bold, this argument is TRUE; if it is not bold, this argument is FALSE.

The FORMAT.FONT() macro function is equivalent to the format font command and applies one of the four current fonts to the selection. It has a similar list of arguments:

=FORMAT.FONT(name_text,size_number,bold,italic, underline,strikeout)

FIGURE 11-1 Enlarge macro sheet

	A
1	enlarge
2	=SELECT("R1C1:R8C9")
3	=REPLACE.FONT(2,"Helv",24,TRUE,FALSE,FALSE,FALSE)
4	=FORMAT.FONT("Helv",24,TRUE,FALSE,FALSE,FALSE)
5	=COLUMN.WIDTH(40)
6	=RETURN()

Now close the macro sheet. Close the file. To close macro sheets and worksheets, depress the ALT or / key, select the file pull-down menu, and choose close. This command closes only the active document. Do not save the changes to the book budget worksheet.

RUNNING A COMMAND MACRO

Now reopen the book budget worksheet and the macro sheet. Be sure the book budget worksheet is the active document. Use the shortcut key (e) designated for this macro by depressing the CONTROL and shortcut keys simultaneously. The macro will enlarge the print and change the column widths of the entire used portion of the worksheet.

A different way to run a command macro is to use the macro run command while the worksheet is the active document. To use this command, depress the ALT or / key, select the macro pull-down menu, and choose run. Select the macro's name from the list box. Depress the ENTER key or choose OK. The macro will run.

This macro will enlarge the print on this particular worksheet. You could record a different macro to be used on worksheets in general.

A MORE GENERAL ENLARGING MACRO

For this macro, we will nearly duplicate the macro above except that we will select the entire worksheet instead of just the used portion of the worksheet. In this way, we will be able to use the macro with any worksheet.

Close the open worksheet but do not save the changes. Leave the macro sheet open. Now open the book budget worksheet again. The print on this worksheet is the normal size.

Make the macro sheet the active document (ALT or /, window, choose the macro sheet). Choose a cell that is unoccupied such as cell D1. Set the recorder (ALT or /, macro, set recorder). Make the library book budget worksheet the active document (ALT or /, window, choose the worksheet). Start the recorder (ALT or /, macro, record) name the macro general and use g as the shortcut key.

Select the entire worksheet. To select the entire worksheet, simultaneously depress the CONTROL, SHIFT, and SPACEBAR keys.

From this point on, the macro is identical to the one above. Use format font to choose a bold font, view the rest of the fonts dialog box by depressing the ALT and o keys simultaneously. Increase the size. Depress the ENTER key or choose OK. Then increase the width of the columns to 40 by using format column width (ALT or /, format, column width). Depress the ENTER key or choose OK.

The last thing that you must do is stop the recorder. Depress the ALT or / key, select the macro pull-down menu, and choose stop recorder. Excel places a RETURN() at the end of the recorded macro; all Excel macros end with a RETURN() macro function.

This macro can now be used with any worksheet to enlarge the print and make it easier to read. Remember that the macro sheet must be open for it to work. Also remember that to use the shortcut key depress CONTROL and g simultaneously.

EDITING A MACRO SHEET

You can edit a macro sheet as you would any worksheet. To replace an entire cell, highlight that cell and type the new information over the old. When the ENTER key is depressed, the new information will replace the old. If you want to modify a cell entry, highlight that cell, depress the EDIT key, the function key F2, and make the corrections in the formula bar. When the ENTER key is depressed, the changes will appear on the macro sheet.

ADDING USER INPUT

You can have the above macro pause to permit user input on the font, size, and style. To do this, edit the macro by placing a question mark after the replace font command (see Figure 11.2). The addition of the question mark will cause the macro to pause, propose the font, size, and style specified, but permit the user to make any changes he or she feels necessary. The user will see a dialog box (see Figure 11.3). The user will be able to make any changes necessary. When the ENTER key is depressed or the OK button selected, the macro will continue.

To make this modification to your macro, you can edit it using the EDIT key, the function key F2. Or, if you prefer, you can create a new macro on the same macro sheet.

FIGURE 11-2 Macro with question mark

	F
1	ask
2	=SELECT("R1:R16384")
3	=REPLACE.FONT?(2,"Helv",24,TRUE,FALSE,FALSE,FALSE)
4	=FORMAT.FONT("Helv",24,TRUE,FALSE,FALSE,FALSE)
5	=COLUMN.WIDTH(40)
6	=RETURN()

Since most of the lines on this macro will be the same as the previous macro, you can copy the macro and then make the changes necessary. To copy a macro, use the edit copy (ALT or /, edit, copy) and edit paste (ALT or /, edit, paste) commands. Give this macro a new name, such as ask, which should be placed on the first line of the macro.

Now, highlight the third cell of the macro which begins with =REPLACE.FONT(). Depress the EDIT key, the function key F2. Then use the ARROW keys and place a question mark after REPLACE.FONT(). Depress the ENTER key.

You will have to name the macro. To name it, depress the ALT or / key, select the formula pull-down menu, and choose define name. Type in the name and the reference, if they are not correctly suggested by Excel. If you select the first cell of the macro which contains its name prior to beginning this process, Excel will suggest this name and location as the macro's name and reference. Then be sure to depress the ALT and c keys simultaneously to indicate that it is a command macro. Then depress the ALT and k keys simultaneously to select a shortcut key such as a. Depress the ENTER key or choose OK. The macro is now ready to run.

Save the macro sheet. To save a macro sheet, depress the ALT or / key to gain access to the menu bar. Select the file pull-down menu. Choose either save or save as.

Now open a worksheet while the macro sheet is open. Depress the CONTROL and shortcut keys simultaneously. The macro should pause to permit you to modify the suggested font, size, and style. To accept the suggestion, simply depress the ENTER key or choose OK. The macro will modify the worksheet as specified.

ALERT()

You can create a dialog box that displays a message to the user. To do this, you will use the ALERT() macro function. The ALERT() macro function has the following format:

=ALERT("Message",type number)

Using the macro that you have been working on, you could insert an ALERT() macro function after the worksheet has been selected. You can either copy the entire macro to another part of the macro sheet (using edit copy and edit paste) and then move the lines below the select macro function down (using edit copy and edit paste or edit insert).

In the blank cell, type:

124 USING MICROSOFT EXCEL

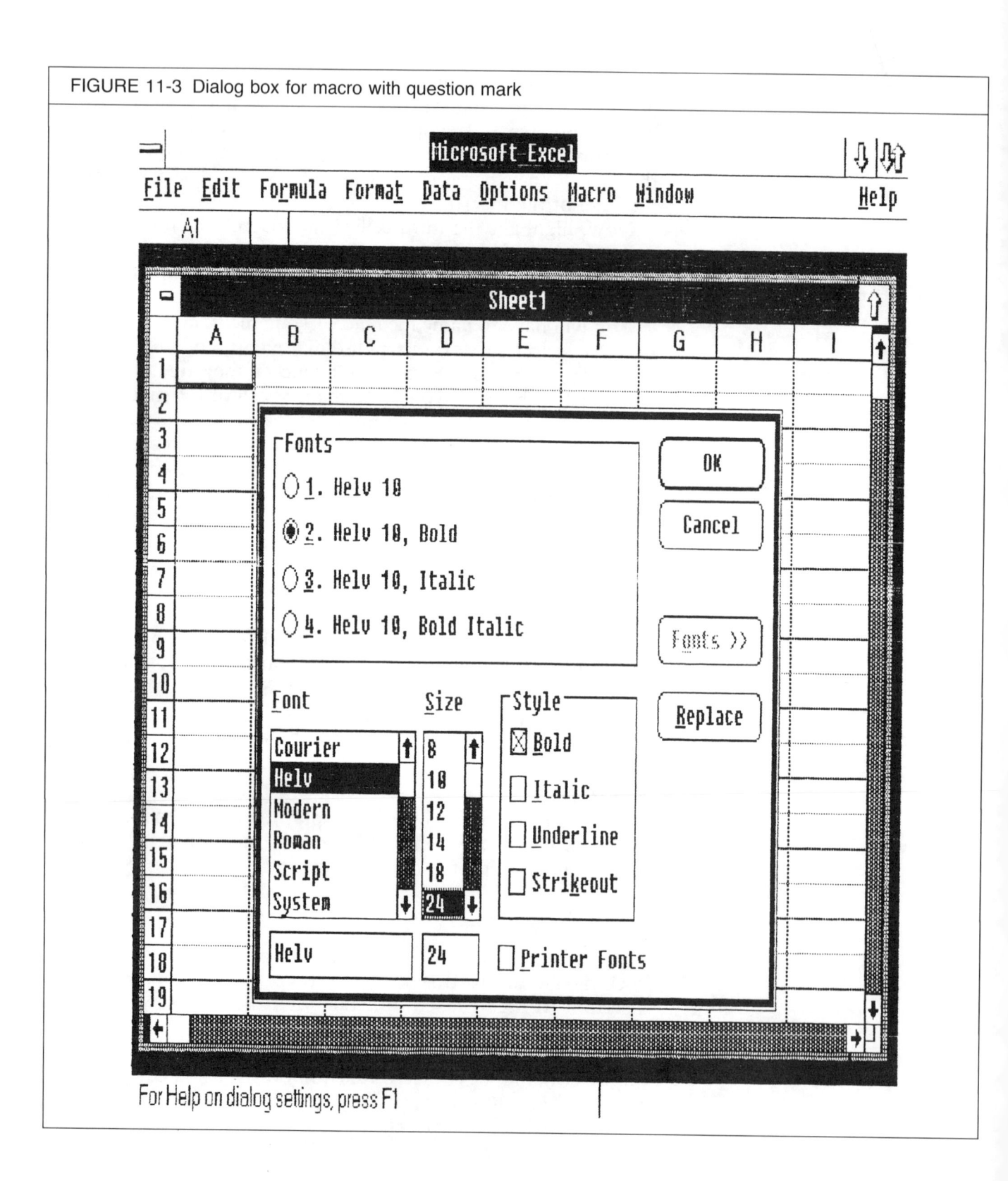

FIGURE 11-3 Dialog box for macro with question mark

= ALERT("MAKE SELECTIONS TO CHANGE DISPLAY",2)

If you have made a new macro for the ALERT() macro function, define its name and shortcut key using formula define name. Be sure to specify that this is a command macro and use a unique shortcut key.

The macro should look like Figure 11.4. Use the macro on a worksheet. As it runs, the macro will beep and a message will be shown alerting the user that display options will be given (see Figure 11.5).

ALERT() MACRO FNCTION TYPE 1

The ALERT() macro function you used only alerts the user that a choice will have to be made. At this point, the user cannot decide not to make any changes on the display unless he or she makes those changes in the format fonts dialog box. There is an easier way: the ALERT() macro function type 1.

Edit the macro just written, changing the ALERT() macro function as follows:

= ALERT("MAKE SELECTIONS TO CHANGE DISPLAY",1)

The macro will be halted, displaying a dialog box which has an OK button and a cancel button. Unfortunately, Excel will not cancel execution of the macro as it is written. It is necessary to include an IF() macro function.

IF(): An IF() macro function tests to see if a logical condition is true

FIGURE 11-4 Macro with ALERT(2)

	H
1	alert
2	=SELECT("R1:R16384")
3	=ALERT("MAKE SELECTIONS TO CHANGE DISPLAY ",2)
4	=REPLACE.FONT?(2,"Helv",24,TRUE,FALSE,FALSE,FALSE)
5	=FORMAT.FONT("Helv",24,TRUE,FALSE,FALSE,FALSE)
6	=COLUMN.WIDTH(40)
7	=RETURN()

126 USING MICROSOFT EXCEL

FIGURE 11-5 Make selections to change display dialog box

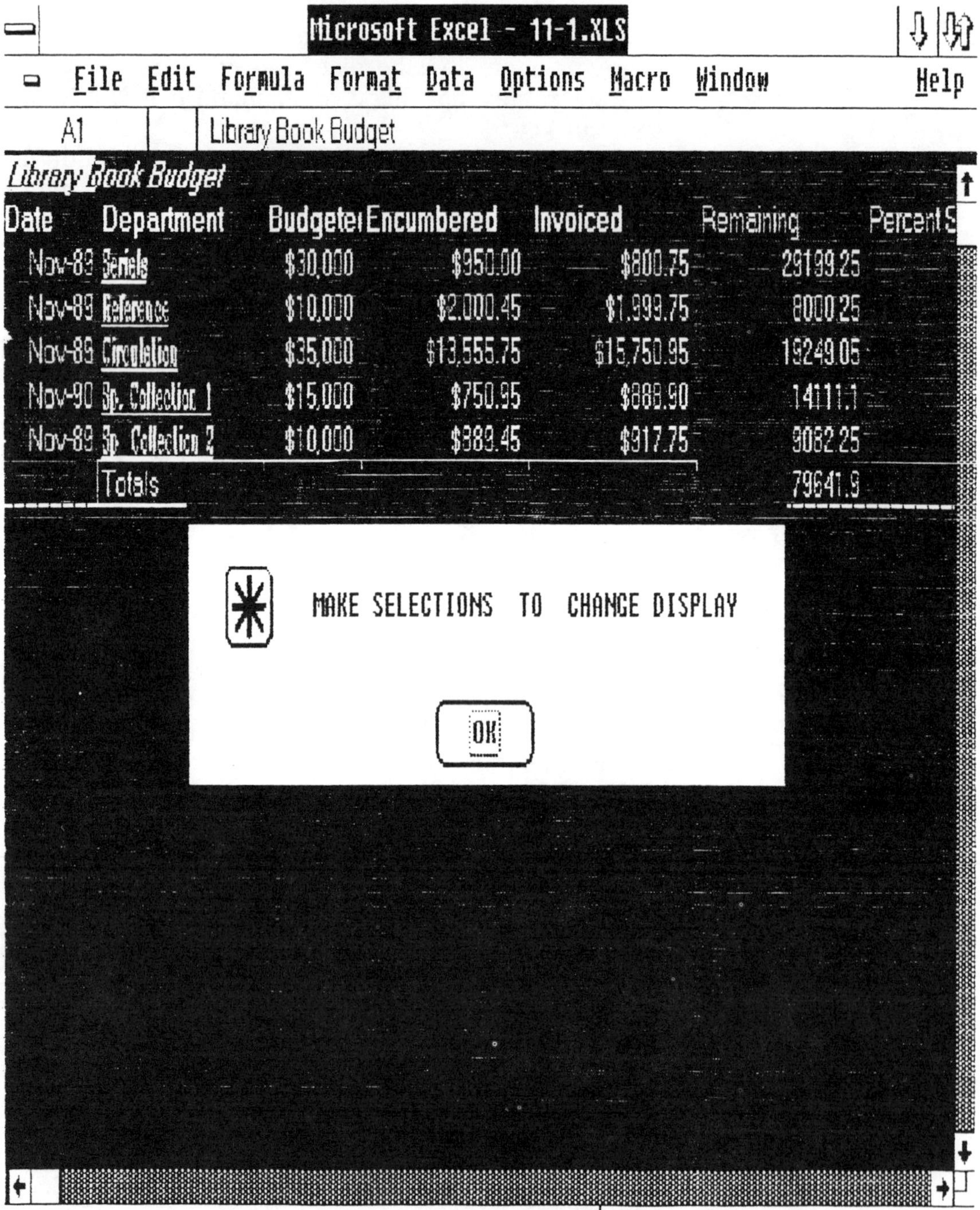

or false, and guides the macro one way if it is true and a different way if it is false. The format for the IF() macro function is:

=IF(logical_test,if_true,if_false)

GOTO(): The macro will use GOTO() macro functions within the IF() macro function. The GOTO() macro function causes the macro to continue operation at the specified cell. Using two GOTO() macro functions, one if the logical value is true, and the other if it is not true, will cause the macro to branch at this point.

Use the edit copy and edit paste commands to either create a new macro on the macro sheet or to modify the existing macro. Then use a TRUE() macro function to test if the alert macro function returned a true or false logical value.

TRUE(): The format of the TRUE() function is:

TRUE()

In the IF() macro function, the TRUE() macro function is used as follows:

=IF(J3=TRUE(),GOTO(J6),GOTO(J9))

The IF() macro function says that if the logical value returned by the ALERT() macro function located in cell J3 is true, continue macro operation in cell J6. If the logical value returned by the ALERT() macro function in cell J3 is not true, continue macro operation in cell J9, which in this macro is a RETURN() macro function and halts the macro. The entire macro looks like Figure 11.6.

When the macro is run on a worksheet, it will be halted and this dialog box will be displayed (see Figure 11.7). If the OK button is chosen, the macro will proceed to display the formula fonts dialog box in which the user will be able to modify or accept the suggested display changes. If the user chooses to cancel macro operation, he or she will leave the macro and be able to continue working on the worksheet.

MESSAGE()

If you find that you have a short message to post but do not want to interrupt the flow of the macro, you can use the MESSAGE() macro function. The MESSAGE() macro function posts a message in the message area of the status bar (the area on the lower left hand

FIGURE 11-6 Macro with ALERT() and IF()

	J
1	cancel
2	=SELECT("R1:R16384")
3	=ALERT("MAKE SELECTIONS TO CHANGE DISPLAY ",1)
4	=IF(J3=TRUE(),GOTO(J6),GOTO(J9))
5	
6	=REPLACE.FONT?(2,"Helv",24,TRUE,FALSE,FALSE,FALSE)
7	=FORMAT.FONT("Helv",24,TRUE,FALSE,FALSE,FALSE)
8	=COLUMN.WIDTH(40)
9	=RETURN()

corner of the display). The format of the MESSAGE() macro function is:

=MESSAGE(logical,"text")

If the logical is true, the text is displayed. The text must be typed in quotation marks.

The message text is displayed until the macro issues another message command. Only one message is displayed at a time, so a new message will replace the old one. If the logical is false, the message area of the status bar is returned to its normal functioning. If you do not want any message displayed in this area, have the logical as true and the message as "" (empty text).

INPUT()

The INPUT() macro function permits the user to have a greater amount of input into the macro. The INPUT() macro function permits the user to select cells, enter cell references, type text or numbers, or choose names or functions. The INPUT() macro function displays a dialog box. The format of the INPUT() macro function is:

=INPUT(prompt,type,title,default,x_pos,y_pos)

The prompt, title, and default must be text; the others must be numbers. In this case, use the INPUT() macro function to allow the user to either choose the default cell selection (the entire worksheet) or detail specific cell references. The form of the INPUT() macro function in this case will be:

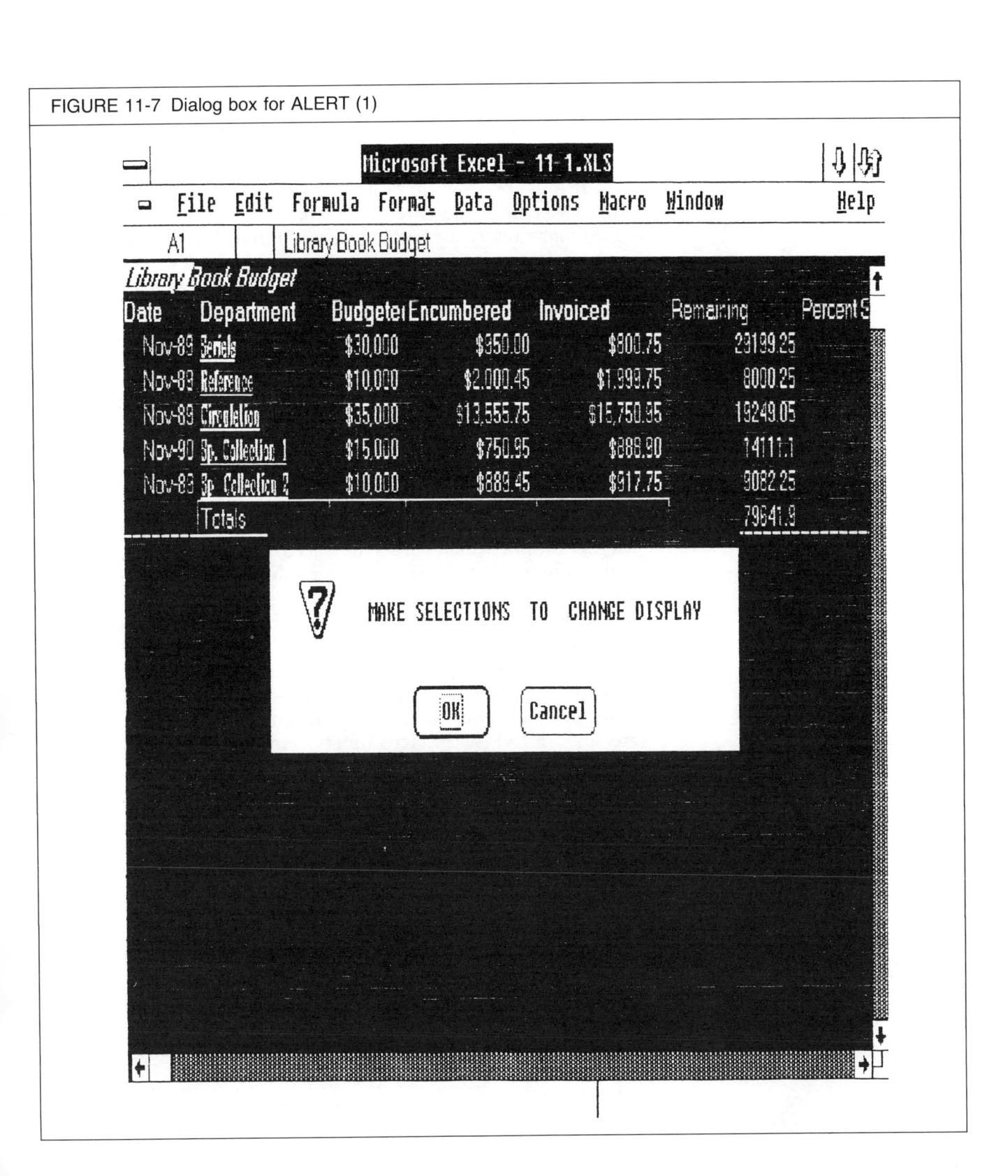

FIGURE 11-7 Dialog box for ALERT (1)

=INPUT("Select range to format",8,"Input", "R1:R16384",0,0)

The prompt (Select range to format) will be displayed in a dialog box. It must be in quotation marks in the INPUT() macro function. The type being entered is a reference, and Excel uses 8 to signal that a reference is going to be entered. The title is the title of the box. It is text and must be in quotation marks. The default in this case is the entire worksheet. The user will be able to accept the default or fill in any other references desired. The final two arguments, for the x and y positions, are used to position the dialog box. If either of them is zero, the box will be centered in that direction.

In this macro we will have to combine the SELECT() macro function with the INPUT() macro function as follows:

=SELECT(INPUT("Select range to format",8, "Input","R1:R16384",0,0))

Modify the line which selects the cells to be formatted to permit the user to enter input. The entire macro should now look like Figure 11.8.

The dialog box produced by the INPUT() macro function looks like Figure 11.9.

Now you may want to modify the column width macro function to permit user input because if the user does not accept the default font, size, and style, the column width of 40 may not be appropriate. Use an INPUT() macro function in this line also:

=COLUMN.WIDTH(INPUT("SELECT WIDTH",1,"WIDTH",40,0,0))

FIGURE 11-8 Macro with one input (select)

	L
1	input
2	=SELECT(INPUT("Select range to format",8,"Input","R1:R16384",0,0))
3	=ALERT("MAKE SELECTIONS TO CHANGE DISPLAY ",1)
4	=IF(L3=TRUE(),GOTO(L6),GOTO(L9))
5	
6	=REPLACE.FONT?(2,"Helv",24,TRUE,FALSE,FALSE,FALSE)
7	=FORMAT.FONT("Helv",24,TRUE,FALSE,FALSE,FALSE)
8	=COLUMN.WIDTH(40)
9	=RETURN()

MACROS **131**

FIGURE 11-9 Input macro function dialog box

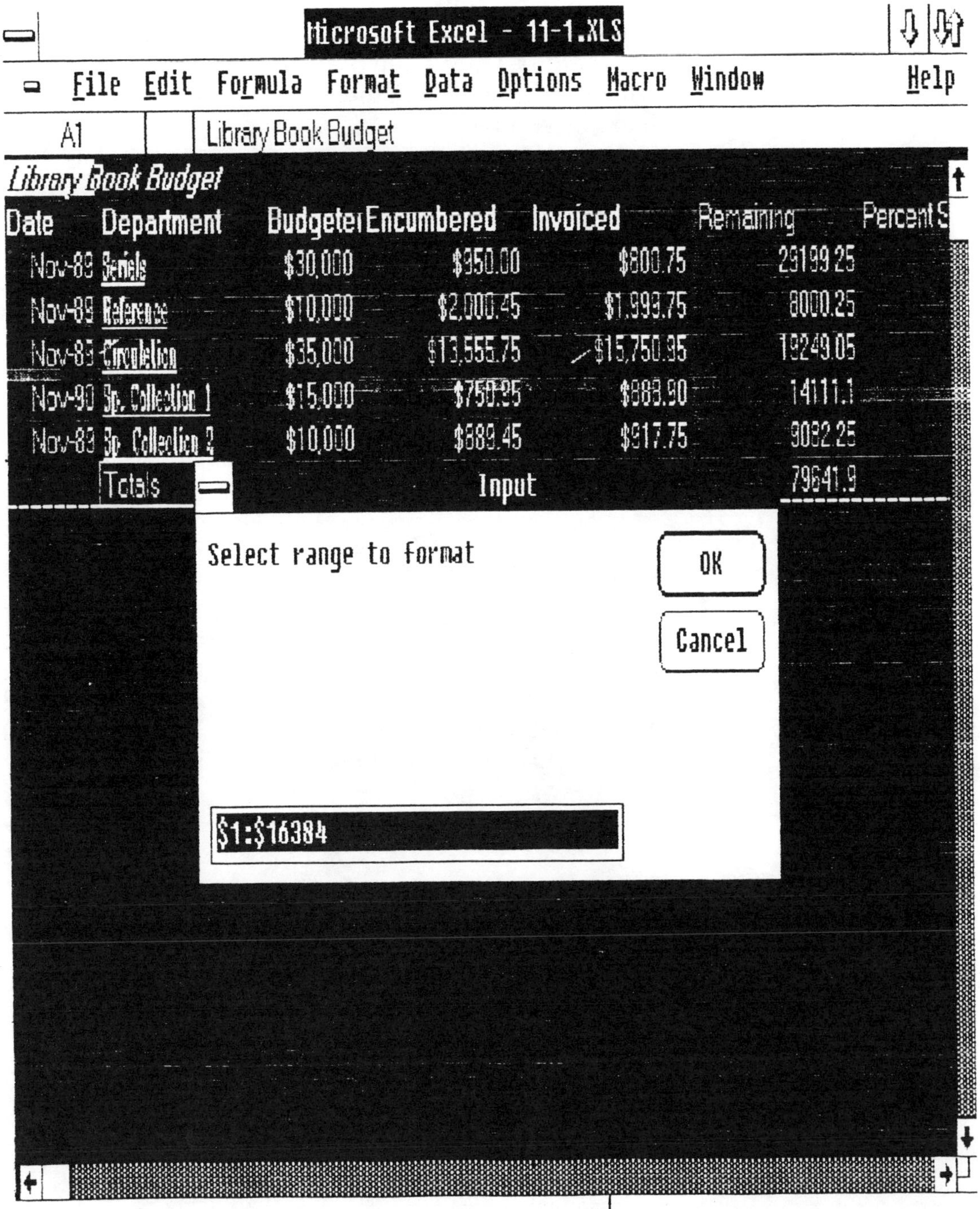

In this case the prompt that appears in the dialog box will be SELECT WIDTH. The type of response expected will be a number, for which Excel uses 1 as the type. The title of the dialog box is WIDTH. The default column width is 40, though a user can type any number. Once again the x and y positions are zero and the box will be centered in both directions. The entire macro will now look like Figure 11.10.

As you run this macro, you may be annoyed at the number of times it pauses. You may want to change the ALERT() macro function to a MESSAGE() macro function. The MESSAGE() macro function will post a message in the message area of the status bar, but the user will not have to respond. Of course changing the ALERT() to MESSAGE() will make it so that the user will not be able to cancel the macro's operation.

If you change the ALERT() macro function to a MESSAGE() macro function, the macro will look like Figure 11.11. Notice that the macro has two MESSAGE() macro functions. The first posts the message in the message area of the status bar. The second returns the status bar to normal operation.

ONKEY() WITH GOTO()

The macro can be modified to permit the user to quit the macro while it is running by pressing the ESCAPE key. To accomplish this, an ON.KEY() macro function should be used. The ON.KEY() macro function tells Excel to do a specified action if a designated key is pressed. In this case, the ON.KEY() macro function is used with a GOTO() macro function as follows:

=ON.KEY("{ESC}",GOTO(R13))

FIGURE 11-10 Macro with two inputs

	N
1	width
2	=SELECT(INPUT("Select range to format",8,"Input","R1:R16384",0,0))
3	=ALERT("MAKE SELECTIONS TO CHANGE DISPLAY ",1)
4	=IF(N3=TRUE(),GOTO(N6),GOTO(N9))
5	
6	=REPLACE.FONT?(2,"Helv",24,TRUE,FALSE,FALSE,FALSE)
7	=FORMAT.FONT("Helv",24,TRUE,FALSE,FALSE,FALSE)
8	=COLUMN.WIDTH(INPUT("SELECT WIDTH",1,"Width",40,0,0))
9	=RETURN()

FIGURE 11-11 Macro with two message functions

	P
1	message
2	=SELECT(INPUT("Select range to format",8,"Input","R1:R16384",0,0))
3	=MESSAGE(TRUE,"MAKE SELECTIONS TO CHANGE DISPLAY ")
4	=IF(P3=TRUE,GOTO(P6),GOTO(P10))
5	
6	=REPLACE.FONT?(2,"Helv",24,TRUE,FALSE,FALSE,FALSE)
7	=FORMAT.FONT("Helv",24,TRUE,FALSE,FALSE,FALSE)
8	=COLUMN.WIDTH(INPUT("SELECT WIDTH",1,"Width",40,0,0))
9	=MESSAGE(FALSE)
10	=RETURN()

Cell R13 contains a RETURN() macro function, which ends macro operation.

In this macro, the MESSAGE() macro function is used to tell the user that pressing ESCAPE will terminate macro operation.

The entire macro looks like Figure 11.12. Create this macro and name it ONKEY using formula define name. Specify that it is a command macro and assign a shortcut key.

Excel has a great number of macro functions. Many of them will be used in the library applications portion of this book. When using a macro function, it is easiest to use the formula paste function command (ALT or /, formula, paste function) and turn on the arguments box so that the function will be displayed with place holders so that you will not miss any of its arguments.

FUNCTION MACROS

A function macro is similar to an Excel function. It computes a value. A function macro must be written; it cannot be recorded because it does not have actions. A function macro is actually a user defined function that can be used as all other Excel functions are used.

An Excel function macro is written on a macro sheet. It begins with the name of the macro in its first cell. After that, the arguments for the macro are defined. Then the formulas that are used to calculate the values are listed. Finally a RETURN() macro function is written; all Excel macros end with a RETURN() macro function.

```
FIGURE 11-12  ONKEY macro

                                    R
 1  onkey
 2  =SELECT(INPUT("Select range to format",8,"Input","R1:R16384",0,0))
 3  =MESSAGE(TRUE,"PRESS ESCAPE TO QUIT")
 4  =ON.KEY("{ESC}",GOTO(R13))
 5
 6
 7
 8  =REPLACE.FONT?(2,"Helv",24,TRUE,FALSE,FALSE,FALSE)
 9  =ON.KEY("{ESC}",GOTO(R13))
10  =FORMAT.FONT("Helv",24,TRUE,FALSE,FALSE,FALSE)
11  =ON.KEY("{ESC}",GOTO(R13))
12  =COLUMN.WIDTH(INPUT("SELECT WIDTH",1,"Width",40,0,0))
13  =RETURN()
```

If you wanted to compute the number of shelves that your library needs for its collection, you could take the number of books in the collection, multiply that number by the average width of a book, and then divide the total by the length of a shelf. If you had to do this process once, you would not need to write a function macro. If you were going to compute the number of shelves needed for the different sections of the library, a function macro would help.

Writing the Function Macro: On a macro sheet, begin by typing the name shelf_space in a cell. In the cell immediately under this, define the argument collection, which will be used to compute the amount of space needed for each of the collections. To define the argument, type the following:

=ARGUMENT("collection")

Remember to enclosed the word collection in quotation marks.
Then write the formula. In this formula it is assumed that the average width of a book is 1.25 inches and the shelf is 24 inches long.

=(collection*1.25)/24

The last line is a RETURN() macro function:

=RETURN(S3)

The S3 refers to the cell whose value is to be returned when the function macro is run (see Figure 11.13).

Name the function macro using formula define name (ALT or /, formula, define name). If the first cell of the macro is highlighted, Excel will suggest that cell's contents as the macro's name. Check the function box at the bottom to indicate that this is a function macro. Then depress the ENTER key or choose OK.

Make a worksheet the active window by either using ALT or /, window, and choosing the worksheet window or by opening a worksheet (ALT or /, file, open worksheet). Then depress the ALT or / key, select the formula pull-down menu, and choose paste function. Excel shows you a list box of functions, beginning with the built-in functions. The function that you wrote will be on the bottom of this list. To get to the bottom, depress the END key. When your function macro is highlighted, depress the ENTER key. The function will appear in the formula bar.

Add the arguments to the formula in the formula bar. For example, type 150000 as the size of the collection. Excel will position this argument in the proper spot in the function. Then depress the ENTER key. Excel will state that 7812.5 shelves are needed for a collection of 150,000 books.

A Second Function Macro: You can modify this macro to permit the user to vary the size of the collection, the width of the average book, and the size of the shelves. To do this, three arguments will be necessary for the function macro.

Once again, you can begin the macro in a separate portion of the macro sheet. In this macro's first cell, type the name: shelf_space2. Then define the three arguments:

= ARGUMENT("collection")
= ARGUMENT("width")
= ARGUMENT("size")

FIGURE 11-13 Shelf space macro

	S
1	shelf_space
2	=ARGUMENT("collection")
3	=(collection*1.25)/24
4	=RETURN(S3)

The arguments must be defined in the exact order in which they will be used in the formula in the macro.

Then the formula to be used is written:

= (collection*width)/size

The RETURN() macro function is written to end the macro:

= RETURN(U5)

The entire macro looks like Figure 11.14.

Use formula define name as you did with the first function macro. Be sure to check the function box because this is a function macro. Then make a worksheet the active document and use the formula paste function command. Use the END key to get to the end of the list, highlight this function, and depress the ENTER key or choose OK.

The function will appear in the formula bar. Add the arguments: collection (indicating the number of books in the collection), the width (indicating the average width of a book), and the size (indicating the size of the shelf). When you depress the ENTER key, Excel will return the result.

This function macro is more flexible than the first: you can determine, for example, that science books are wider than poetry books, and will thus take up more shelf space. You can decide that because your library's collection is growing rapidly in business that you will only use 16 inches of each shelf in that area.

FIGURE 11-14 Modified shelf space macro

	U
1	shelf_space(collection,size,width)
2	=ARGUMENT("collection")
3	=ARGUMENT("width")
4	=ARGUMENT("size")
5	=(collection*width)/size
6	=RETURN(U5)

SUMMARY

In this chapter, you have:

1. learned about macros;
2. opened and used a macro sheet;
3. recorded a command macro;
4. run a command macro;
5. edited a command macro;
6. added user input to a command macro;
7. used the ALERT() macro function;
8. used the IF() macro function;
9. used the TRUE() macro function;
10. learned about the MESSAGE() macro function;
11. used the INPUT() macro function;
12. used the ONKEY() macro funcation;
13. used the GOTO() macro function;
14. written function macros;
15. learned to document macros;
16. learned to debug macros.

DOCUMENTING MACROS

It is a good idea to document your macros. To document a macro, you can use the column next to it to write comments to explain what was done and why. You could also use notes for the same purpose. For example, you could define each of the arguments so that if you forget what each refers to, you can check.

DEBUGGING MACROS

Sometimes a macro does not work exactly as desired. A malfunctioning program is said to have bugs. To help debug a macro, Excel offers a STEP() macro function which moves through the macro one step at a time so that you can see exactly where the macro is malfunctioning. To use the STEP() macro function, insert it before the portion of the macro that you want to step through. This macro function can be placed in the cell right below the macro's name. If the macro does not have a blank line above or in it, you can move the cells of the macro down (ALT or /, edit, insert down).

Save the macro sheet. To save a macro sheet, use file save or file save as.

REVIEW

To review this chapter, we will construct a command macro that allows the user to choose a file to be opened and then change the display. To do this, you can either use the macro recorder since it is a command macro or you can write the macro yourself.

Start in a blank area of the macro sheet you have been using. If you are using the macro recorder, start it by depressing the ALT or / key, selecting the macro pull-down menu, and choosing start recorder. Then make a worksheet the active document by using the window command. Then start the macro recorder by depressing the ALT or / key, selecting the macro pull-down menu, and choosing the record command. Name the macro, check the command box, and give it a shortcut key. Then depress the ENTER key or choose OK.

Start by depressing the ALT or / key to gain access to the menu bar. Then select the file pull-down menu. Choose the open dialog box. In the box, change the directory to B if that is where your data disk is usually kept. Use the list box to choose a file such as books.

Complete the macro by depressing the ALT or / key, selecting the macro pull-down menu, and choosing to stop the recorder.

Now look at the recorded macro by making the macro sheet the active window.

This macro is very specific: it opens the books worksheet on drive B. You can edit the macro to make it more general. To edit a macro, highlight a particular cell and depress the EDIT key, the function key F2. Then make changes to the line in the formula bar. When you depress the ENTER key, the changes will be reflected in the macro.

Change the third line of the macro to make it more general. The new macro function will look like this:

= OPEN?()

The function tells Excel to open a file, and since the command is followed by a question mark and then nothing in the parentheses, the user will see the file open dialog box. From the list box, he or she can choose the appropriate file.

Now clear the cell with the RETURN() macro function. We will be branching to a macro that was created in the first part of this chapter, the onkey macro. To branch to another macro, use a GOTO() macro function:

= GOTO(onkey)

This portion of the macro will now look like Figure 11.15.

The macro will now branch to the onkey macro, which will be used to modify the display of the selected worksheet. A RETURN() macro function is not needed at this point because the macro does not end here. It ends with the onkey macro, which is concluded with a RETURN() macro function.

Try the macro: depress the CONTROL key and the shortcut key simultaneously. Alternatively, you could depress the ALT or / key, select the macro pull-down menu, and choose the run dialog box.

FIGURE 11-15 Directory macro with GOTO (ONKEY)

	W
1	directory
2	=DIRECTORY("B:\")
3	=OPEN?()
4	=GOTO(onkey)

Then select this macro from the list box. Choose a file to work with.

Save the macro sheet using file save or file save as. If you use file save, the new macro sheet will replace the previous one. On the other hand, you could use file save as and give this macro sheet a unique name.

12 FURTHER CUSTOMIZATION

Excel permits the user to customize its display in many ways, some of which have been previously discussed. In addition, Excel has the options workspace command, the file save as command, and the control panel to permit customization.

OPTIONS WORKSPACE

The options workspace command permits the user to control the entire Excel session. These controls include fixing a number of decimal places, changing the column and row heading designations, determining whether the scroll bars, formula bar, and status bar will be displayed, and designating an alternative key to be used to gain access to the menu bar (see Figure 12.1).

The first option is determining the number of fixed decimal places. This option may seem similar to the format number command, but there is a significant difference. Using the options workspace command changes the value entered into a cell into a decimal number; the cell formatted for two decimal places only changes the display of that number. For example, if you enter 1222 into a cell when the options workspace fixed decimal places is set to two, the stored value will be 12.22. If you enter the same number (1222) into a cell formatted for two decimal places using format number, the stored value will be 1222 while the displayed value will be 1222.00.

Using this command actually changes the number that you are entering into a decimal if no decimal point is specified. It may be good to use this command if all your numbers will contain a fixed number of decimal points, but it may cause a great deal of confusion. Use this option with a great deal of caution.

There are also four display options. The first is R1C1 which effects the row and column designations. The default for Excel and most other spreadsheets is to have columns named with letters and rows named with numbers. Alternatively, you could have Excel use numbers for both. This format is often used by programmers.

The next three options determine whether the scroll bars, formula bar, and status bar will be displayed. Suppressing the display of these bars will increase the amount of the worksheet displayed.

Throughout this book, you have been told that you can gain access to the menu bar by depressing either the ALT or / keys. If you want to designate a different key as the alternative menu key (other than the / key), you can designate it here. Excel has the / key

FIGURE 12-1 Options workspace dialog box

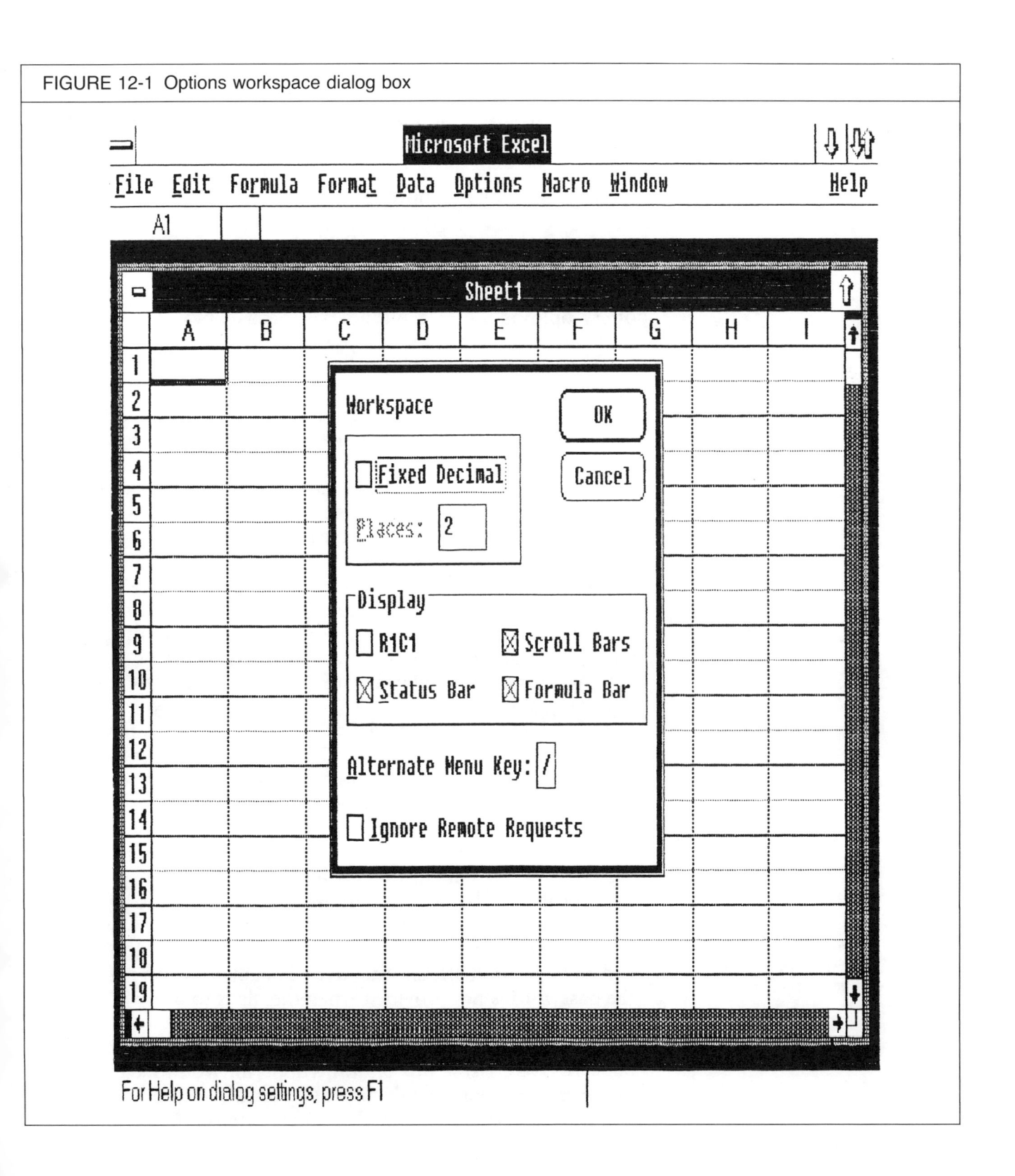

as the default because Lotus 1-2-3 uses that key to gain access to menus.

The final option, ignore remote requests, is only applicable if you are using Excel within a Windows environment using Dynamic Data Exchange using Excel as a temporary server. If this is not the case, Excel will ignore this option.

FILE SAVE AS

The file save as command has been used often in this book, but it offers options which have not yet been explored. Depress the ALT or / key, select the file pull-down menu, and choose save as. Then depress the ALT and o keys simultaneously (see Figure 12.2).

Using this command, you can easily save an Excel worksheet to be used by programs other than Excel. The normal file format is the one used by Excel and it is the default.

Another option included is to save the file as text, which is used to transfer data to word processing programs. Columns are separated by tabs and rows by carriage returns. Only the displayed text and values are saved.

It should be noted that if you are importing text files into Excel, the data will be imported into a single column. The contents of the single file can then be separated into several columns using the data parse command (ALT or /, data, parse).

CSV format is similar to text format except that commas separate columns.

To be able to read an Excel worksheet with Microsoft Multiplan or Excel for the Apple Macintosh, save the file in SYLK.

Excel can read and write Lotus release 1A and 2 files as well as Symphony files. Use the WKS format to save to Lotus release 1A or Symphony; use WK1 format to save to Lotus release 2.

The DIF format is used to transfer data to programs that require the DIF format. One of these programs is Visicalc.

Excel also reads and writes dBase files. The DBF2 format is used to transfer information to dBase 2; the DBF3 format is used to transfer information to dBase 3.

Another option offered is to save a document with a password. If the password is not provided when the file is to be opened, it will not be opened.

The final option is to create a backup file whenever the document is saved. Using this option will permit you to keep the two most recent versions of a document on disk. The backup document will have the same name with a .BAK extension.

FURTHER CUSTOMIZATION **143**

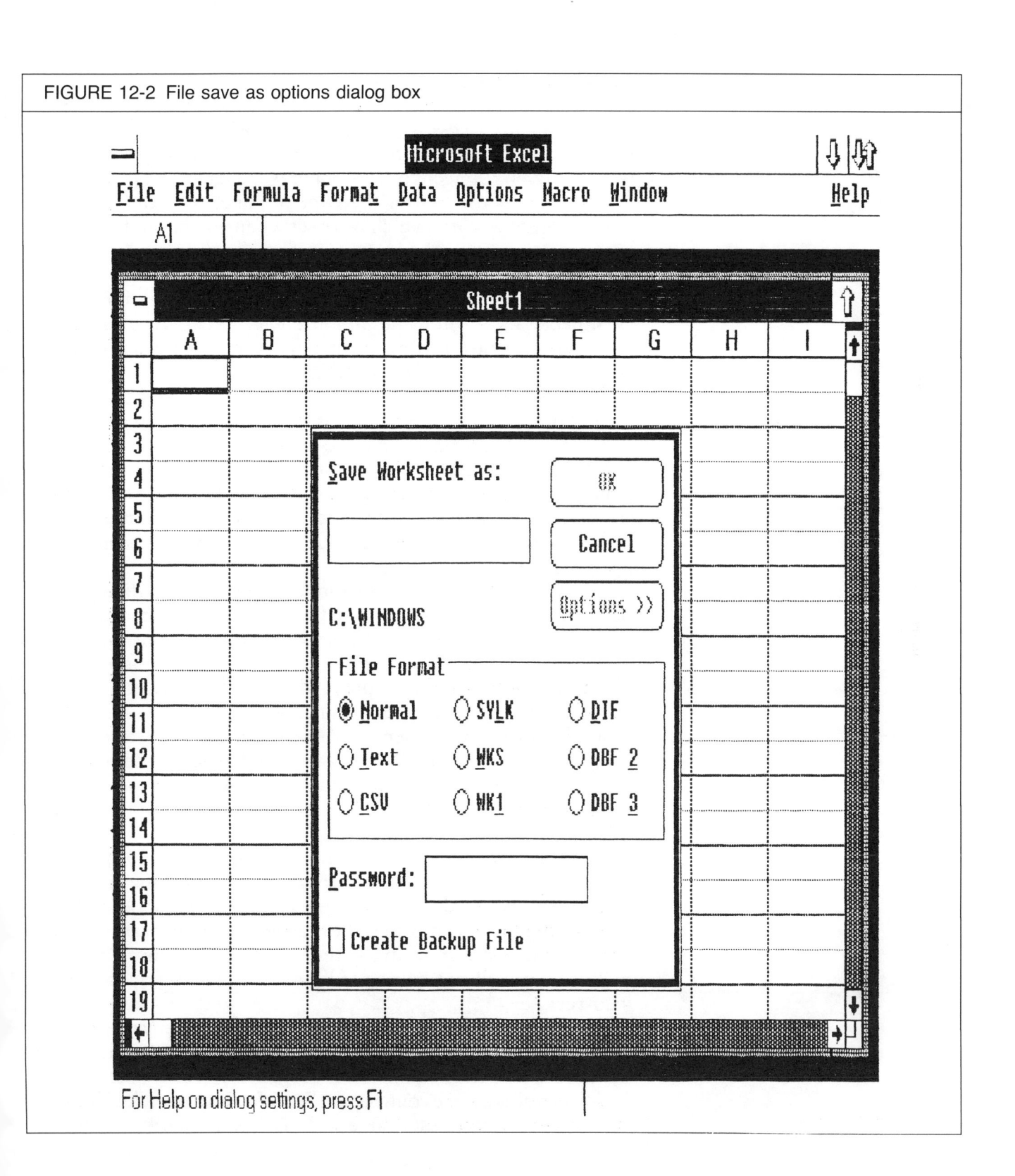

FIGURE 12-2 File save as options dialog box

CONTROL PANEL

Screen settings and colors can be adjusted by using Excel's control panel. To gain access to the control panel, depress the ALT or / key, depress the SPACEBAR, and choose the run dialog box. From this dialog box, select control panel (see Figure 12.3).

On the initial screen of the control panel, you can adjust the system time and date (which were set when you booted the system or was set automatically by your system's built-in clock). You can also adjust how fast the cursor blinks at the insertion point in the formula bar. Furthermore, you can change the speed of the double click necessary when using a mouse with Excel. To make any of these adjustments, TAB to the proper section (or point using the mouse) and then use the ARROW keys.

From the initial control panel dialog box, you can gain access to several other dialog boxes. The first is the installation dialog box, which is used to install (or remove) printers and fonts.

You can also gain access to the setup portion of the control panel. This is used to configure your system without having to reinstall Excel. This set of options includes setting up the system's default printer and its output modes. It also permits the user to set up a communications port.

The final option available from the control panel dialog box is being able to change the displayed screen colors. Use the preferences option (depress ALT and p simultaneously) from the control panel to modify screen colors.

The portions of the display whose colors can be modified include: screen background, application workspace, window background, window text, menu bar, menu text, active (selected) title bar, inactive (unselected) title bar, title bar text, active border, inactive border, window frame, and scroll bars. The adjustments to each of these areas include hue, brightness, and color (see Figure 12.4).

Using the preferences section can also permit you to specify the border width surrounding windows. When adjusting the border widths, the larger the number typed, the wider the border.

Warning beeps can also be turned off. Though warning beeps may be annoying, not having them can be even more annoying because you will not be warned by a beep when you depress an incorrect key.

You can also adjust the mouse options if you are using a mouse. You can tell Excel which mouse button will be used and how fast the mouse pointer will move on the display.

You can also use the control panel's preferences to make changes in the country setting used in Excel. This command modifies the

FURTHER CUSTOMIZATION **145**

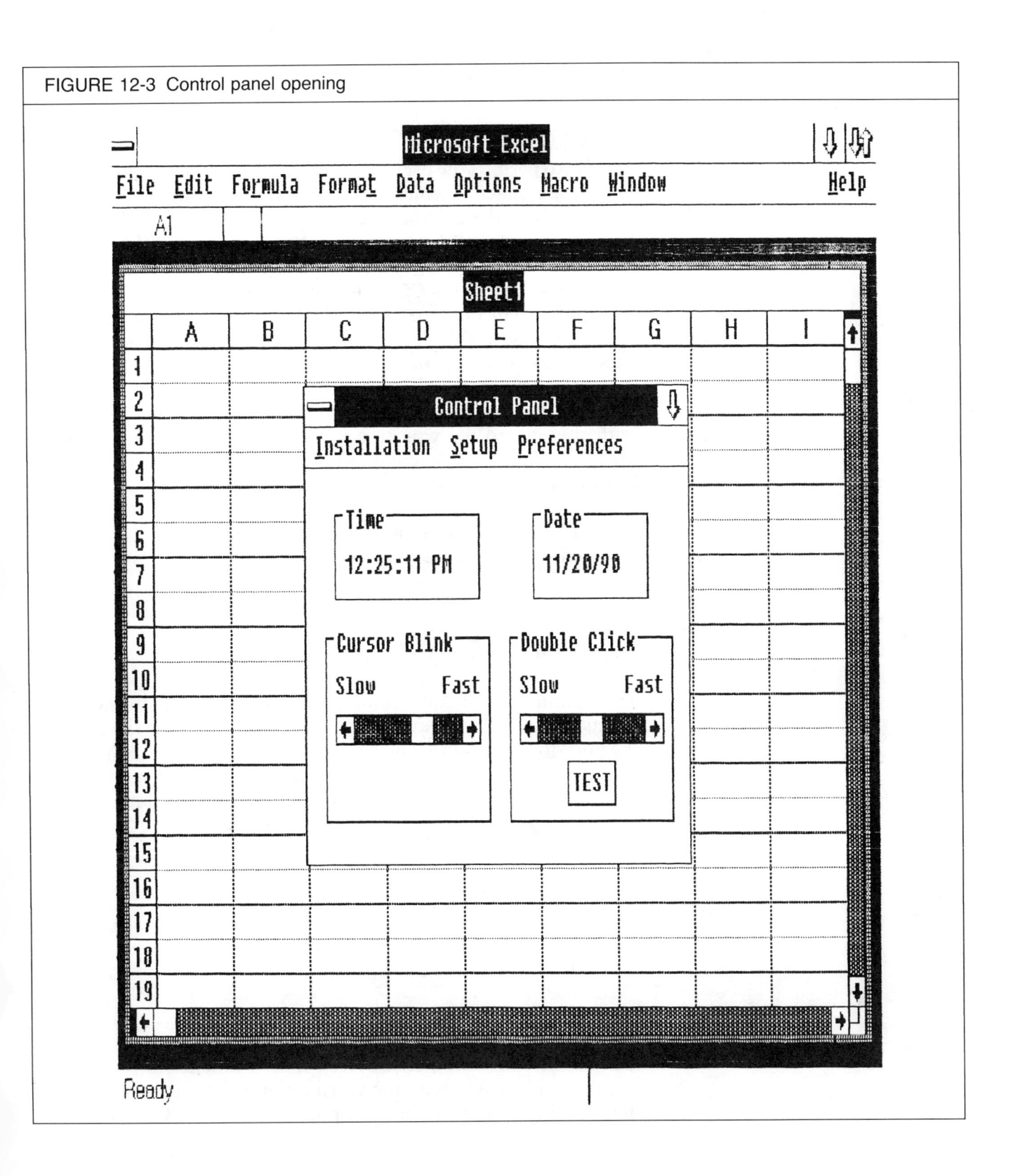

FIGURE 12-3 Control panel opening

country, time and date formats, leading zeros, and currency symbols.

CUSTOM MENUS

Excel also permits the user to customize menus. To do this, the user must write macros which either create a new menu bar or add commands to the existing menus.

If you found that the people who use Excel in your library often need to enlarge the display of documents, you may want to consider adding an enlargement command to the format menu. To do this, begin by opening a new macro sheet. To open a new macro sheet, depress the ALT or / key, select the file pull-down menu, and choose new. Choose macro.

On the new macro sheet, begin to write a macro by giving it a name. In the sample, the macro was named addcommand, because with this macro we will be adding a command to a pull-down menu. The first macro command is ADD.COMMAND(), which has the following format:

ADD.COMMAND(menu_bar_id,menu_position,menu_reference)

To use this command, type:

=ADD.COMMAND(1,"Format",C1:D2)

This command will add a command to the first menu bar, which is the full menus for worksheets and macros. Format is the name of the pull-down menu to which this will be added. The cell references indicate where on the macro sheet to find the name of the command to be added and the name of the command macro to be executed when this command is chosen.

The next line is:

=SHOW.BAR()

This command shows the menu bar as modified.
The final line is:

=RETURN()

All macros end with a RETURN() macro function..

Cell C1 is filled in with the word Enlarge. This is the command that will be seen on the format pull-down menu. Cell D1 is:

FURTHER CUSTOMIZATION **147**

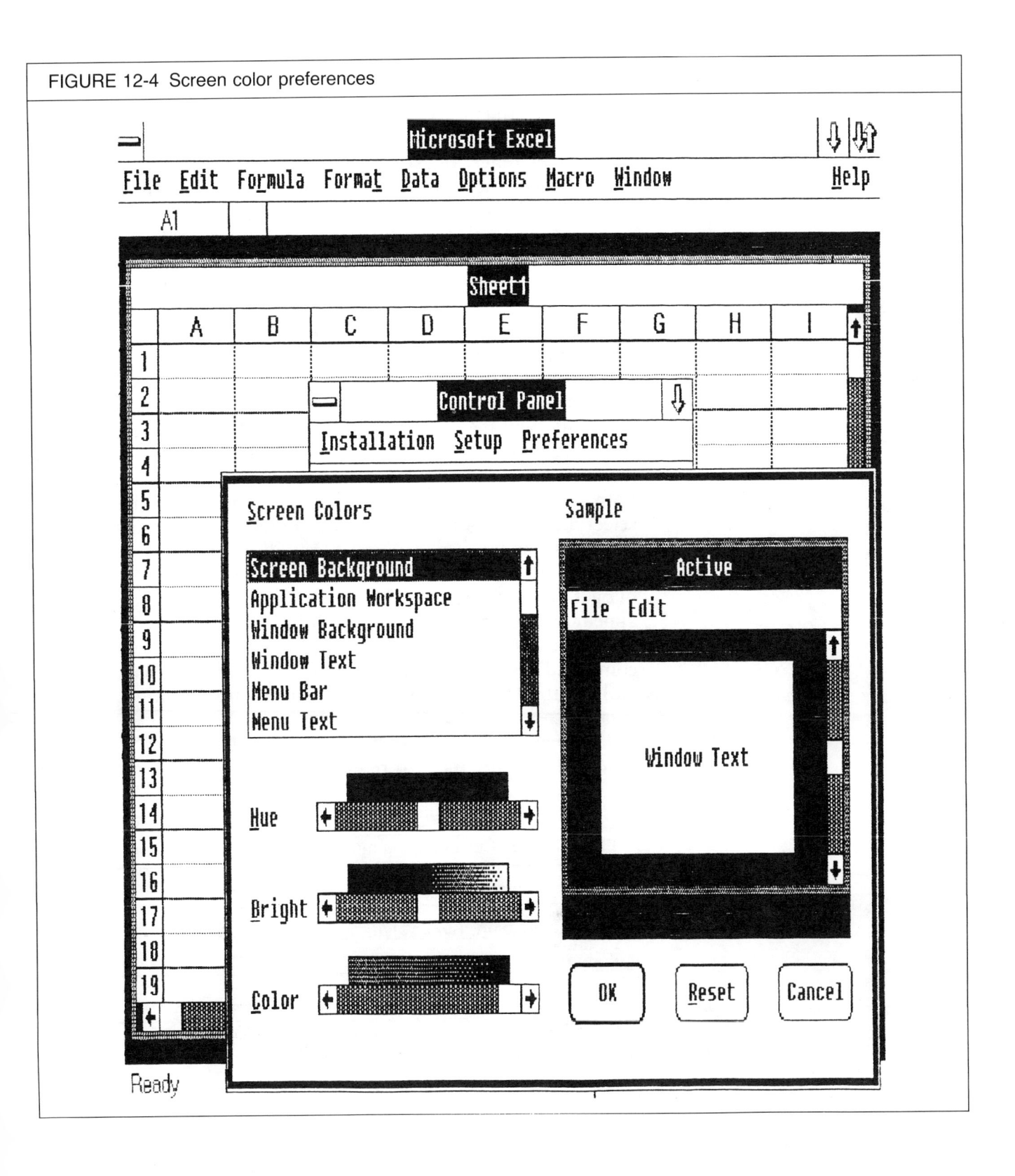

FIGURE 12-4 Screen color preferences

sample.xlm!general

The name of the macro sheet on which the command will be found is sample.xlm; the name of the macro is general. Since this is an external reference, an exclamation point (!) follows the name of the macro sheet. The entire used portion of the macro sheet will look like Figure 12.5.

Notice that Enlarge has an ampersand before the l. When the command is added to the pull-down menu, the l will be underlined, and can be used to invoke the command as in all other Excel pull-down menus.

Name the macro, using formula define name. Indicate that it is a command macro and specify a shortcut key. Now, when both macro sheets are open and the CONTROL and shortcut keys are depressed simultaneously, the macro will run and the enlarge command will be added to the format pull-down menu. Because both macro sheets have to be open for the command to be added to the pull-down menu, you may want to save the workspace with both sheets in it. To save a workspace, depress the ALT or / key, select the file pull-down menu, and choose save workspace. When you open the workspace, both files will open.

Open the worksheet that has the circulation department's book budget. Then depress the CONTROL and shortcut keys. It may appear that nothing has happened, but depress the ALT or / key, select the format pull-down menu, and notice that the enlarge command has been added (see Figure 12.6). Choose that command and see that the circulation department's book budget has been enlarged.

The menu reference portion of the ADD.COMMAND() macro function has only the two required columns, but it can use three

FIGURE 12-5 Custom menu macro sheet

	A	B
1	addcommand	
2	=ADD.COMMAND(1,"Format",C1:D2)	
3	=SHOW.BAR()	
4	=RETURN()	

	C	D
1	En&large	sample.xlm!general
2		
3		
4		

FIGURE 12-6 Enlarge on pull-down format menu

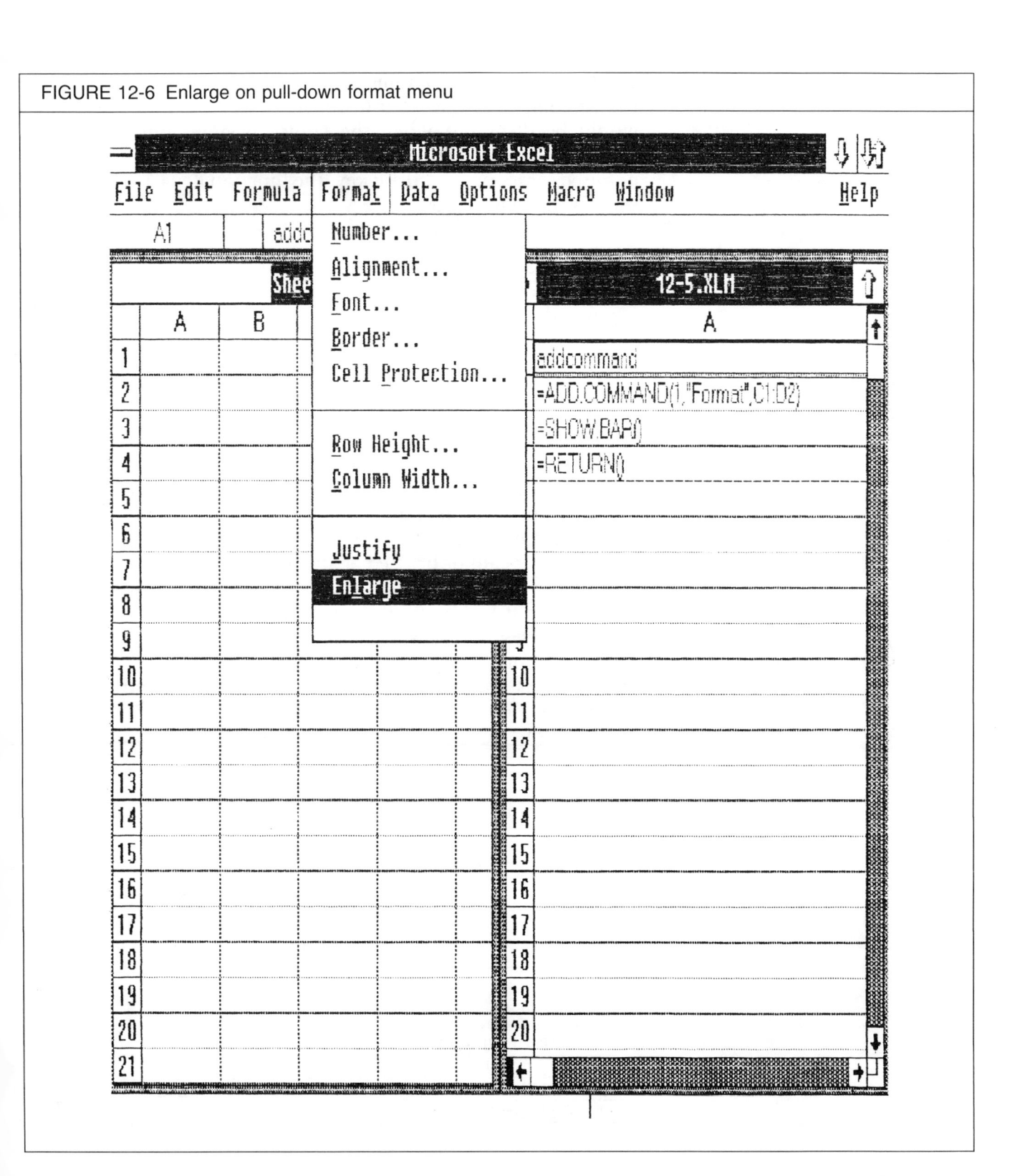

additional optional columns. The third column is left blank. The fourth column can be used to record status bar messages, which would be displayed when the choice is highlighted. The final column can be used for custom help messages. If the final column is not used, pressing the HELP key, the function key F1, will lead the user to the help index.

ENABLING AND DISABLING COMMANDS

You can enable or disable a command by using the following command:

ENABLE.COMMAND(menu_bar_id,menu_position, command_position,state)

If the state is true, the command is able to be used; if the state is false, the command will not be able to be used. if the command cannot be used the menu choice will have a grayed background.

Once the enlarge command has been used to enlarge the entire worksheet, it cannot be used again. The addcommand macro can be modified using the ENABLE.COMMAND() to gray the enlarge option once it has been used (see Figure 12.7).

The enlarge macro, as it has been written, does not operate like other Excel pull-down menu commands. In this macro, the entire worksheet is enlarged, but in most Excel commands, the user selects a portion of the worksheet and then invokes the command. To make this command like all the others, the macro has to be modified.

Just one line of the macro needs to be edited: the SELECT() macro function on the second line. This line has been changed to:

=SELECTION()

FIGURE 12-7 ADD.COMMAND with ENABLE.COMMAND to gray it

	A
7	addcommand
8	=ADD.COMMAND(1,"Format",C7:D8)
9	=SHOW.BAR()
10	=ENABLE.COMMAND(1,"Format","Enlarge",FALSE)
11	=RETURN()

This command takes whatever cells have been selected and applies the rest of the macro to them.

If you want to keep the original macro and create another version of it, you can use edit copy and edit paste to copy it. Then change the name of the macro on the first line. In the sample the name was changed to selectenlarge, since the new macro will enlarge only selected portions of the worksheet. Then modify the second line using the SELECT() macro function. The new macro looks like this Figure 12.8. Use formula define name to name the macro. Indicate that it is a command macro, and assign a shortcut key. Remember to modify the macro that calls this macro (in cell D2 of the other macro sheet); the cell will now be:

sample.xlm!selectenlarge

Then, save this macro sheet using file save or save as. If you are assigning a new name to the sheet, save the workspace using the new macro sheet.

ADDING MENUS

In addition to adding commands to existing menus, you can create your own menus in Excel. To add a menu, use the ADD.MENU() macro function:

ADD.MENU(menu_bar_id,menu_reference)

Excel begins with six menu bars; you can add up to 15 new menu bars.

FIGURE 12-8 Selectenlarge macro

	D
10	selectenlarge
11	=SELECT()
12	=REPLACE.FONT(3,"Helv",24,TRUE,FALSE,FALSE,FALSE)
13	=FORMAT.FONT("Helv",24,TRUE,FALSE,FALSE,FALSE)
14	=COLUMN.WIDTH(40)
15	=RETURN()

DELETING MENUS AND COMMANDS

Excel permits you to delete both built-in and custom menus and commands. To do this, you will have to use the following commands in a macro:

DELETE.MENU(menu_bar_id,menu_position)
DELETE.COMMAND((menu_bar_id,menu_position, command_position)

Instead of graying the enlarge command once it was used, you could have deleted it using DELETE.COMMAND().

RENAMING COMMANDS

Excel permits you to rename both built-in and custom commands. To do this, use the RENAME.COMMAND() macro function:

RENAME.COMMAND(menu_bar_id,menu_position, command_position,name)

Name refers to the new name of the command.

CHECKMARKS

Similarly, a checkmark can be placed beside a command.

CHECK.COMMAND(menu_bar_id,menu_position, command_position,state)

If the state is true, a check mark will appear; if the state is false, no check mark will appear.

CUSTOM DIALOG BOXES

Excel also permits the user to create custom dialog boxes. These user created dialog boxes function exactly like the built-in Excel dialog boxes. These dialog boxes can be used to quickly access data from within a macro, enter data easily (if the dialog box is used with a data form), and check data. Dialog boxes can be created on a macro sheet or by using the Excel dialog editor.

For example, you could group together some of the more popular print settings into one dialog box. The macro would have the following lines to gain access to the dialog box:

```
print document
 = DIALOG.BOX(B8:H21)
 = RETURN()
```

The first line of the macro is its name. The second line opens the dialog box whose coordinates on the macro sheet are from cell B8 to cell H21. The macro ends with a RETURN() macro function, as all Excel macros do.

The portion of the macro sheet referred to contains 7 columns as follows:

B: Type of item, indicated by a number
C: X coordinate of the dialog box
D: Y coordinate of the dialog box
E: Width of item in the dialog box
F: Height of item in dialog box
G: Text
H: Init/Result suggested

If columns C, D, E, and F are left empty, Excel will center the dialog box and place the items in it.

Column B, which refers to the number of the type of item, has 20 different item types. These types include the OK and cancel buttons, text and text boxes, integer and number boxes, and check, group, and list boxes. Refer to the Microsoft Excel Functions and Macros Manual for a complete list of item types and numbers. The top cell of this column should remain blank or refer to a custom help topic.

Column G, which contains text, can include the ampersand. The use of the ampersand will underline the letter after the sign, and this letter in conjunction with the ALT key, can be used to quickly move around a dialog box.

Column H contains the suggested responses. Its use is optional.

Figure 12.9 shows a macro sheet to create a dialog box for print settings. Name this macro using formula define name. Indicate that it is a command macro and assign a shortcut key. When the CONTROL and shortcut keys are depressed simultaneously, you will see the custom dialog box (see Figure 12.10).

DIALOG EDITOR

Another way to create custom dialog boxes is to use the dialog editor. To gain access to the dialog box editor, depress the ALT or /

FIGURE 12-9 Print settings dialog box macro sheet

	A	B	C	D
1	print document			
2	=DIALOG.BOX(B8:H21)			
3	=RETURN()			
4				
5				
6		item	x	y
7				

	E	F	G	H
1				
2				
3				
4				
5				
6	width	height	text	init/result
7				
8				
9			PRINT MENU	
10			&Header	
11				title
12			&Footer	
13				page and page num
14			&Row and Columns	
15				TRUE
16			&Gridlines	
17				TRUE
18			&Copies	
19				1
20			OK	
21			CANCEL	

Rows 8–21 column A/B:
	A	B
8		
9	title	5
10	header text	5
11	header	6
12	footer text	5
13	footer	6
14	row and columns text	5
15	row and column	13
16	gridline text	5
17	gridlines	13
18	copies text	5
19	copies	7
20	ok button	1
21	cancel button	2

key and then depress the SPACEBAR. From the pull-down menu, select run. Then choose dialog editor. You will be confronted with a blank dialog box.

In this dialog box, you can place command buttons, option buttons, check boxes, text, edit boxes, group boxes, list boxes, and icons. Depress the ALT key to gain access to the menu bar, and then select the item pull-down menu. From this menu choose buttons, and you will be able to choose from 4 types of buttons. Choose OK by simply depressing the ENTER key.

The OK button will appear in the dialog box. You can move this button by using the ARROW keys. When you have placed it where you want, depress the ENTER key. The OK button will be moved to the specified location. If you are using a mouse, drag the button to the desired location.

Repeat the above procedure for the cancel button. Place it under the OK button.

Now depress the ALT key and select item text. Type the words

FIGURE 12-10 Custom dialog box

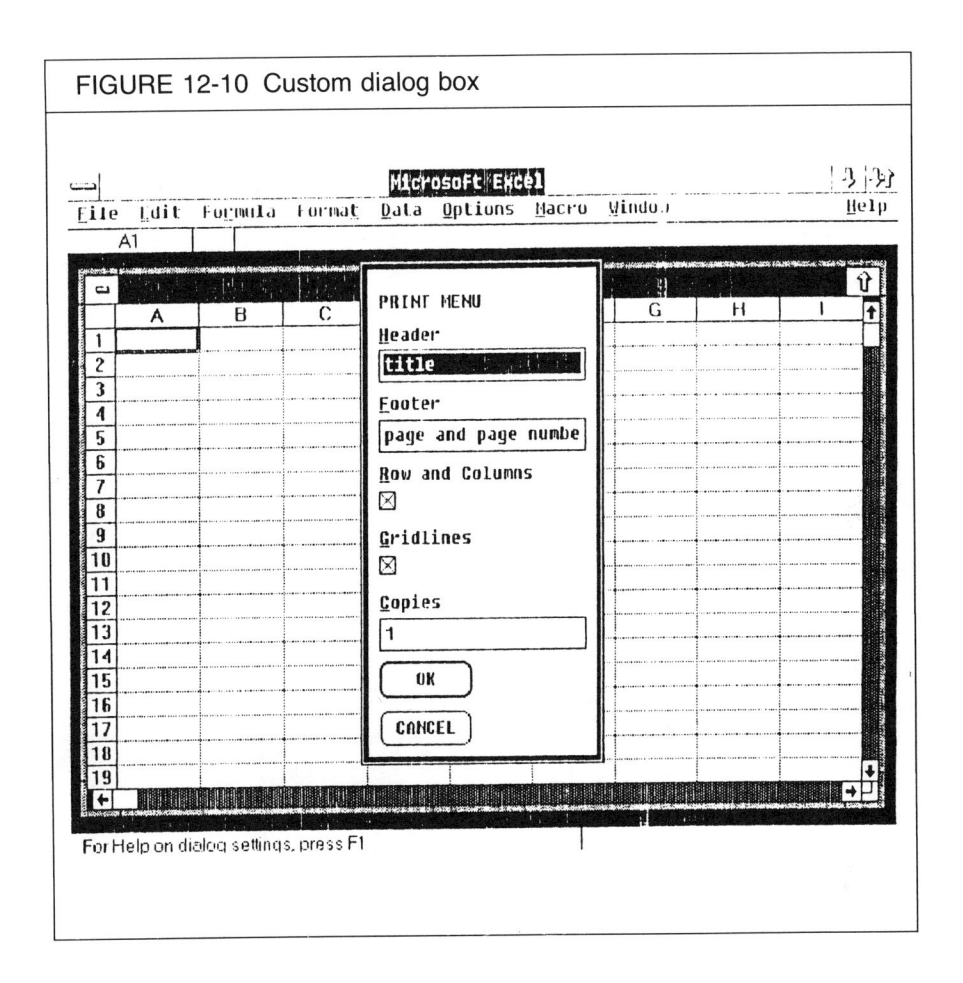

Print Menu. Now move the title of the dialog box to the upper left-hand position.

Add text for the words Header, Footer, and Copies as well as edit text and edit integer boxes as appropriate next to the appropriate text.

Add more text for Column and Row Headings and Gridlines. Then add check boxes next to each using item buttons check boxes. The entire dialog box should look like Figure 12.11. It should be noted that using the ampersand (&) before the letter to be underlined will allow you to move around the dialog box by depressing the ALT and underlined keys simultaneously.

The dialog editor permits you to resize items. To resize an item, select it and use the SHIFT and ARROW keys simultaneously. With a mouse, drag a side or corner of the item.

FIGURE 12-11 Dialog box from dialog box editor

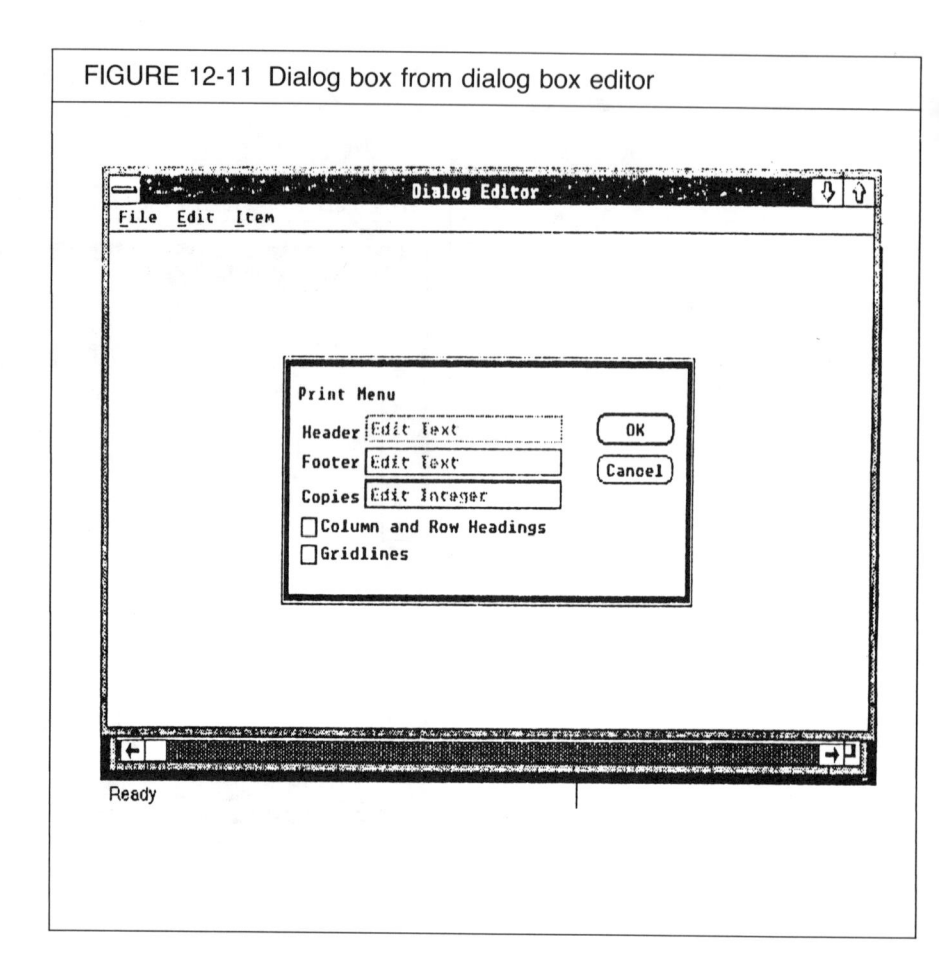

You can also size and place an item within a dialog box by using the edit info command. Depress the ALT key, select the edit pull-down menu, and choose the info dialog box. In this dialog box you can adjust the X and Y coordinates, as well as the width and height of the selected item.

The dialog box must now be copied from the dialog editor to the clipboard. To copy the dialog box to the clipboard, depress the ALT key, select the edit pull-down menu, and choose the select dialog dialog box. Choose the edit copy command. Alternatively, you could depress the ALT key, select the file pull-down menu, and choose exit. Excel will ask if you want to save the dialog box. Then go to a blank portion of a macro sheet. Depress the ALT or / key, select the edit pull-down menu, and choose paste. The dialog box that you created will be translated into macro code on the macro sheet. It will look like a macro that you created (see Figure 12.12). Save the macro sheet so that the dialog box can be used.

FIGURE 12-12 Macro sheet dialog box from dialog box editor

	A	B	C	D	E	F
1		111	70	320	144	
2	5	4	8			Print Menu
3	5	8	34			Header
4	6	60	29	160		
5	5	8	53			Footer
6	5	8	75			Copies
7	5	8	93			Text
8	13	8	93			Check Box
9	13	8	111			Check Box
10	5	24	95			Column and Row Headings
11	5	24	113			Gridlines
12	1	248	26	64		OK
13	2	248	53	64		Cancel
14	6	60	50	160		
15	6	60	71	160		
16	7	60	72	160		

REVIEW

To review the customizing features learned in this chapter, construct a macro that creates a new pull-down menu that will offer the user a faster way to select fonts. To begin, you will have to write or record and edit several macros.

Three macros will have to be created: the first to change the font to script, the second to modern, and the third to Roman. If these fonts are not available for your configuration, choose three other fonts. When you select the font to be modified, do not choose the first of the list of available fonts because this is the default font and will modify every entry throughout the worksheet that is not already specified with a different font.

To record a macro, open a macro sheet (ALT or /, file, new, macro). Set the macro recorder (ALT or /, macro, set recorder) while highlighting the cell that you want the macro to begin recording in. Then change to a worksheet (ALT or /, window, and highlight the worksheet). Select to record the macro (ALT or /, macro, record) and assign a name and shortcut key. Specify that this is a command macro. When ENTER is depressed or OK chosen, the macro recorder will be started.

Select cells (the number and position of the cells selected does

SUMMARY

In this chapter, you have:

1. learned about options workspace;
2. learned more about file save as;
3. learned about the control panel;
4. added a custom command to a menu;
5. disabled a command;
6. learned about adding menus;
7. learned about deleting menus and commands;
8. learned to rename commands;
9. learned to add and delete checkmarks;
10. learned about using the dialog editor.

not matter since the macro will be edited) to have fonts changed in. Then change the font by depressing the ALT or / key, selecting format, and choosing the fonts dialog box. Choose one of the four available fonts other than the first one and then depress the ALT and o keys simultaneously. Choose the script font from the list box and then depress ENTER or choose OK.

Complete the recording of the macro by depressing the ALT or / key, selecting macro, and choosing to stop recorder. The macro has now been recorded. Make the macro sheet the active window (ALT or /, window, and choose the macro sheet). The macro has been recorded, but must be modified: the line beginning with:

+SELECT(cell references)

must be changed to:

=SELECTION()

This will allow the user to select cells to be used with the new menu command. To edit a macro cell, highlight the cell, depress the EDIT key (the function key F2), and make the appropriate changes. Alternatively, you could highlight the cell and type the new command. Then depress the ENTER key.

Repeat this process for the other two macros. You can change the other two fonts listed in the available fonts list for the other two macros. Then be sure to edit each as indicated above. The three macros will look like Figure 12.13.

Save the macro sheet. In the sample, the macro sheet was saved as sample3.xlm.

Now you have to write a brief macro that will create the new menu. Open a new macro sheet and begin by writing the name of the macro; in the sample the macro was named addmenu. Then use the ADD.MENU() macro function:

ADD.MENU(1,B14:C17)

This command adds the new menu to menu bar 1 (the full worksheet and macro menu bar) and refers to cells B14 to C17 for the information for the menu.

The next line tells Excel to show the menu bar:

=SHOW.BAR()

FIGURE 12-13 Macros for three fonts

	A
10	script
11	=SELECTION()
12	=REPLACE.FONT(2,"Script",10,FALSE,FALSE,FALSE,FALSE)
13	=FORMAT.FONT("Script",10,FALSE,FALSE,FALSE,FALSE)
14	=RETURN()

	B
10	modern
11	=SELECTION()
12	=REPLACE.FONT(2,"Modern",10,FALSE,FALSE,FALSE,FALSE)
13	=FORMAT.FONT("Modern",10,FALSE,FALSE,FALSE,FALSE)
14	=RETURN()

	C
10	roman
11	=SELECTION()
12	=REPLACE.FONT(4,"Roman",10,FALSE,FALSE,FALSE,FALSE)
13	=FORMAT.FONT("Roman",10,FALSE,FALSE,FALSE,FALSE)
14	=RETURN()

This command will show the modified menu bar. The final line of the macro is:

= RETURN()

This macro, as all others, ends with a RETURN() macro function.
Cells B14 through C17 begin with the name of the menu in cell B14. The name is Font&s. The ampersand (&) indicates that the s

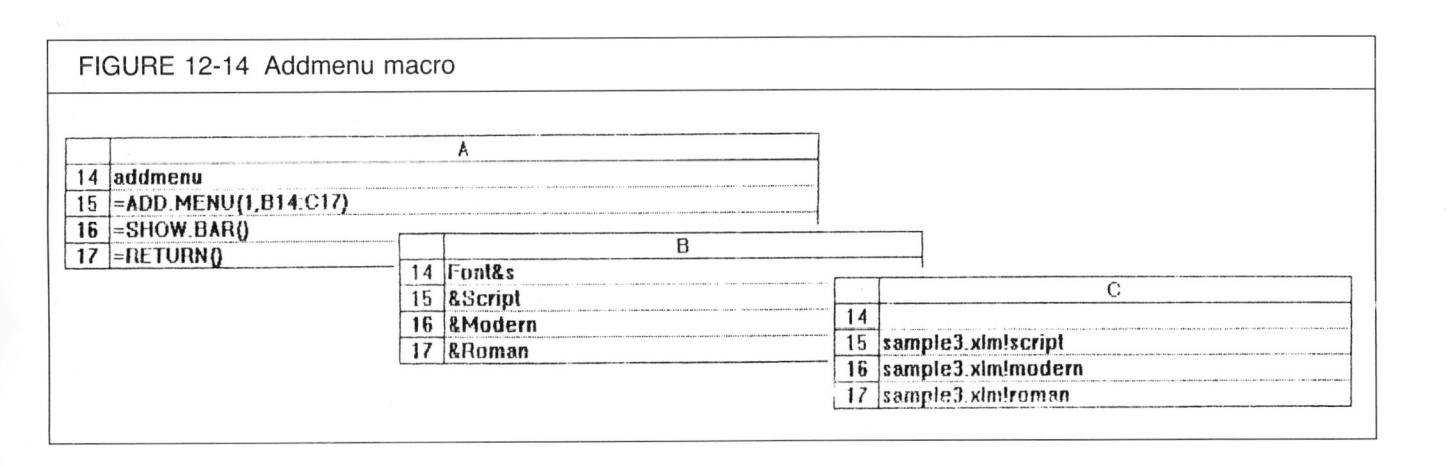

FIGURE 12-14 Addmenu macro

	A
14	addmenu
15	=ADD.MENU(1,B14:C17)
16	=SHOW.BAR()
17	=RETURN()

	B
14	Font&s
15	&Script
16	&Modern
17	&Roman

	C
14	
15	sample3.xlm!script
16	sample3.xlm!modern
17	sample3.xlm!roman

160 USING MICROSOFT EXCEL

FIGURE 12-15 Fonts pull-down menu

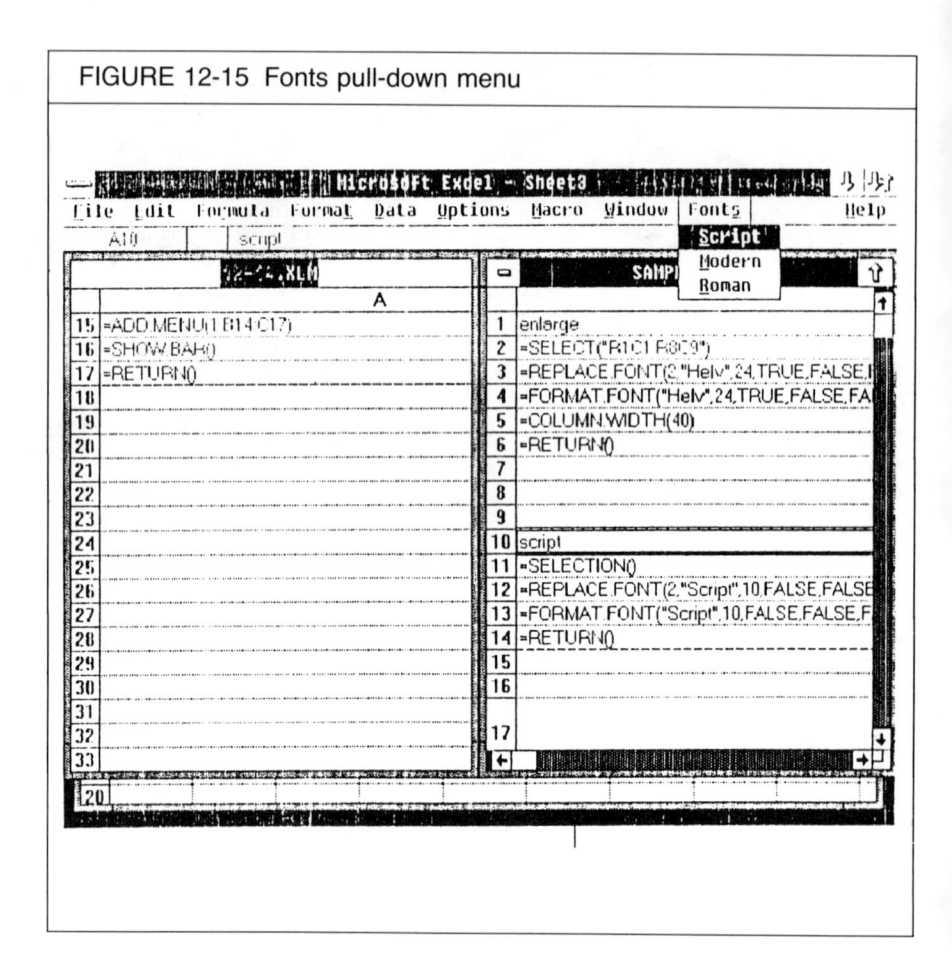

will be underlined and can be used to quickly get to the newly created menu. The rest of the cell reference is as displayed in Figure 12.14.

Name the macro by placing the cellpointer on the name of the macro and depressing ALT or /, selecting the formula pull-down menu, and choosing define name. Define the name, indicate that it is a command macro, and specify a shortcut key.

Save the macro sheet. You may want to save the workspace so that when you open the workspace both macro sheets will be opened; both must be open in order for the macro to add the new menu option and function properly.

Now make a worksheet the active document and use the shortcut key to start the macro. Notice that the menu bar has been modified and the fonts pull-down menu is now available (see Figure 12.15). You can use this menu as you would any other pull-down menu: select the cells to be modified, depress the ALT or /

key, select the fonts pull-down menu, and choose the font. Then depress ENTER. The selected cells' fonts will be modified.

There is a limitation to this command as it is written: it will modify all the cells that have been formatted with the changed fonts. This pull-down menu is best used on worksheets that have not had any fonts specified.

PART II

LIBRARY APPLICATIONS

If you have worked through the first portion of this book, you have learned to construct and use a budget worksheet and databases as well as the techniques of charting data. In the process, you have learned a great deal about Excel, its commands, and macros.

The second portion of this book takes what you have learned one step further by applying the techniques to unique library situations. In this section, Excel will be used to provide an online periodicals list, a method for keeping track of workers' time, creating and using library maps, and bibliographic instruction in the form of a review of the card catalog and in creating quizzes. The applications are used to illustrate various techniques and to open up the possibilities of Excel.

13 PERIODICALS LIST

A library can place its periodicals holdings into an Excel file. Users can then search this file on the computer. The database should be set up utilizing notes for the library's holdings since the title of the journal will probably be too large to permit the title and holdings information to be displayed simultaneously.

PERIODICALS DATABASE

To set up the database, use the first column for the title of the journal. With the title selected, depress the ALT or / key to gain access to the menu bar. Then select the formula pull-down menu. Choose the note dialog box. Type a note in the dialog box specifying the holdings of the library, the location of the back issues if that is relevant for your library, and any other information that you want the user to be able to access. Do not depress the ENTER key while typing the information in the formula note box: depressing the ENTER key is identical to selecting the OK button and will close the formula note box.

Use separate columns of the worksheet for each piece of information by which you will want to be able to search the list. One of these pieces of information will be the subject heading. Use the second column for the subject heading assigned to each journal.

You can sort the list by title to have the journal titles in alphabetical order. Select the entire database excluding the field names and then depress the ALT or / key, select data, and then choose the sort dialog box. Specify the title column as the sort key and ascending order. Then depress the ENTER key or choose OK; the database will be sorted into alphabetical order by title.

Select the entire database, including the headings for each of the columns (in the example, only two columns were used: Title and Subject). With the entire database selected, depress the ALT or / key, select data, and choose set database. Excel will name the selected area database.

Then copy the field names to a separate part of the worksheet: this will be the criteria range. To copy the field headings, select them and then depress the ALT or / key, select the edit pull-down menu, and choose copy. Then select a portion of the worksheet to the right of the periodicals list. Depress the ENTER key or depress the ALT or / key, select edit, and choose paste. Either way, the headings will be copied.

Select the field headings just copied and a single row under them. Depress the ALT or / key, select data, and choose set criteria. The criteria range has now been specified. This criteria range will be used in the macro.

Copy the subject field name to a portion of the worksheet to the right of the periodicals list and criteria range (ALT or /, edit, copy and ALT or /, edit, paste). This will be the extract range, which will be used to extract subject headings.

With this heading selected, depress the ALT or / key, select data, and choose the extract dialog box. In this dialog box specify the unique characteristic: this will permit Excel to only select each subject heading once from the list.

Once the unique subject headings have been selected, sort them alphabetically. Select them and then use data sort (ALT or /, data, sort). You will now have n alphabetical list of all the subject headings used in your periodicals list.

Select the alphabetical list of subjects and name it subject. To name the list, depress the ALT or / key, select formula, and choose define name. The name will be used in the macro.

DIALOG EDITOR

Use the dialog editor to create a custom dialog box that will ask the user if she or he is interested in discovering if the library has a particular title or if he or she wants to search by subject to discover what journals are held in a particular subject.

The dialog box will use text, a text box, a linked list box, which will permit the user to either type in a subject or choose the subject from the list of subjects, and an OK button. The finished dialog box will look like Figure 13.1.

The macro code is displayed in Figure 13.2. To transfer the dialog box from the dialog editor to the macro sheet, exit the dialog editor (ALT, file, exit). Then save the dialog box to the clipboard. When you open a macro sheet, find an unused area and paste the information from the clipboard on to the macro sheet. Excel will translate what was on screen into the required macro code.

Notice that the dialog box has the t in title and the s in subject underlined: in the macro code the ampersand is used preceding these letters.

Cell F7 will have to be filled in manually: the dialog editor does not know where to look for the subjects to be displayed in the linked list box. Since the range was named, type !subject in this cell. The exclamation point (!) tells Excel that the list will be found on the currently active worksheet; the worksheet with the periodicals list will be the active worksheet when the macro is run.

BOX MACRO

When the macro is run, the user will first see the custom dialog box, but before the box is displayed the macro will have to perform

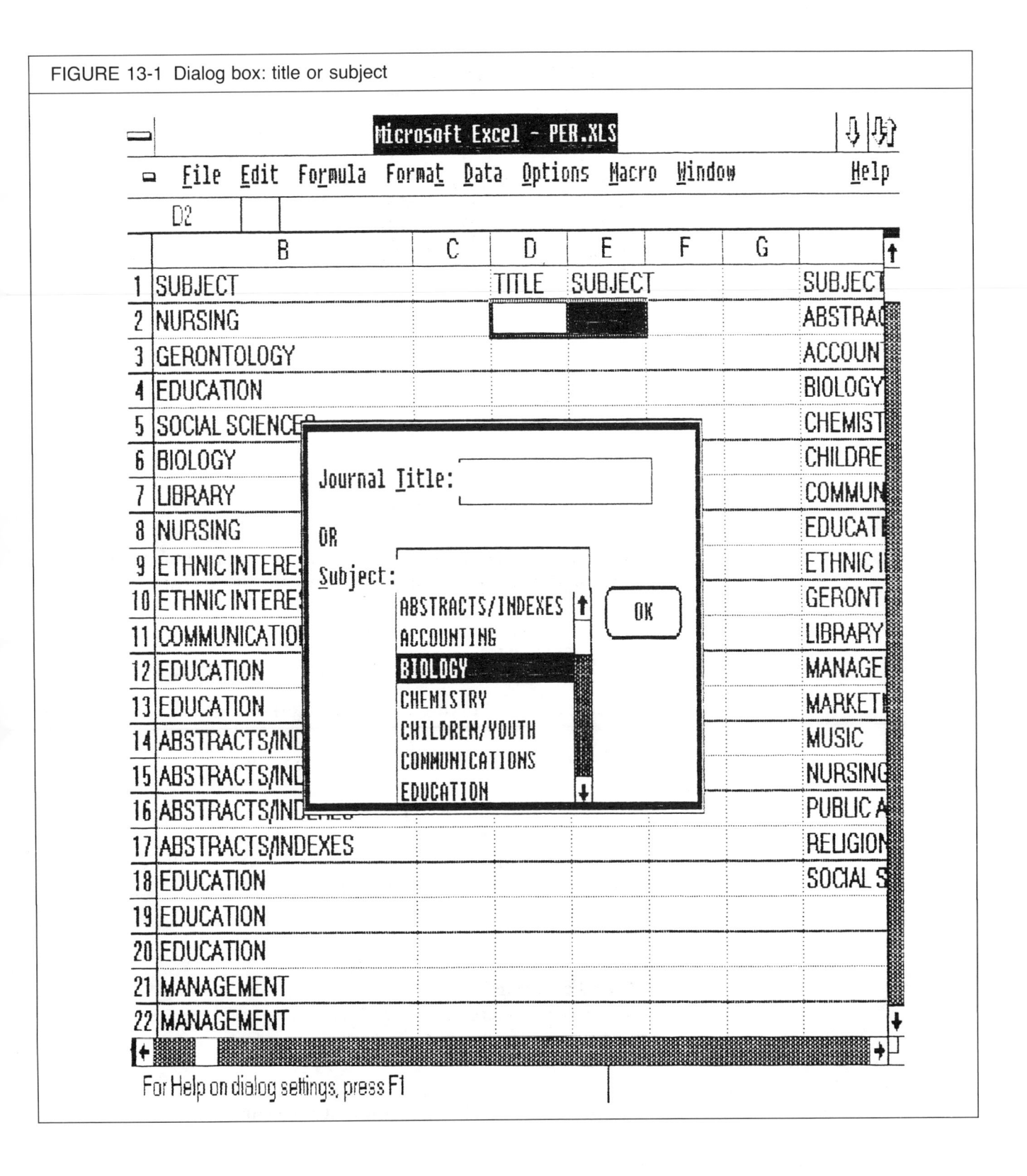

FIGURE 13-1 Dialog box: title or subject

FIGURE 13-2 Macro for dialog box

	A	B	C	D	E	F
1		111	70	320	144	
2	5	8	12			Journal &Title:
3	6	124	11	160		
4	5	8	35			OR
5	6	72	46	160		
6	5	8	50			&Subject
7	16	72	62	160	84	!subject
8	1	244	61	64		OK

a few functions. First, in order for there not to be a default value in either the title or subject portion of the dialog box, the macro must use the SET.VALUE() macro function to set the cells in the dialog box to blank cells:

=SET.VALUE(G3:G5,"")

Then the macro must select and clear the second line of the criteria range so the macro will search for only the title or subject specified.

=FORMULA.GOTO(D2:E2)
=CLEAR(1)

At this point, the dialog box and criteria range are ready for user input.

The next line of the macro displays the dialog box:

=DIALOG.BOX(A1:G8)

Then the macro continues with a macro which will determine if a title or subject is to be searched:

=GOTO(decide)

DECIDE MACRO

The decide macro uses an IF() macro function to determine whether the macro should continue operation with the title or subject macro.

=IF(G3<>"",GOTO(title),GOTO(subject))

Cell G3 is where the dialog box will record the user's input if a specific title is entered. The IF() macro function states that if cell G3 is not empty, continue operation with the macro named title. If cell G3 is empty, continue operation with the macro named subject.

TITLE MACRO

The title macro starts by copying the title entered in the dialog box to the criteria range:

=FORMULA(PER.XLM!G3,!D2)

The exclamation point (!) in the middle of the PER.XLM reference describes the location of this information as an external reference. The exclamation point (!) before the reference to cell D2 indicates its location on the active worksheet (the worksheet containing the periodicals list).

Once the information is in the criteria range, the DATA.FIND() macro function is issued:

=DATA.FIND(TRUE)

Excel will now try to match the title entered by the user to a title on the periodicals list.

If a match is found, not only does the title have to be displayed, but also the information in the note:

=SHOW.INFO(TRUE)

The macro then details which information is to be shown in the displayed information window using the DISPLAY() macro function.

=DISPLAY(FALSE,TRUE,FALSE,FALSE,FALSE, FALSE,0,0,TRUE)

The general form of the DISPLAY() macro function is:

=DISPLAY(cell,formula,value,format,protect,names, precedents,dependents,note)

Since the user will only need to view the name of the journal (which is in the formula portion) and the note, those are the only two arguments which are noted as true. An INPUT() macro function is used to pause the macro for the user to see the information currently on screen and it posts a message:

=INPUT("Press any key to continue. Then depress enter or choose OK",3,,190,190)

Type 3 input boxes have only an OK button (no cancel button is included). The location of this box will be in the lower right hand corner of the display.

Once the ENTER key is depressed or the OK button chosen, the information window is taken off screen and the input is evaluated:

=SHOW.INFO(FALSE)
=IF(A26<>"",GOTO(box),GOTO(A26))

If the response to the INPUT() macro function was anything other than an empty cell (in other words, if a key was pressed), the macro branches to the box macro. If no key was pressed, the macro loops back to the same input box.

SUBJECT MACRO

If the user chooses to search the list by subject, the box macro branches to the subject macro. This macro begins by copying the response to the criteria range:

=FORMULA(PER.XLM!G3,!E2)

In this case, the response is copied into the portion of the criteria range specifying the subject.

The macro then invokes the DATA.FIND() macro function and tells Excel to show the information window:

=DATA.FIND(TRUE)+SHOW.INFO(TRUE)

This line combines two lines from the title macro: it is possible to combine two macro commands on the same line by linking them with a plus sign (+).

The next macro line tells Excel what information to display in the information window. This information is identical to that detailed in the title macro:

=DISPLAY(FALSE,TRUE,FALSE,FALSE,FALSE,FALSE,0,0,TRUE)

This line is followed by an INPUT() macro function:

> =INPUT("Do you want to see more? Press y for yes or n for no",2,,190,190)

Because the user is searching by subject, he or she might want to explore more journals on the same subject.

The macro then has to examine the user's response and branch in different directions depending on that response:

> =IF(A38="y",GOTO(A41),GOTO(box))

Cell A41 contains a command to continue finding journals that match the criteria and is branched to if the user wants to continue viewing journal titles on the selected subject. If the user does not want to continue, the macro loops back to the box macro.

The macro can continue displaying journals on the selected subject:

> =DATA.FIND.NEXT()
> =SHOW.INFO(TRUE)
> =GOTO(A38)

This creates a loop; cell A38 contains the INPUT() macro function which pauses the macro and asks the user if he or she wants to see more.

The entire macro looks like Figure 13.3.

Name each of the macros using formula define name (ALT or /, formula, define name). Specify that each is a command macro and specify a shortcut key for each.

Once all the macros have been thoroughly tested, you can name the box macro AUTO_OPEN. Save the macro sheet (ALT or /, file, save). Then hide the macro sheet (ALT or /, window, hide). Finally save the workspace (ALT or /, file, save workspace). When the workspace is opened, both the macro sheet and the worksheet will be opened, the macro sheet will be hidden, and the box macro will automatically start.

	A
10	box
11	=SET.VALUE(G3:G5,"")
12	=FORMULA.GOTO(D2:E2)
13	=CLEAR(1)
14	=DIALOG.BOX(A1:G8)
15	=GOTO(decide)
16	
17	decide
18	=IF(G3<>"",GOTO(title),GOTO(subject))
19	=RETURN()
20	
21	title
22	=FORMULA(PER.XLM!G3,!D2)
23	=DATA.FIND(TRUE)
24	=SHOW.INFO(TRUE)
25	=DISPLAY(FALSE,TRUE,FALSE,FALSE,FALSE,FALSE,0,0,TRUE)
26	=INPUT("Press any key to contniue. Then depress enter or choose OK",3,,,190,190)
27	=SHOW.INFO(FALSE)
28	=IF(A26<>"",GOTO(box),GOTO(A26))
29	=RETURN()
30	
31	
32	
33	
34	subject
35	=FORMULA(PER.XLM!G5,!E2)
36	=DATA.FIND(TRUE)+SHOW.INFO(TRUE)
37	=DISPLAY(FALSE,TRUE,FALSE,FALSE,FALSE,FALSE,0,0,TRUE)
38	=INPUT("Do you want to see more? Press y for yes or n for no",2,,,190,190)
39	=SHOW.INFO(FALSE)
40	=IF(A38="y",GOTO(A41),GOTO(box))
41	=DATA.FIND.NEXT()
42	=SHOW.INFO(TRUE)
43	=GOTO(A38)
44	=RETURN()

FIGURE 13-3 Subject memo

14 TIME

Often a library has many part-time or student workers who seem to come and go. It is often quite a task to keep track of exactly when the worker has come and gone. Excel can be used to keep track of a worker's time.

First set up a separate worksheet to keep track of the time for each of the workers. The first column of each can be headed IN; the second column headed OUT, and the third headed TOTAL. Only three columns will be used on each of the worksheets for keeping track of the time. Widen each of the columns to accommodate the information; a column width of 20 works well. To widen the columns, select them by holding down the SHIFT key while using the ARROW keys or by using the EXTEND key, the function key F8. If you are using a mouse, click on and drag the column letters. When the columns have been selected, depress the ALT or / key, select the format pull-down menu, and choose column width. In the column width dialog box, indicate the new width of the columns.

Name the first cell in the A column IN; name the first cell in the second column OUT. To name a cell, select it and depress the ALT or / key, select formula, and choose define name. These names will be used in the macro which will be written.

Now format the first two columns, which will be used for recording the arrival and departure times, to record the date and time. To select the format, select the two columns and then depress the ALT or / key, select the format menu, and choose number. From the format number dialog box choose the date and time format. Depress the ENTER key or choose OK to complete the formatting.

Repeat the formatting for the third column, but instead of choosing date and time as the format, choose time. Once again, depress the ENTER key or choose OK.

Cells A1, B1, and C1 will have the column headings; the row under these three will have to be filled in with something to allow the macro to work properly. The asterisk can be used.

FORMULAS TO COMPUTE TOTAL TIME

Cell C3 requires a formula that will subtract the arrival time from the departure time to compute the total amount of time worked. You could use a simple formula like:

=B3-A3

This formula can be copied down the column using the edit copy and edit paste commands, but at times the results will not be as desired. Undesired results will be displayed if any cell in either the A or B column has something other than a number.

To avoid this problem, you could write a more complicated formula such as:

= IF(AND(ISNUMBER(B3),ISNUMBER(A3)),B3-A3," ")

This formula combines several functions. The AND function tells Excel to test the two indicated cells (B3 and A3) to see if they are numbers. If both are numbers, the AND function returns true.

The IF function states a logical condition. In this case the logical condition is stated with the AND function. If the logical condition is true, Excel will place the remainder of the subtraction of the contents of cell A3 from the contents of cell B3 in the cell in which the formula has been written. If the logical test is false (in this case if either of the tested cells is not a number), Excel will leave the cell in which the formula has been written blank.

This formula can be copied using edit copy and edit paste, and Excel will adjust the relative cell addresses. Unfortunately, there is another possible problem: the subtraction can possibly result in a number that is less than zero. This will occur before a person's departure time is recorded. To avoid this problem, the above formula can be modified:

= IF(AND(ISNUMBER(B3),ISNUMBER(A3),B3-A3 > 0),B3-A3," ")

This formula prevents the possibility of negative numbers in the totals column by introducing another argument in the AND function. This argument tests whether or not the subtraction of the contents of cell A3 from cell B3 will be greater than zero. If this test also results in true (using the AND function, all the tests must be true for the function to return TRUE), the formula will return the remainder of the subtraction. Otherwise, the formula will return a blank cell.

This formula can also be copied using edit cut and edit paste. The relative cell addresses will be adjusted automatically by Excel.

Save this worksheet. Use file save as repeatedly, assigning a unique name for each of the worksheets that will be used for each of the employees who will be using this method of recording his or her time. Then close all the open worksheets.

MACRO SHEET

Open a macro sheet using file new macro sheet. This macro sheet will contain a number of connected short macros. Briefly, one macro will be used to show a custom dialog box. A macro will test the responses made in the dialog box to see whether the user wants to record an arrival or departure time. Two macros will open a designated worksheet and record the arrival or departure time. The final macro will tell Excel what to do in the event of an error.

CUSTOM DIALOG BOX

Before actually writing the dialog box macro, construct a dialog box using the Excel dialog editor. To begin the dialog editor, depress the ALT or / key, depress the SPACEBAR, and then choose run. From this dialog box choose dialog editor.

When this command is run, you will see an empty dialog box. Using the dialog editor commands, you can create a dialog box by placing various items of text, buttons, and edit boxes in the dialog box. After everything has been placed to your satisfaction, you can save the custom dialog box to the clipboard. When you select an empty area on the macro sheet, you can paste the dialog box on to the macro sheet. Excel will convert the dialog box into the required code.

To use the dialog editor, first depress the ALT key to gain access to the menu bar. The menu bar for the dialog editor is similar to that for the rest of Excel though it only has three menu choices: file, edit, and item. Select the item pull-down menu. This pull-down menu has six choices: button, text, edit box, group box, list box, and icon. Choose group box.

A group box is chosen because only one item in a group box can be chosen at a time. In this group box you will have two option buttons: arrival and departure. The item chosen in the group box will determine whether an arrival or departure time will be recorded on the active worksheet.

Next choose item button (ALT, item, button). From the button dialog box choose option button. An option button will appear in the dialog box. Move this button with either the ARROW keys and then the ENTER key or by dragging it with the mouse. With the option button active, type &Arrive. This text will replace the text on screen. The ampersand is used to underline the A so that a user can select this item with the ALT and underlined letter.

With the option button selected, you can simply depress the ENTER key to create another option button in the group box. Repeat the process of typing text to replace the on screen text. This time type &Departure. The D will be underlined.

176 USING MICROSOFT EXCEL

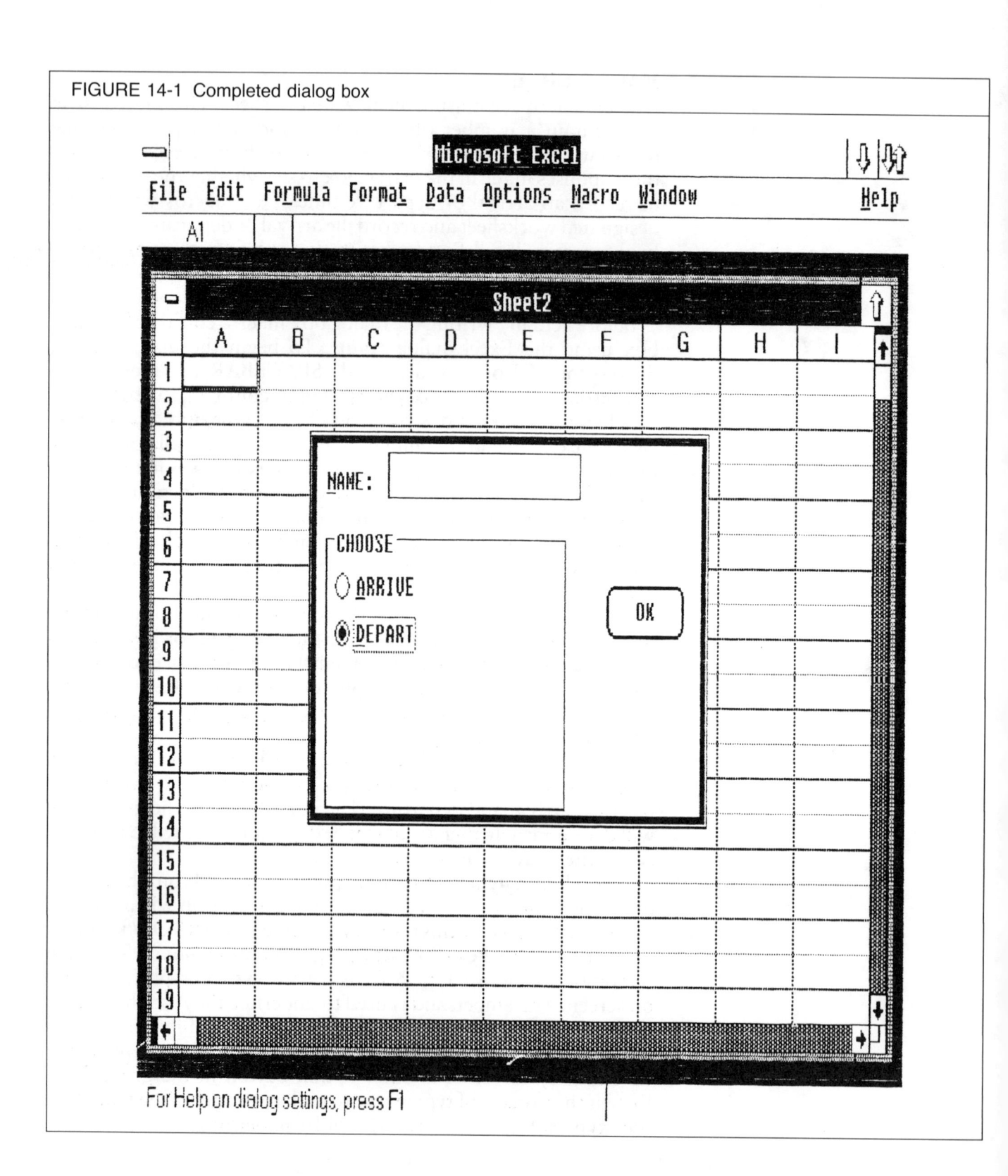

FIGURE 14-1 Completed dialog box

Depress the ALT key again and select item button. This time choose an OK button. Move the OK button to the side of the group box. It is not necessary to have a cancel button: once the user makes his or her selection, an OK button is all that is required.

So far, the user has not designated the name of the worksheet to be opened. Select item text (ALT, item, text). Move it over the group box and then type &Name:. The N will be underlined. Now select item edit box (ALT, item, edit box). From this dialog box choose text edit. A text edit box will appear. Move this box next to Name (see Figure 14.1).

The dialog box is now complete; save it. To save the custom dialog box, depress the ALT key, select the file pull-down menu, and choose exit. Excel will ask if you want to save the created dialog box to the clipboard. Save it to the clipboard.

Then make the macro sheet active and select a cell away from all other items; the dialog box will require many rows and seven columns. Then depress the ALT or / key, select the edit pull-down menu, and choose paste. Excel will translate the dialog box you have created into the code required for a dialog box (see Figure 14.2).

DIALOG BOX MACRO

A macro can now be used to display the created dialog box. The first line of the macro is used for its name: Box. Then the macro removes the previous response from the name text edit box. It does this by using a SET.VALUE() macro function:

=SET.VALUE(G57,"")

Cell G57 is where the response filled in to the name text edit box is placed. By using the SET.VALUE() macro function, the next user

FIGURE 14-2 Dialog box macro code

	A	B	C	D	E	F	G
50		111	68	320	144		
51	14	8	32	200	111	CHOOSE	
52	11	0	0				2
53	12	16	47		18	&ARRIVE	
54	12	16	65		18	&DEPART	
55	1	243	55	64		OK	
56	5	8	9			&NAME:	
57	6	60	4	160			

will see a blank box. If you do not use this command, the user may forget to change the default name, and then will have his or her arrival or departure time recorded on the incorrect worksheet. Using the SET.VALUE macro function, if the user forgets to fill in a name, the macro will detect an error and go to the error macro.

The next lines display the custom dialog box and checks for an error in the response:

=DIALOG.BOX(A50:G57)
=ERROR(TRUE,error)
=GOTO(test)
=RETURN()

The ERROR() macro function tells Excel that if an error is detected proceed to the macro named error. If an error is not detected, the macro continues with the test macro (GOTO(text)).

The entire dialog box macro is displayed in Figure 14.3.

OPEN MACRO

The open macro uses a value obtained in the dialog box macro to determine which file is to be opened. Then the macro instructs Excel to move the active cell to the cell named IN on the active worksheet.

=FORMULA.GOTO(!IN)

The next line uses a SELECT.END() macro function. The SELECT.END() macro function moves the cellpointer to the edge of the occupied cells in the direction specified. In this case the direction is down and the function is:

=SELECT.END(4)

FIGURE 14-3 Box macro

	A
60	BOX
61	=SET.VALUE(G57,"")
62	=DIALOG.BOX(A50:G57)
63	=ERROR(TRUE,error)
64	=GOTO(test)
65	=RETURN()

The cellpointer is now on the last occupied cell, but you will want to move the active cell one more cell down. To do this, use the FORMULA.GOTO() macro function:

= FORMULA.GOTO("r[1]c")

This moves the active cell down one row but keeps it in the same column. The R1C1 style of cell reference is used because a relative reference is desired.

The next line uses a NOW() macro function to record the serial number of the date and time; since the cell was formatted to display the date and time, the actual date and time will be displayed.

= FORMULA(NOW())

Using the NOW() function in conjunction with the FORMULA() macro function converts the NOW() function to a constant value. Otherwise, every time the worksheet was recalculated the NOW() function would change its value.

Then the worksheet is closed and saved using a CLOSE() macro function:

= CLOSE(TRUE)

The user is then given a message, which is posted using an ALERT() macro function. The ALERT() macro function tells the user that the arrival time has been recorded on the named worksheet and tells the user to depress the ENTER key or choose OK to continue. The macro then loops to the dialog box macro (see Figure 14.4).

FIGURE 14-4 Open macro

	A
1	OPEN
2	=OPEN(G57)
3	=FORMULA.GOTO(!IN)
4	=SELECT.END(4)
5	=FORMULA.GOTO("r[1]c")
6	=FORMULA(NOW())
7	=CLOSE(TRUE)
8	=ALERT("Arrival time has been recorded on "&G57&" Depress enter or choose OK to continue")
9	=GOTO(BOX)
10	=RETURN()

CLOSE MACRO

The close macro is very similar to the open macro. First it opens the worksheet the user specified in the dialog box. Then it goes to the cell named OUT on the active worksheet. It also uses the SELECT.END(4), FORMULA.GOTO("r[1]c"), FORMULA(NOW()), and CLOSE(TRUE) macro functions. An ALERT() macro function is also used to notify the user that the departure time has been recorded on the specified worksheet and the user is instructed to depress the ENTER key or choose OK to continue. This macro also loops to the dialog box macro.

The entire close macro is displayed in Figure 14.5.

TEST MACRO

The test macro tests the responses specified in the custom dialog box to determine if the user wants to record an arrival or departure. This macro uses an IF() macro function to test the contents of cell G52 on the macro sheet. A 1 in this cell indicates that the user wants to record an arrival; a 2 in this cell indicates that the user wants to record a departure. The entire test macro is seen in Figure 14.6.

ERROR MACRO

The error macro will be called whenever an error is encountered by Excel. It uses an ALERT() macro function to post a message telling the user that an error has been encountered. This ALERT() macro function has two buttons: an OK and cancel button. The macro then tests to see which button was chosen using an IF() macro function. If the OK button is chosen, the macro displays the dialog box again; if the cancel button is chosen, the macro is halted (see Figure 14.7).

Each of the macros must be named using formula define name. If

FIGURE 14-5 Close macro

	B
1	CLOSE
2	=OPEN(G57)
3	=FORMULA.GOTO(!OUT)
4	=SELECT.END(4)
5	=FORMULA.GOTO("r[1]c")
6	=FORMULA(NOW())
7	=CLOSE(TRUE)
8	=ALERT("Departure time has been recorded on "&G57&" Depress enter or choose OK to continue")
9	=GOTO(BOX)
10	=RETURN()

FIGURE 14-6 Test macro

	A
20	test
21	=IF(G52=1,GOTO(OPEN),GOTO(CLOSE))
22	=RETURN()

you select the first cell of the macro before depressing the ALT or / key to gain access to the menu bar, Excel will display the first cell as the macro's name and reference. Specify that each is a command macro and give each a shortcut key.

Test all the macros to be certain that they work flawlessly. Then use formula define name a second time on the dialog box macro. In addition to naming this macro box, name it AUTO_OPEN. Whenever the macro sheet is opened, this macro will automatically run.

FIGURE 14-7 Error macro

	B
60	error
61	=ALERT("An error has been encountered. Depress enter or choose OK to try again. Choose CANCEL to qui
62	=IF(B61=TRUE,GOTO(BOX),HALT())
63	=RETURN()

15 MAPS

Excel can be used to direct your patrons to different parts of the library. To do this, you must first draw the map on a worksheet and then create macros on a macro sheet.

DRAWING THE MAP

To draw the map, first change the column widths of the active worksheet to 1. This will make the macros work uniformly and properly. To change column widths, depress the ALT or / key, select format, and choose column width.

Then you will probably want to eliminate the gridlines and column and row headings. This will create a blank display on which to draw. To eliminate the display of gridlines and column and row headings, depress the ALT or / key, select options, choose display, and select gridlines and column and row headings. The display will now be without these features.

You are now ready to draw an outline of your library. Use the split vertical (|) for vertical lines; use the underline (_) for horizontal lines. You can then use the same keys and some of the others to denote interior features of your library. These features can include pillars, stacks, reference desks, etc.

You will probably want to scale the library's floor plan so that it will fit on one screen. This will aid in the display of directions when the map is used.

A library map may look like Figure 15.1.

BEGINNING THE MACRO

The beginning of the macro moves the cellpointer to the position on the map that the user is actually at. To move the cellpointer, the macro uses a FORMULA.GOTO() macro function:

=FORMULA.GOTO(J9)

Because the map no longer has gridlines and column and row headings, you should place your cellpointer in the proper location on the map and note its location on the formula bar. On the other hand, you could place the cursor in the proper spot on the worksheet and then name the cell using formula define name. This way, you could use the cell's name instead of its address.

The next line in the macro displays a dialog box:

=DIALOG.BOX(B1:I4)

FIGURE 15-1 Library map

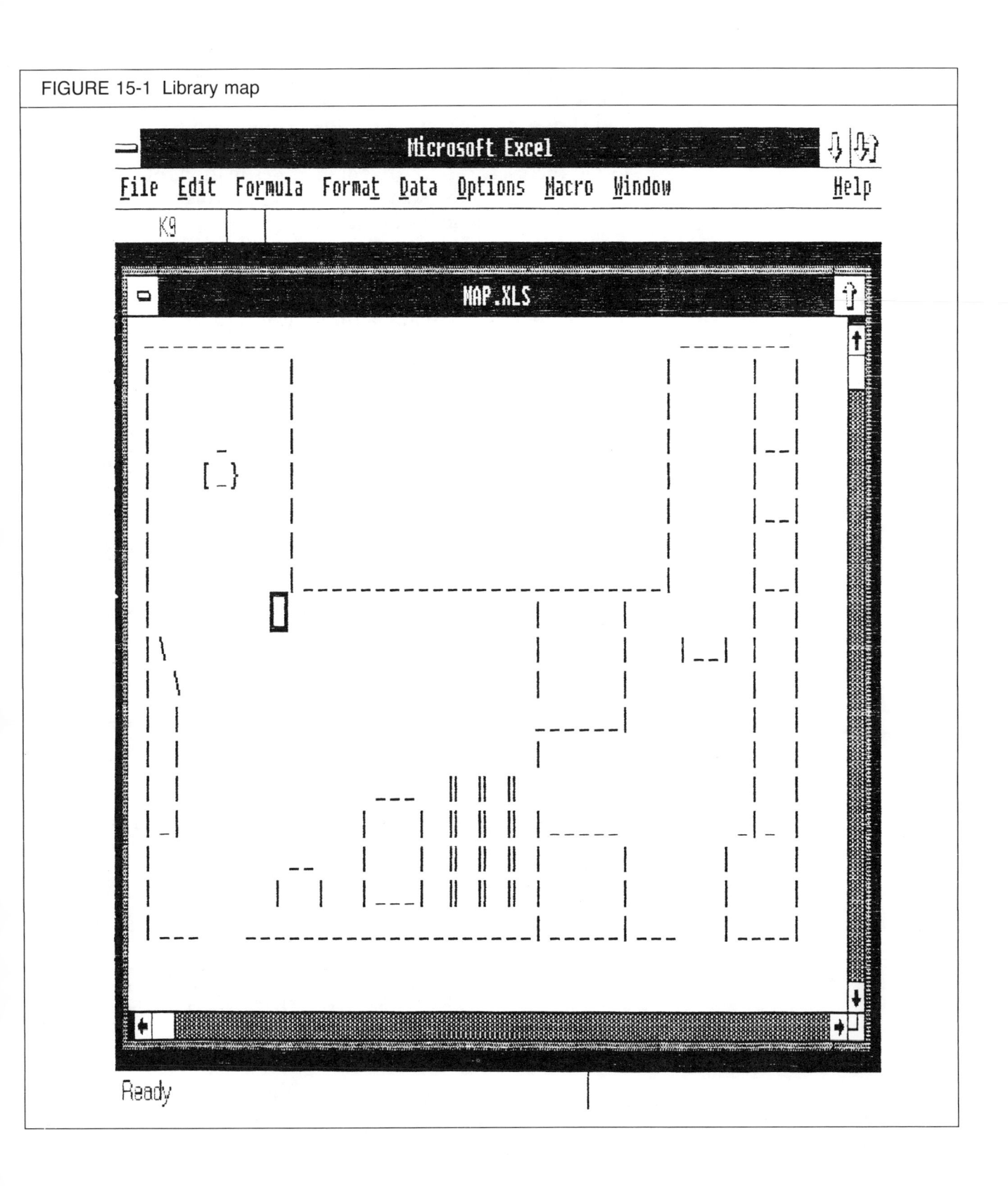

This dialog box can be created using the dialog editor. To use the dialog editor, depress the ALT or / key, depress the SPACEBAR, and choose run. Then choose the dialog editor.

In the blank dialog box that appears, place text (ALT, item, text) to tell the user to select the desired destination, place a list box (ALT, item, list box, standard list box) in which the destinations will be listed, and an OK button (ALT, item, button, OK). When complete, exit the dialog editor, saving the dialog box, and then paste it on the active macro sheet (ALT or /, edit, paste).

The dialog box will not be usable as it is: it has a list box but nothing to be listed in it. On the same macro sheet, create a list of the destinations to which users will be directed. The names of the destinations cannot be long: the list box will only display a limited number of characters at a time. A little experimenting might help. Because of the limits of the CHOOSE() macro function which will be used, only twelve destinations can be designated. When the list is ready, select the entire list. Put it in alphabetical order using date sort; then name the list using formula define name. The name specified will be inserted in the dialog box just created. In the sample, the name destination was used. The entire dialog box macro code looks like Figure 15.2.

The dialog box will look like Figure 15.3.

When the user chooses an item from the list box, its number on the destination list will be placed in cell H2. The next macro

FIGURE 15-2 Dialog box macro code: list box

	A
1	start
2	=FORMULA.GOTO(J9)
3	=DIALOG.BOX(B1:I4)
4	=CHOOSE(H2,card(),circd(),COPY(),ent(),micro(),perd(),rel(),refst(),rest(),sp(),stack(),study())
5	=BEEP()
6	=WAIT(NOW()+0.0007)
7	=DIALOG.BOX(K1:Q4)
8	=CLOSE(FALSE)
9	=OPEN("map.xls",0,TRUE)
10	=start()

	B	C	D	E	F	G
1		111	68	320	144	
2	15	40	44	160	84	Destinations
3	5	16	10			Where do you want
4	1	244	72	64		OK

function chooses the correct subroutine to execute depending on the number of the destination in cell H2. This is accomplished with a CHOOSE() macro function:

=CHOOSE(H2,card(),circd(),copy(),ent(),micro(), perd(),ref(),refst(),rest(),sp(),stack(),study)

The CHOOSE() macro function will pick the subroutine that corresponds to the number of the item in the list box. The subroutines are listed in the same order in both the list and the CHOOSE() macro function.

SUBROUTINES

Each destination has its own subroutine; each subroutine must be written separately. Each relies on the SET.VALUE() and FOR() macro functions. The SET.VALUE() macro function sets a value in a specified cell on the macro sheet; the FOR() macro function executes a loop.

The SET.VALUE() macro function sets a value in a cell on the macro sheet that is used in the FOR() macro function. There will be four of these cells needed, one for each direction: nend (for north end), send (south end), eend (east end), and wend (west end). These will tell Excel how many times to execute the loop in the FOR() macro function.

The FOR() macro function also uses a range named count. This range counts the number of times the loop has been executed; when the count number is equal to the end number in the FOR() macro function, the loop stops and the macro continues to the next line.

The FOR() macro function has the following format:

=FOR(counter,start,stop,step)

For example, to have the macro execute a subroutine four times, the macro function would be:

=FOR("count",1,send,1)

This assumes that the cell named send contains the value 4.

Subroutines for Directions: Each of the named subroutines will rely on subroutines for the four directions that a user can go: north,

186 USING MICROSOFT EXCEL

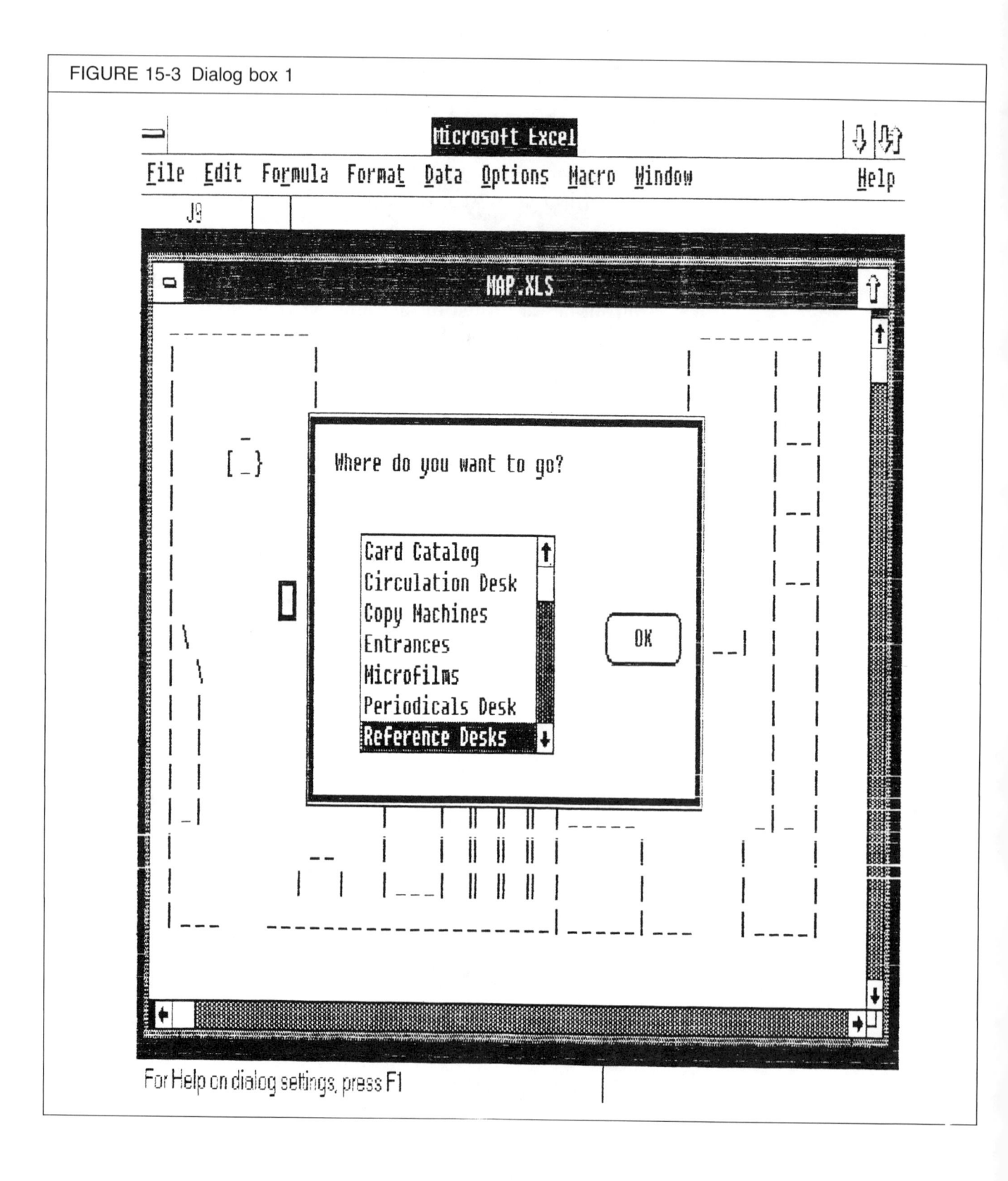

FIGURE 15-3 Dialog box 1

south, east, and west. Each of these subroutines uses FORMULA.GOTO() and FORMULA() macro commands to move the cellpointer and to put a line in the active cell.

The south() subroutine has the following lines:

=FORMULA.GOTO("r[1]c")
=FORMULA("|")
=RETURN()

The first line uses the R1C1 style of reference to move the cellpointer one cell down. This cell is then filled in with the split vertical (|). Then the subroutine returns control to the calling macro.

The north() subroutine is similar, except the FORMULA.GOTO() macro function is slightly changed:

=FORMULA.GOTO("r[-1]c")

This moves the cellpointer up one cell.

The east() subroutine has the following lines:

=FORMULA.GOTO("rc[1]")
=FORMULA("_")
=RETURN()

This subroutine is similar to the one above, except that it moves the cellpointer one cell right.

The west() subroutine is similar, except the line using the FORMULA.GOTO() macro function is slightly different:

=FORMULA.GOTO("rc[-1]")

This line moves the cellpointer one cell to the left.

Card() Subroutine: If the user chooses to find the directions to the card catalog from the list box, the number 1 would appear in cell H2 on the macro sheet. The CHOOSE() macro function would then tell Excel to execute the card() subroutine (see Figure 15.4). This subroutine uses SET.VALUE() macro functions to set the values in the cells named send (south end) and eend (east end). Then a loop is set up using FOR() macro functions. Each loop executes one of the directional subroutines. Each loop is concluded with a NEXT() macro function. When the entire subroutine is complete, a RETURN() macro function returns control to the original macro.

Perd() Subroutine: If the user chooses the periodicals desk as the desired destination, the number 6 would appear in cell H2. The CHOOSE() macro function would then execute the perd() subroutine (see Figure 15.5).

This subroutine, like the card() subroutine, uses the SET.VALUE() macro function to prepare for the loops executed by the FOR() macro functions.

Ref() Subroutine: The ref() subroutine is slightly different: this library has two reference desks and the subroutine directs the user to both of them. First one desk is pointed out; then directions to the other are shown. When the first reference desk is reached, a BEEP() macro function is used to alert the user that a reference desk has been reached. Then, with those directions still on screen, the macro directs the user to the other reference desk (see Figure 15.6).

RETURNING TO THE MACRO

Whichever destination is chosen, once the subroutine called by the CHOOSE() macro function has finished, Excel returns control to the calling macro. The next line is used to alert the user that the destination has been reached: it sounds a note using a BEEP() macro function:

=BEEP()

Then the macro is told to wait for about a minute to allow the user a chance to study the directions given. This is accomplished with a WAIT() macro function:

=WAIT(NOW()+.0007)

The NOW() function tells Excel the serial number of the current date and time; .0007 is approximately 1 minute.

After waiting for one minute, the macro continues to the next line:

=DIALOG.BOX(K1:Q4)

This is a dialog box which uses only text and an OK button. The dialog box can be easily created using the dialog editor. To run the dialog editor, depress the ALT or / key, depress the SPACEBAR, and then choose run. From the dialog box, choose dialog editor.

FIGURE 15-4 Card() subroutine

	A
24	card()
25	=SET.VALUE(send,6)
26	=FOR("count",1,send,1)
27	=south()
28	=NEXT()
29	=SET.VALUE(eend,5)
30	=FOR("count",1,eend,1)
31	=east()
32	=NEXT()
33	=RETURN()

FIGURE 15-5 Perd() subroutine

	B
24	perd()
25	=SET.VALUE(send,4)
26	=FOR("count",1,send,1)
27	=south()
28	=NEXT()
29	=SET.VALUE(eend,18)
30	=FOR("count",1,eend,1)
31	=east()
32	=NEXT()
33	=SET.VALUE(send,1)
34	=FOR("count",1,send,1)
35	=south()
36	=NEXT()
37	=SET.VALUE(eend,14)
38	=FOR("count",1,eend,1)
39	=east()
40	=NEXT()
41	=SET.VALUE(send,1)
42	=FOR("count",1,send,1)
43	=south()
44	=NEXT()
45	=RETURN()

FIGURE 15-6 Ref() subroutine

	C
24	ref()
25	=SET.VALUE(send,7)
26	=FOR("count",1,send,1)
27	=south()
28	=NEXT()
29	=SET.VALUE(eend,1)
30	=FOR("count",1,eend,1)
31	=east()
32	=NEXT()
33	=BEEP()
34	=FORMULA.GOTO(J9)
35	=SET.VALUE(send,4)
36	=FOR("count",1,send,1)
37	=south()
38	=NEXT()
39	=SET.VALUE(eend,18)
40	=FOR("count",1,eend,1)
41	=east()
42	=NEXT()
43	=SET.VALUE(send,1)
44	=FOR("count",1,send,1)
45	=south()
46	=NEXT()
47	=SET.VALUE(eend,12)
48	=FOR("count",1,eend,1)
49	=east()
50	=NEXT()
51	=SET.VALUE(nend,3)
52	=FOR("count",1,nend,1)
53	=north()
54	=NEXT()
55	=RETURN()

Create the dialog box and then exit the dialog editor, saving the dialog box. Paste it onto the active macro sheet.

The dialog box will look like Figure 15.7.

The macro code for this dialog box is shown in Figure 15.8.

If you would prefer, you could use an ALERT() macro function to post a message to the user. The format for the ALERT() macro function is:

=ALERT("message",type)

Using the ALERT() macro function forces you to have an icon in the displayed message area. Type 2 will display an asterisk; type 3 will display an exclamation point.

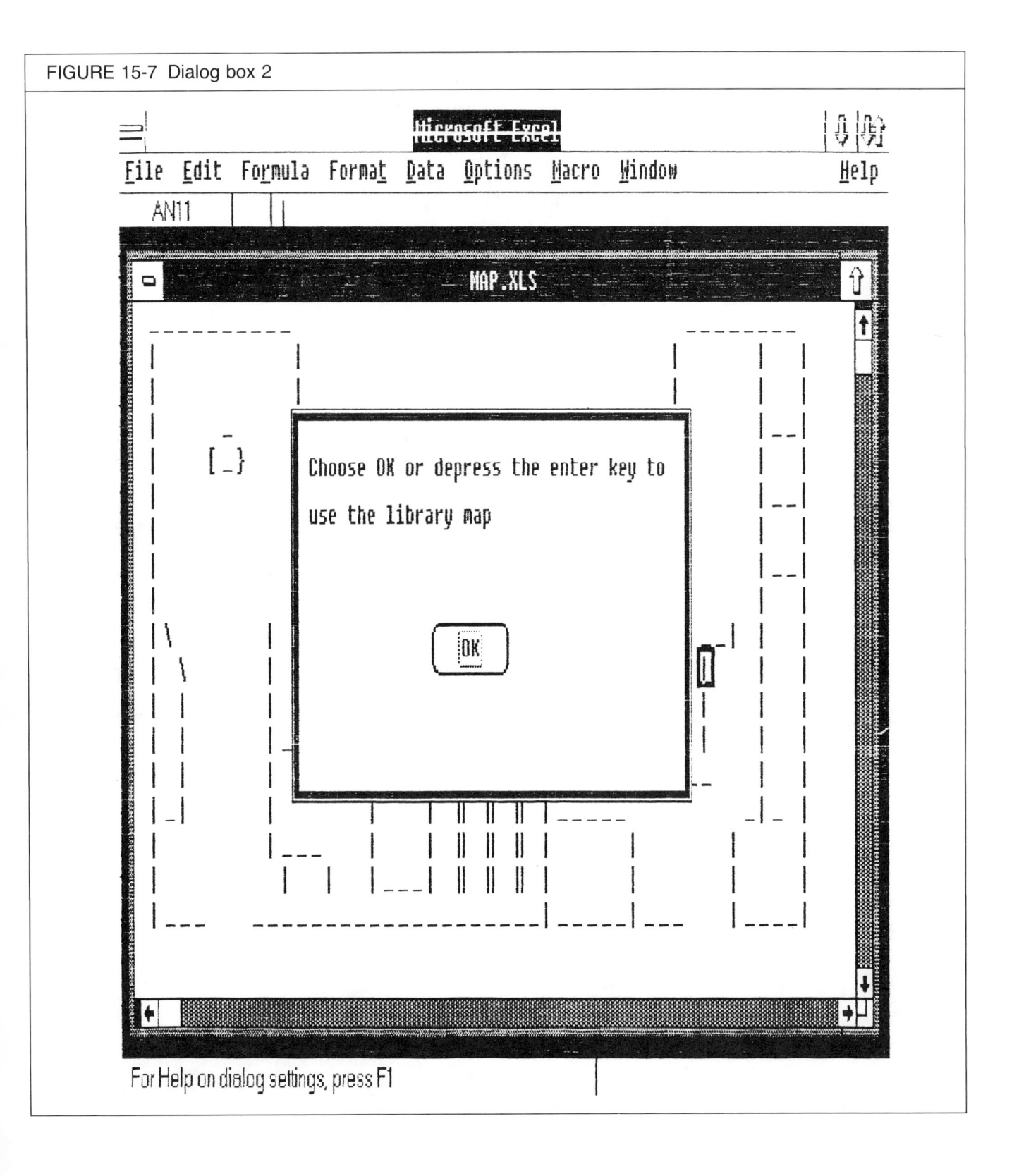

FIGURE 15-7 Dialog box 2

NEXT USER

The map must then be made ready for the next user. To do this, you can close and not save the active worksheet. Then you can reopen the map worksheet:

= CLOSE(FALSE)
= OPEN("map.xls",0,TRUE)

The logical value of false in the CLOSE() macro function tells Excel not to save the current worksheet, but simply to close it. The OPEN() macro command opens the specified worksheet (in quotation marks since it is text), tells it to update neither external nor remote references, and makes the file read only.

The final line returns the macro to its beginning:

= start()

NAMING AND SAVING

Name the macro twice: once start() so that the macro can repeat itself, once AUTO_OPEN so it will automatically open when the macro sheet is opened. Save the macro sheet and the worksheet separately (ALT or /, file, save or save as). Then hide the macro sheet (Alt or /, window, hide). Save the workspace (ALT or /, file, save workspace). When the workspace is opened, the map will be displayed, the macro sheet will be hidden, and the macro will automatically execute.

FIGURE 15-8 Active macro sheet

	K	L	M	N	O	P
1		111	68	320	144	
2	5	8	12			Choose OK or depress the enter
3	5	8	30			use the library map
4	1	111	79	64		OK

16 CATALOG CARDS

Excel can be used to reinforce a lesson in which library users are taught what information is on a library's catalog card. To reinforce the lesson, a worksheet having reproductions of catalog cards must be created in addition to a macro sheet containing macros.

THE WORKSHEET

The worksheet should contain three catalog cards: an author, title, and subject card, all for the same book. Each of the cards should be in completely separate portions of the worksheet so that when one card is being viewed by the user, the others cannot be seen.

Before entering the information for the cards, use options display to remove the gridlines and row and column headings from the display. To use options display, depress the ALT or / key, select the options pull-down menu, and choose display. Turn off the gridlines and row and column headings checkboxes.

When entering the information for the cards, you may want to align the cells on the call number. To align the contents of a cell, select the cell and then depress the ALT or / key, select format, and choose align. You may also wish to vary the height of some of the blank rows to permit all the information to be seen on screen at one time as well as to insure that the macros will place INPUT() messages that do not overlap the cards. To vary a row height, select the row and then depress the ALT or / key, select format, and choose row height.

Name each of the cards, using formula define name. First select the entire width of the screen for each of the cards that you wish displayed when one of the cards is viewed. This will mean that some blank cells might be selected. This is necessary so that when the FORMULA.GOTO() macro function is used in the macro, the user will see the entire card. Once the proper area has been selected for each of the cards, depress the ALT or / key, select formula, and choose name. Define the name of the cards: author, title, and subject. These names will be used in the macros.

THE MACRO SHEET

The macro sheet is composed of a number of short macros, many using custom dialog boxes. In addition, the ALERT() and INPUT() macro functions are used.

To create custom dialog boxes, it is easiest to use the dialog editor. To gain access to the dialog editor, depress the ALT or / key. Depress the SPACEBAR. Finally choose the run dialog box. From this dialog box choose to run the dialog editor.

The dialog boxes created for this macro rely on group boxes with option buttons. Only one option button can be chosen in each group and the macros analyze the choices made and branch accordingly.

The ALERT() macro function is used to post messages to the user. These messages are posted and do not need a response. If a response is needed, the macro uses the INPUT() macro function. It then tests the response and branches according to whether or not the correct answer was entered.

Beginning Macro: The set of macros begins with a short macro that requests the name of the user. The name entered here will be used in some of the messages.

=INPUT("Type your name",2,"INPUT",,190,190)

The INPUT() macro function posts the message in a box located in the lower right hand corner of the screen, indicated by the X and Y positions 190 and 190. The input box is titled Input. The 2 indicates that the response will be text. The two commas preceding the location of the box indicate that there is no default response to this query.

When the name has been typed and the ENTER key depressed or OK chosen, the macro proceeds to the next line which tells Excel to continue the macro with the macro named box.

=GOTO(Box)

The GOTO() macro function is used to tell Excel to continue macro operation with a different named macro.

Box Macro: The box macro uses a custom dialog box to allow the user to decide on which type of catalog card he or she wishes to review (see Figure 16.1). The dialog box created with the dialog editor is displayed in Figure 16.2. The macro uses the following line to display the dialog box:

=DIALOG.BOX(A10:G19)

After the user selects one type of card and either depresses the ENTER key or chooses the OK button, the macro will test to see which choice was made. The choice is in cell G15 on the macro sheet, and the macro uses a CHOOSE() macro function to choose which direction to branch.

=CHOOSE(G15,GOTO(author),GOTO(title),GOTO(subject))

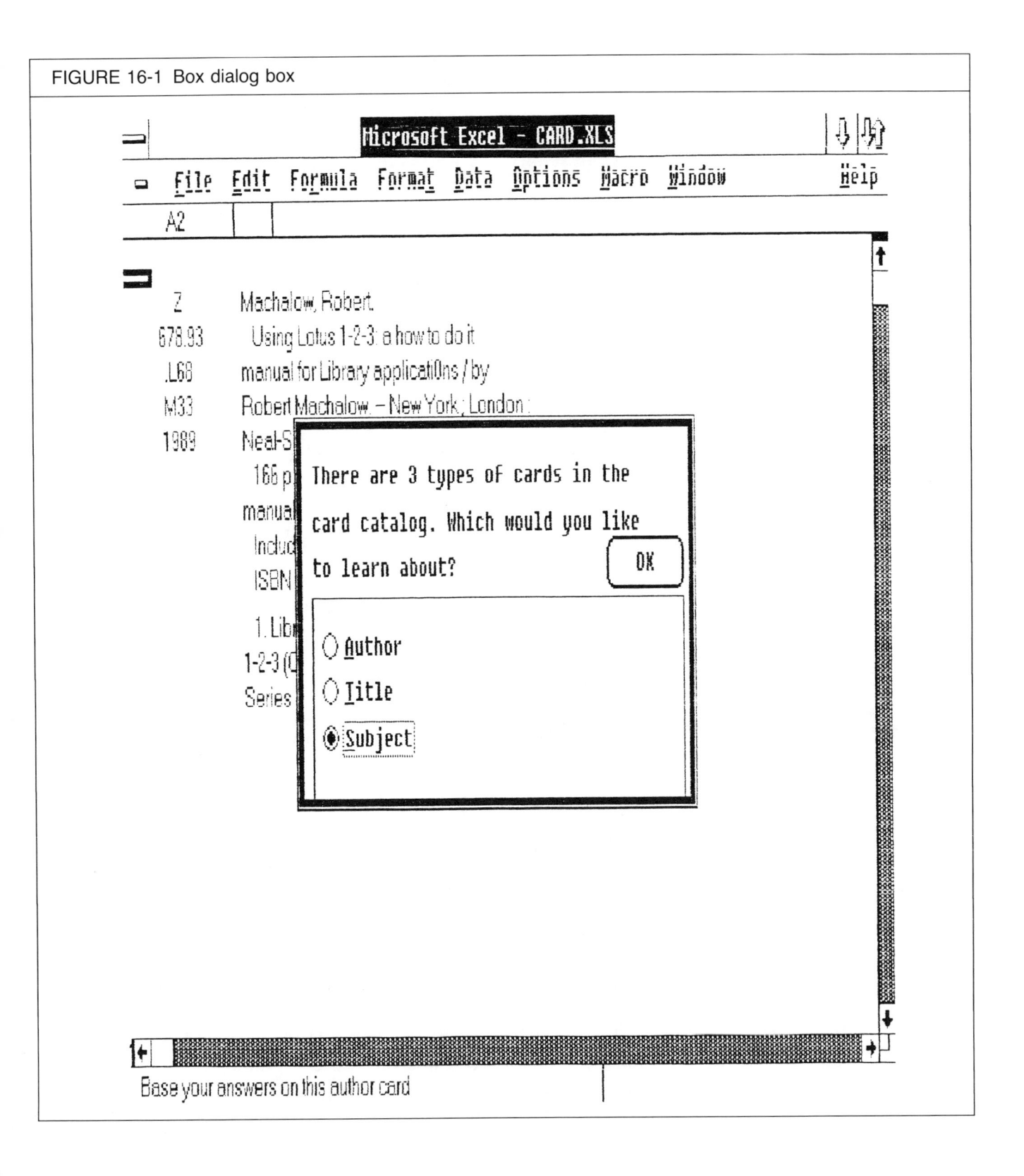

FIGURE 16-1 Box dialog box

There are 3 types of cards in the card catalog. Which would you like to learn about?

○ Author
○ Title
◉ Subject

Base your answers on this author card

FIGURE 16-2 Dialog box formula

	A	B	C	D	E	F
10		111	68	320	144	
11	5	8	12			There are 3 types of cards in the
12	5	8	30			card catalog. Which would you like
13	5	8	48			to learn about?
14	14	8	60	308	135	
15	11	0	0			
16	12	16	75		18	&Author
17	12	16	93		18	&Title
18	12	16	111		18	&Subject
19	1	252	42	64		OK

Thus, if a 1 is in cell G15 the macro will branch to a macro named author; if a 2 is in cell G15 the macro will branch to a macro named title; if a 3 is in cell G15 the macro will branch to a macro named subject.

AUTHOR MACROS

If the user desires to review the contents of the author catalog card, the author macro is branched to. This macro begins by making the author card the visible portion of the worksheet:

= FORMULA.GOTO(!author)

A FORMULA.GOTO() macro function is used because the cellpointer is being moved. The named range is used rather than a cell location. The exclamation point (!) indicates that the named range is on the active worksheet.

At this point, the author card is displayed in reverse video (white letters on a black background). To remedy this situation, you have to move the active cell:

= FORMULA.GOTO("R[1]C")

This moves the active cell down one cell and restores the display to its normal look.

The macro proceeds by setting the default value in the dialog box to 1, an incorrect answer. Since the dialog box will be using a group box with option buttons, the default would be the last chosen button which may be a correct answer; by setting the

FIGURE 16-3 Author's name dialog box

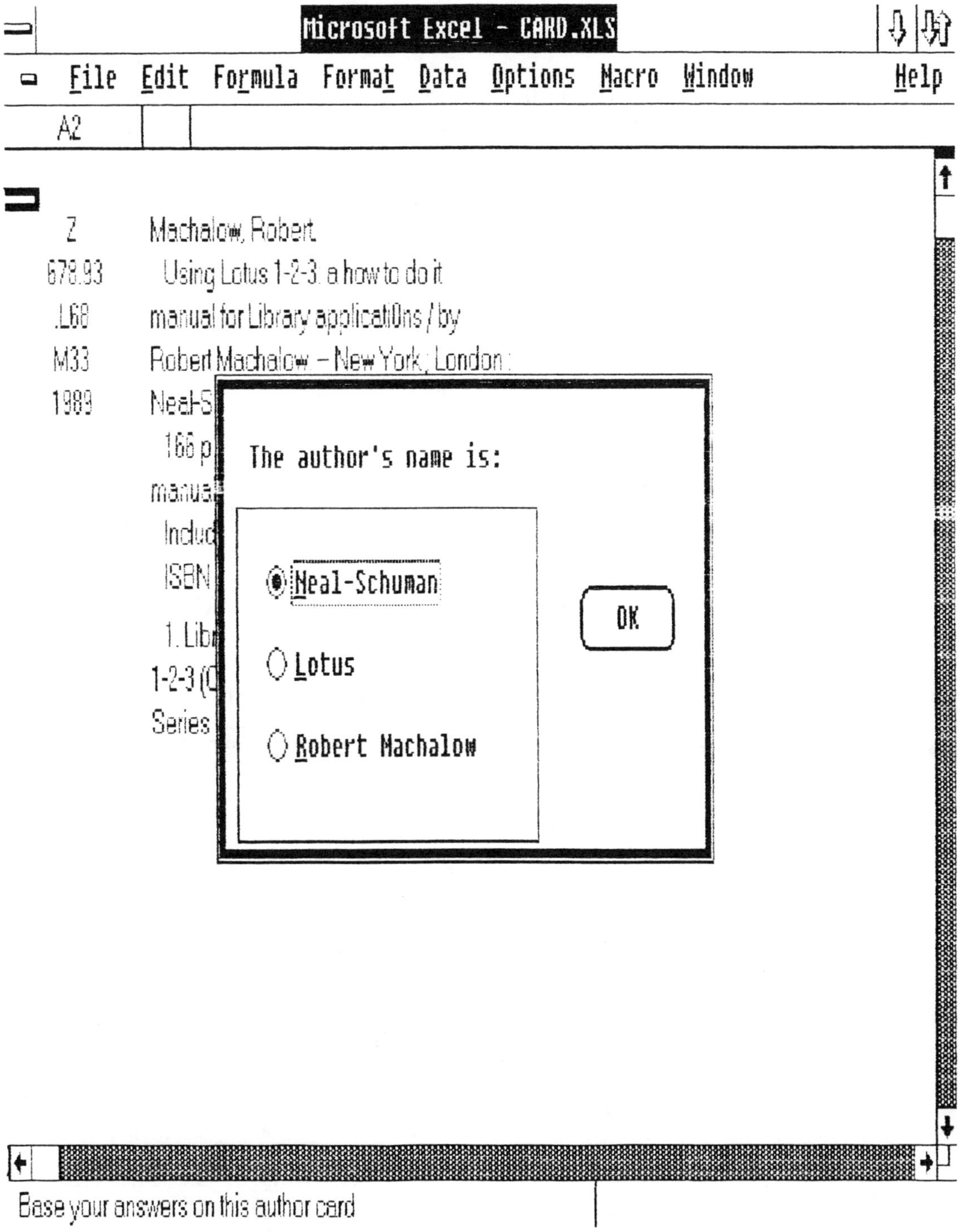

```
Microsoft Excel - CARD.XLS
File  Edit  Formula  Format  Data  Options  Macro  Window          Help
A2
```

      Z   Machalow, Robert
   678.93   Using Lotus 1-2-3: a how to do it
    .L68   manual for Library applications / by
    M33   Robert Machalow – New York; London :
    1989   Neal-S
              166 p   The author's name is:
             manua
             Includ
             ISBN   ⦿ Neal-Schuman   [OK]
             1. Libr
             1-2-3 (○ Lotus
             Series
                        ○ Robert Machalow

Base your answers on this author card

default to an incorrect answer the user will have to think rather than simply depress the ENTER key or choose the OK button.

=SET.VALUE(H33,1)

Then the macro posts a message in the message area in the bottom left corner of the screen using a MESSAGE() macro function:

=MESSAGE(TRUE,"Base your answers on this author card")

Then the dialog box is displayed (see Figure 16.3). This dialog box is displayed using this macro command:

=DIALOG.Box(B30:H37)

The dialog editor created this custom dialog box using this code in Figure 16.4.

The response will be in cell H33, and a CHOOSE() macro function is used to branch the macro:

=CHOOSE(H33,GOTO(ErrorAU),GOTO(ErrorAU), GOTO(author2))

The CHOOSE() macro function will branch to an error macro if one of the incorrect answers is chosen and to an author2 macro if the user selects the correct answer.

Error Macro: The error macro, branched to in the event of an incorrect choice, begins with an ALERT() macro function:

FIGURE 16-4 Dialog box code for author's name

	B	C	D	E	F	G
30		111	68	320	144	
31	14	8	32	200	111	
32	5	16	15			The author's name is:
33	11	0	0			
34	12	28	51		18	&Neal-Schuman
35	12	28	77		18	&Lotus
36	12	28	103		18	&Robert Machalow
37	1	236	62	64		OK

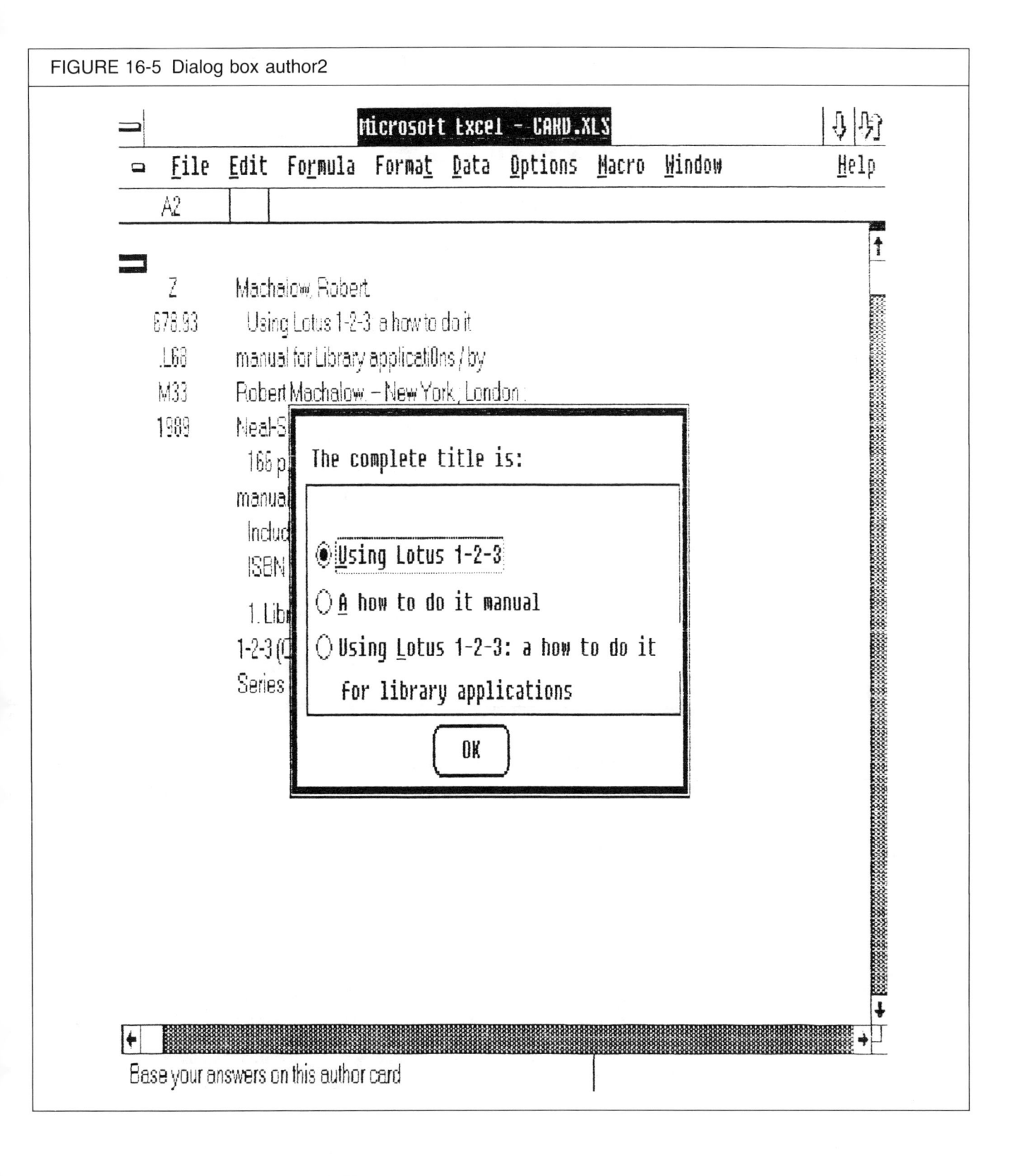

FIGURE 16-5 Dialog box author2

The complete title is:

● Using Lotus 1-2-3
○ A how to do it manual
○ Using Lotus 1-2-3: a how to do it for library applications

OK

Base your answers on this author card

= ALERT("Try again "&A2,2)

This macro function posts a message and uses the response to the INPUT() macro function used at the beginning requesting the user's name. The macro then branches back to the author macro:

= GOTO(author)

Author2 Macro: The author2 macro is similar to the author macro: it uses a custom dialog box, but first it sets the default value to an incorrect choice (see Figure 16.5). The macro code created by the dialog editor is shown in Figure 16.6. This macro also uses a CHOOSE() function to branch either to the ErrorAu macro or to author3.

The entire macro is:

= SET.VALUE(H43,1)
= DIALOG.BOX(B41 { H48)
= CHOOSE(H43,GOTO(ErrorAU),GOTO(ErrorAu), GOTO(author3))

Author3 Macro: The author3 macro begins with an INPUT() macro function which gives some information about the author card and then asks for input from the user (see Figure 16.7). The INPUT() function specifies the text to be posted and the type of response expected, in this case a number:

= INPUT("Message",1)

An IF() macro function then tests the response: if 1989 is

FIGURE 16-6 Dialog box code for author2

	B	C	D	E	F	G
41		111	68	320	144	
42	14	8	22	311	97	
43	11	0	0			
44	12	16	45		18	&Using Lotus 1-2-3
45	12	16	63		18	&A how to do it manual
46	12	16	81		18	Using &Lotus 1-2-3: a how to do it
47	1	112	121	64		OK
48	5	36	101			for library applications
49	5	12	11			The complete title is:

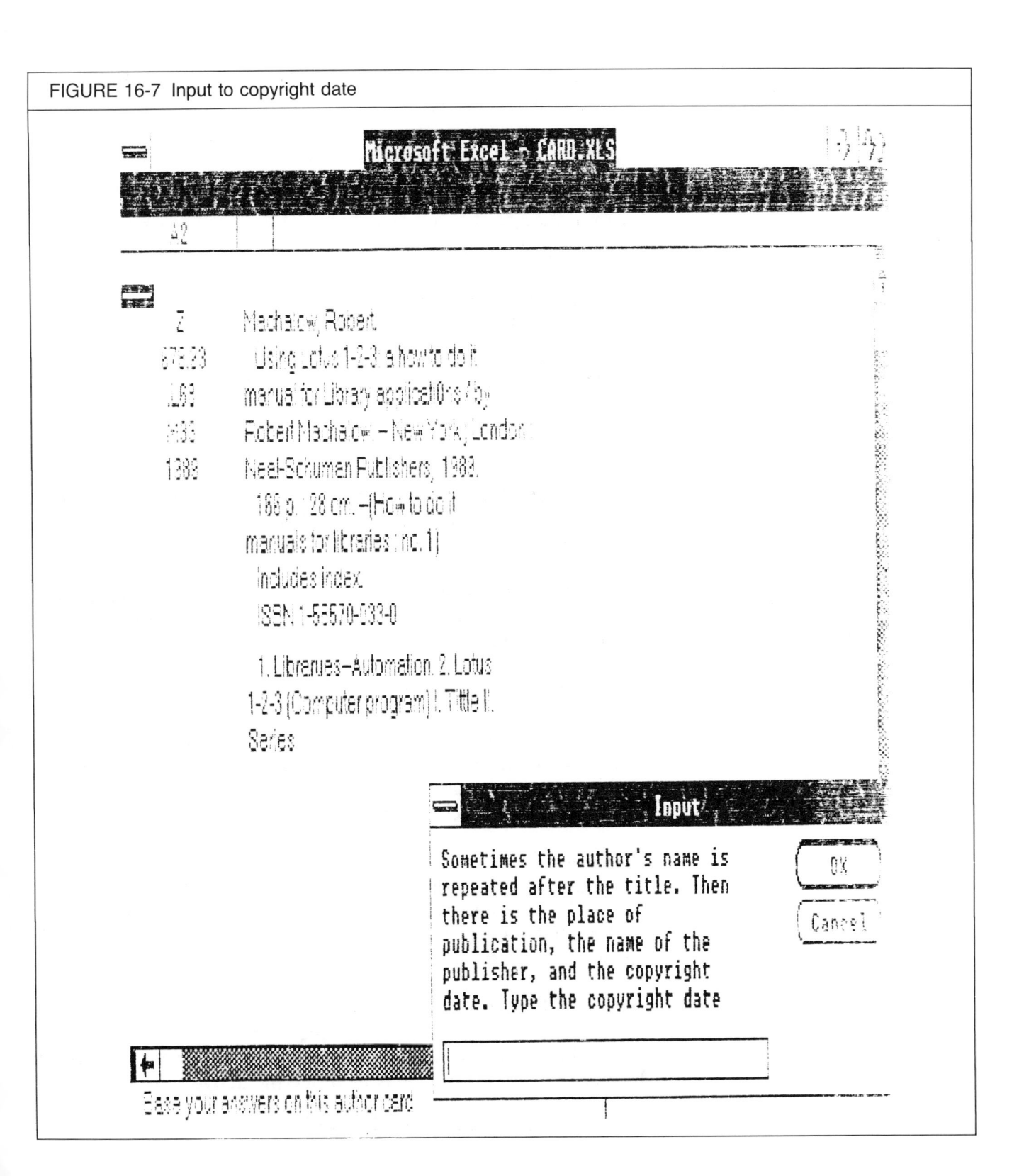

FIGURE 16-7 Input to copyright date

entered, the macro branches to the macro named author4; otherwise, the macro branches to the ErrorAU macro.

=IF(A52=1989,GOTO(author4),GOTO(ErrorAU))

Author4: The author4 macro simply posts a message using an ALERT() macro function see Figure 16.8). Then it tells Excel to continue operation with the author5 macro.

=ALERT("Message",3)
=GOTO(author5)

Author5 Macro: This macro also uses an ALERT() macro function to post a message, but this message allows the user to choose to continue the review of the contents of catalog cards or to quit the lesson.

=ALERT("You have now reviewed the author card. Choose OK to continue or Cancel to stop",1)
=IF(A62=TRUE,GOTO(Box),GOTO(Stop))

Stop Macro: The stop macro removes the message from the lower left hand corner of the display and halts the macro's operation. It has just two lines:

=MESSAGE(FALSE)
=HALT()

The message must have a logical value of false so Excel messages will function normally. Otherwise, the posted message will remain on screen until Excel is exited.

TITLE MACRO

If the user decides to review the contents of a title card, the box macro branches to the title macro. This macro begins with a FORMULA.GOTO() macro command which displays the title card:

=FORMULA.GOTO(!title)

Since the display is in reverse video (white print on a black background), the macro has to move the active cell:

=FORMULA.GOTO("R[1]C")

FIGURE 16-8 Alert message from author4

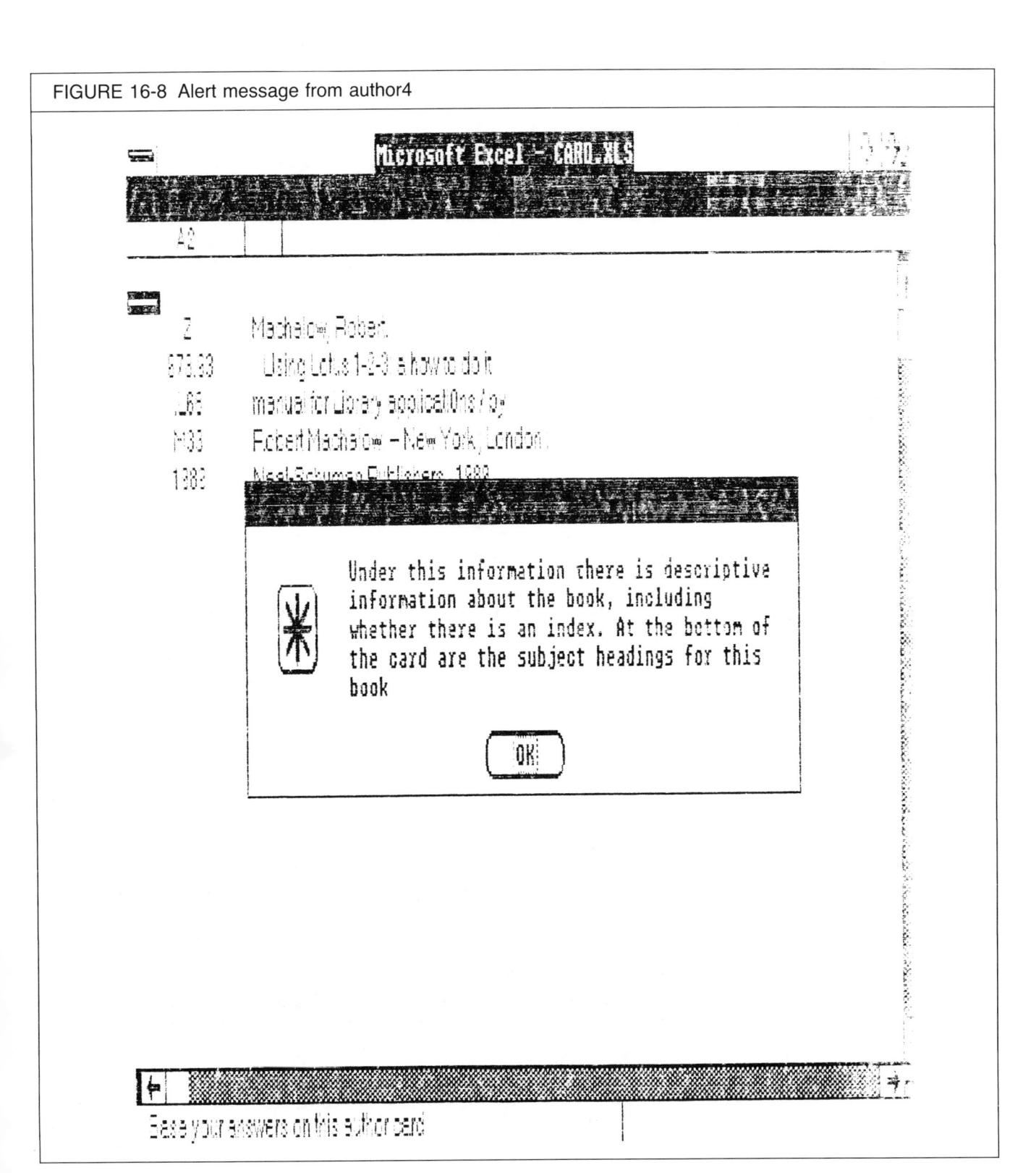

> Under this information there is descriptive information about the book, including whether there is an index. At the bottom of the card are the subject headings for this book

Then the message in the lower left hand corner of the display is changed:

=MESSAGE(TRUE,"Base your answers on this title card")

Then ALERT() macro functions are used to post messages:

=ALERT("The title is on the top line of the title card",2)
=ALERT{"After that, the card is identical to the author card",2)

A custom dialog box is then displayed, asking the user if she or he wants to review one of the types of cards or quit the program (see Figure 16.9). The dialog editor can be used to create the macro code (see Figure 16.10). The macro uses the following line to display the dialog box:

=DIALOG.BOX(B79:H87)

Then the macro uses a CHOOSE() macro function to branch:

=CHOOSE(H81,GOTO(author),GOTO(title),
    GOTO(subject),
    GOTO(stop())

SUBJECT MACRO
The subject macro is identical to the title macro except that it uses a GOTO() macro function to tell Excel to continue macro operation at cell A80, which is where the title macro used the DIALOG.BOX() macro function to display the above custom dialog box. Of course, the MESSAGE() and FORMULA.GOTO() macro functions are slightly altered.

NAMING THE MACROS
Each of the macros must be named using formula define name. Specify that each is a command macro and specify a shortcut key for each of them. After testing all the macros separately and together, you can name the opening macro, which calls for the user's name, AUTO_OPEN. Naming the macro AUTO_OPEN means that it will automatically execute each time the macro sheet is opened.

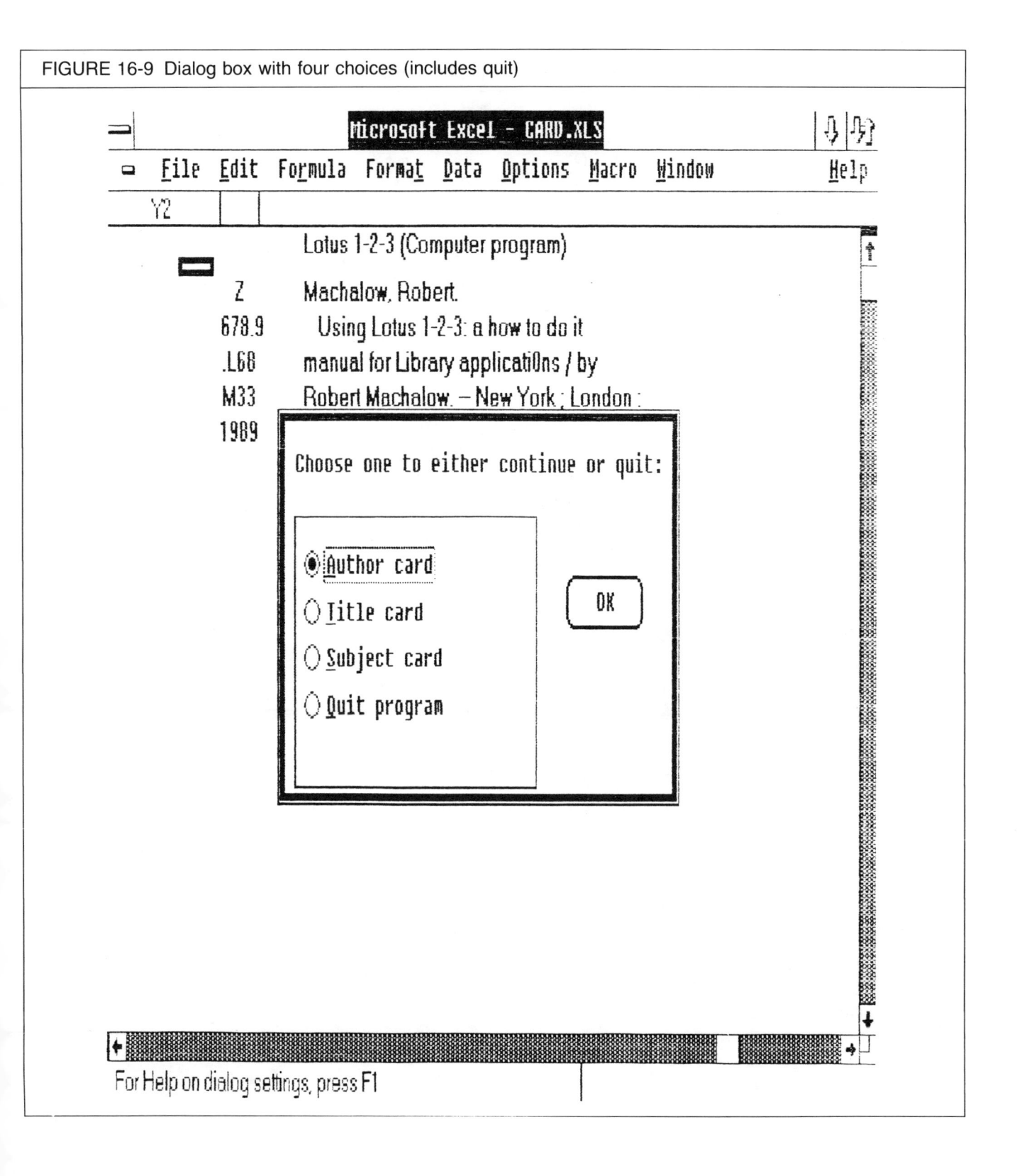

FIGURE 16-9 Dialog box with four choices (includes quit)

FIGURE 16-10 Dialog box code

	B	C	D	E	F	G
79		111	68	320	144	
80	14	8	32	200	111	
81	11	0	0			
82	12	16	47		18	&Author card
83	12	16	65		18	&Title card
84	12	16	83		18	&Subject card
85	12	16	101		18	&Quit program
86	1	232	60	64		OK
87	5	8	11			Choose one to either continue or quit

SAVING

Save the macro sheet and the worksheet separately. Then make the macro sheet the active sheet and hide it using window hide. Then save the workspace. When the workspace is opened, the worksheet will be displayed and the macro sheet hidden. If the AUTO_OPEN macro name was used, the macro will begin as soon as the workspace is opened.

17 QUIZZES

Excel has several interactive commands that can be used to create quizzes. These quizzes rely on INPUT() and DIALOG.BOX() macro functions. A subroutine can be used to keep track of the number of correct answers the user has given. The questions in this chapter are used to demonstrate the types of questions that can be constructed using Excel.

INPUT() MACRO FUNCTION

The INPUT() macro function permits the posting of a message to the user and pauses the macro for the user to furnish input. The type specified in the INPUT() macro function defines the expected input.

The form of the INPUT() macro function is:

=INPUT(prompt,type,title,default,x_position,y_position)

The prompt is what the user will see on the screen; in the case of a quiz, the prompt will be the question. The prompt must be surrounded by quotation marks.

The type specifies the type of response to be entered. Excel permits seven different data types to be specified and these types can be combined to permit the user to enter one of many different data types. In the case of a quiz, only 3 data types will be used: number (data type 1), text (data type 2), and logical (data type 4). If your library uses the Library of Congress classification system, reference (data type 8) can also be used.

The title is the title of the input box; in the case of a quiz, the title of each can be the number of the question. The title must be surrounded by quotation marks. If no title is specified, Excel uses "Input".

The x and y positions determine where on the display the input box will be displayed. If these are omitted, the input box will be centered by Excel.

CORRECT SUBROUTINE

Each time the user answers a question correctly, a range named total will be increased by 1. To accomplish this, a subroutine has to be written; in the example, this subroutine is named correct(). When a subroutine is executed, the macro goes to the subroutine, executes it, and then returns control to the calling macro. The correct() subroutine is:

=SET.VALUE(total,total+1)
=RETURN()

The SET.VALUE() macro function increases the value of the range named total by 1. After that, the correct() subroutine returns to the macro that called it.

BEGINNING THE MACRO

The macro begins by resetting the value in the cell named total to zero:

=SET.VALUE(total,0)

Then it uses an INPUT() macro function to solicit the name of the user:

=INPUT("Name:",2)

The data type in this case is 2, which is text. The rest of the arguments for the INPUT() macro function are optional. Since they are not specified, the input box will be centered; the title of the input box will be Input.

Question 1: INPUT() Data Type 1: The first question uses the INPUT() macro function to solicit a number:

=INPUT("The card catalog in this library is divided into ____ parts",1,"Question 1")

Figure 17.1 displays this INPUT():
The response, a number, will be analyzed by the next line of the macro:

=IF(A4=2,correct())

In other words, if the response is 2, execute the correct subroutine, increasing the total by 1. Then the macro will continue operation with the next question. If the answer is not correct, the macro will simply continue operation with the next question without executing the correct() subroutine.

Question 2: INPUT() Data Type 2: The second question also uses the INPUT() macro function, but this time a textual response is solicited:

=INPUT("To get help from a librarian, go to the _____", 2,"Question 2")

QUIZZES **209**

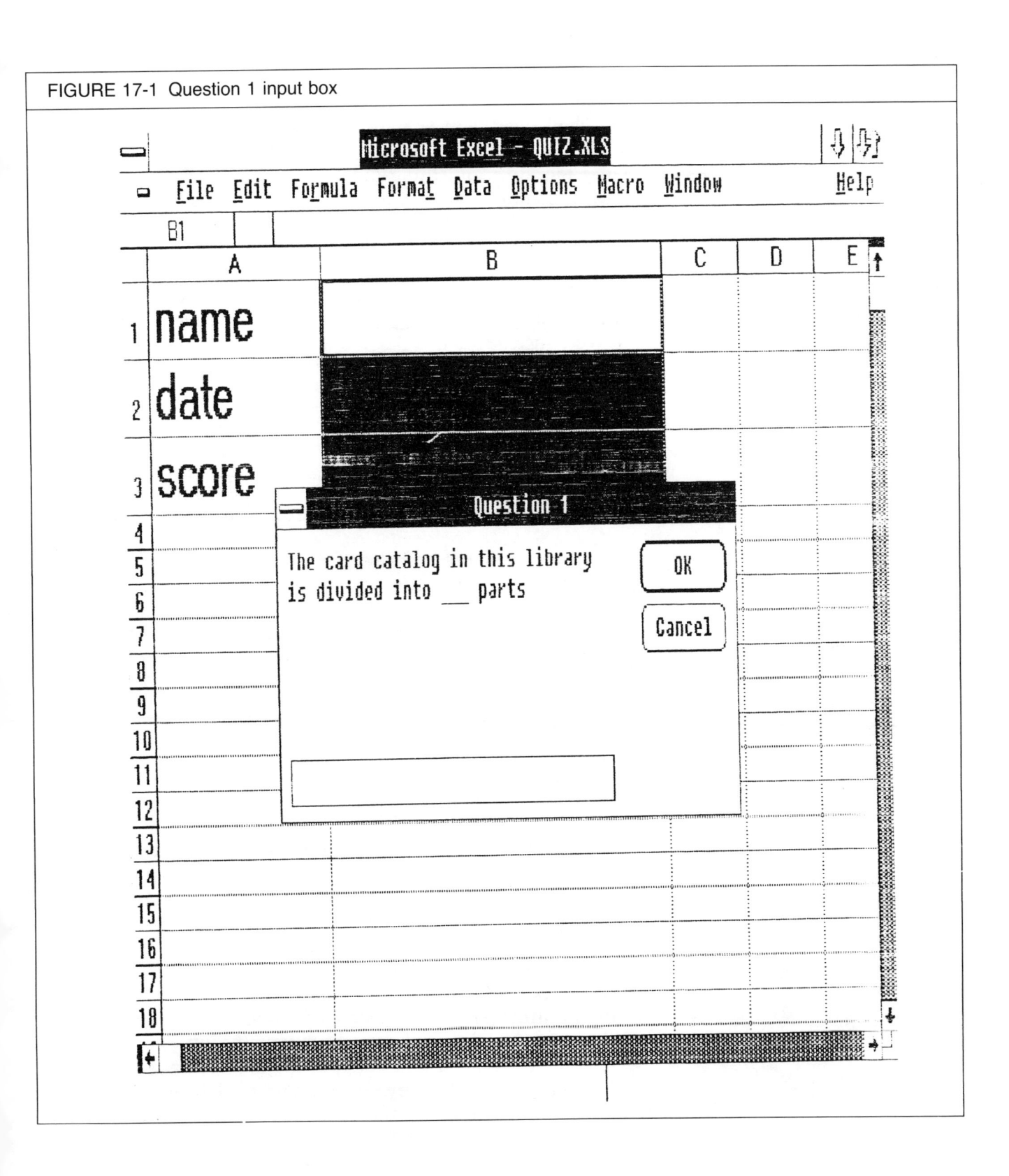

FIGURE 17-1 Question 1 input box

The input box displayed by this function is seen in Figure 17.2. The answer to be checked by Excel is textual; textual responses offer a few challenges. A user may or may not capitalize an entire response, or he or she may capitalize the first letter of each word. To avoid marking something incorrectly, an IF() macro function is used in conjunction with a LOWER() function as follows:

= IF(LOWER(A6) = "reference desk",correct())

The LOWER() function changes the user's response to all lower case so that it will be, if spelled correctly, equivalent to the correct answer. Instead of using a LOWER() function, an UPPER() or PROPER() function could have been used; the capitalization of the correct answer would then have to be modified. The textual response for the correct answer has to be in quotation marks. Once again, a correct answer invokes the correct() subroutine.

Question 3: INPUT() Data Type 4: The third question uses the INPUT() macro function to solicit a logical (true or false) response:

= INPUT("True or False: The fine for overdue books
is 10 cents per day per book",4,"Question 3")

The input box displayed by this function is seen in Figure 17.3.
The response, which must be either true or false, is evaluated by the next line of the macro:

= IF(A8 = FALSE,correct())

If the user responded that the statement was false, the correct() subroutine is called.

Question 4: Dialog Box with True and False Buttons: In a similar manner, a dialog box can be used for a true or false question. To create the dialog box, it is easiest to use the dialog editor. To gain access to the dialog editor, depress the ALT or / key, depress the SPACEBAR, and choose the run dialog box. From this dialog box choose the dialog editor.

In the example, this dialog box uses text, an OK button and a Cancel button. The buttons were edited to make them TRUE and FALSE respectively. To change the text on the button, type the new text while the button is selected in the dialog editor.

Exit the dialog editor by depressing the ALT key and selecting file. Choose exit and save the dialog box created to the clipboard.

FIGURE 17-2 Question 2 input box

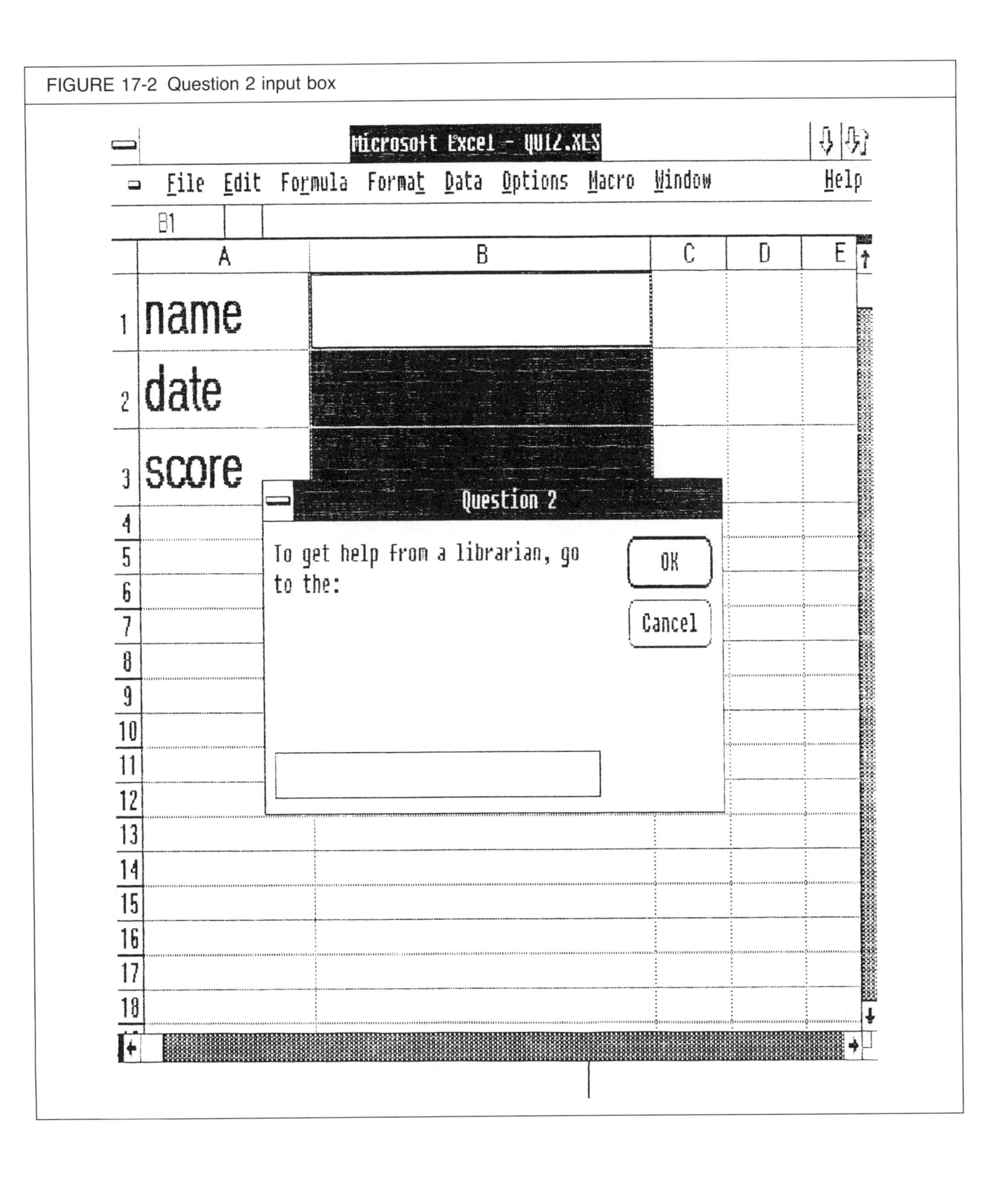

Microsoft Excel - QUIZ.XLS

File Edit Formula Format Data Options Macro Window   Help

B1

	A	B	C	D	E
1	name				
2	date				
3	score				

Question 2

To get help from a librarian, go to the:

[OK]

[Cancel]

QUIZZES **211**

FIGURE 17-3 Question 3 input box

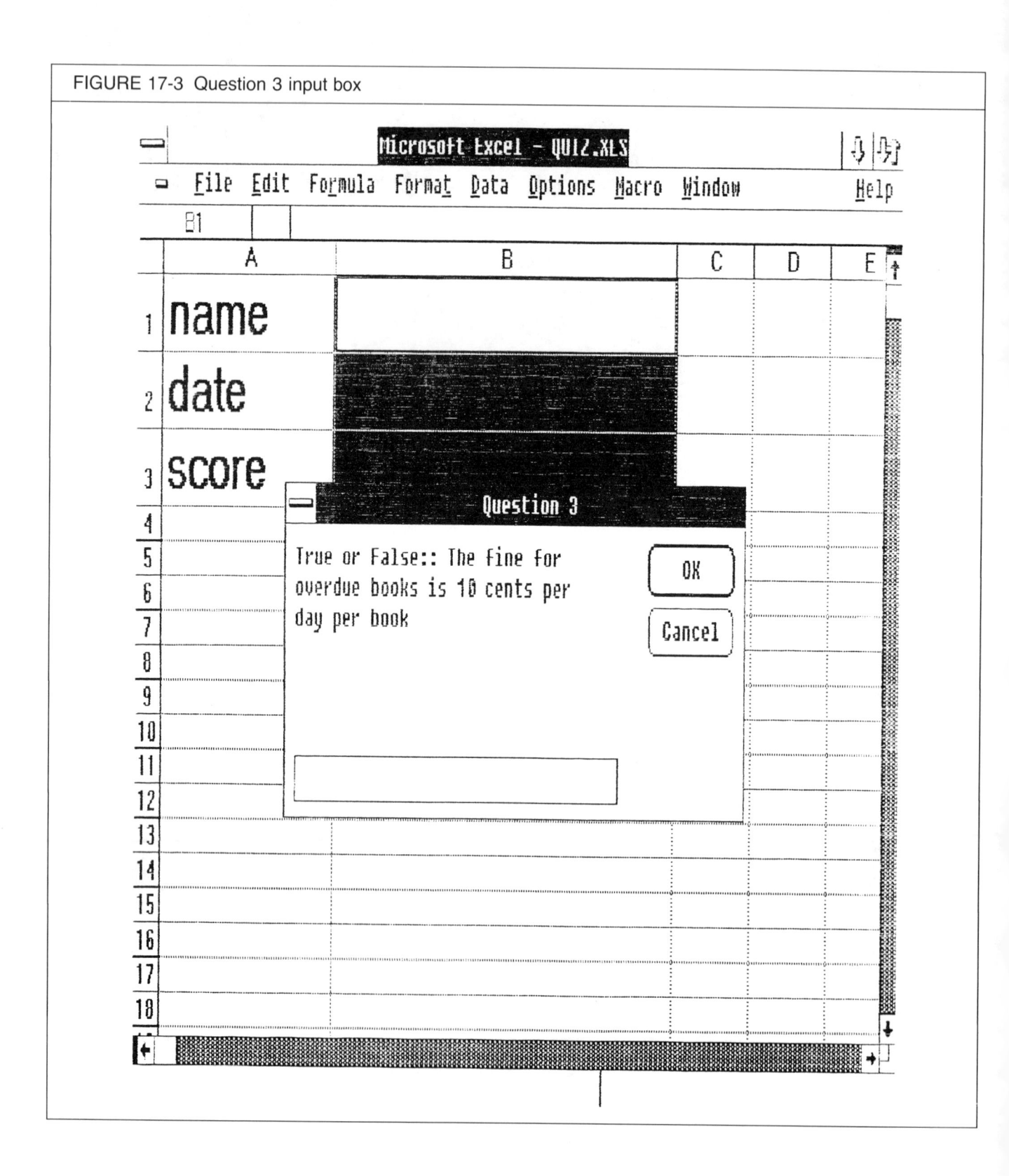

Microsoft Excel - QUIZ.XLS

	A	B	C	D	E
1	name				
2	date				
3	score				

Question 3

True or False:: The fine for overdue books is 10 cents per day per book

[OK]
[Cancel]

FIGURE 17-4 Dialog box: true/false

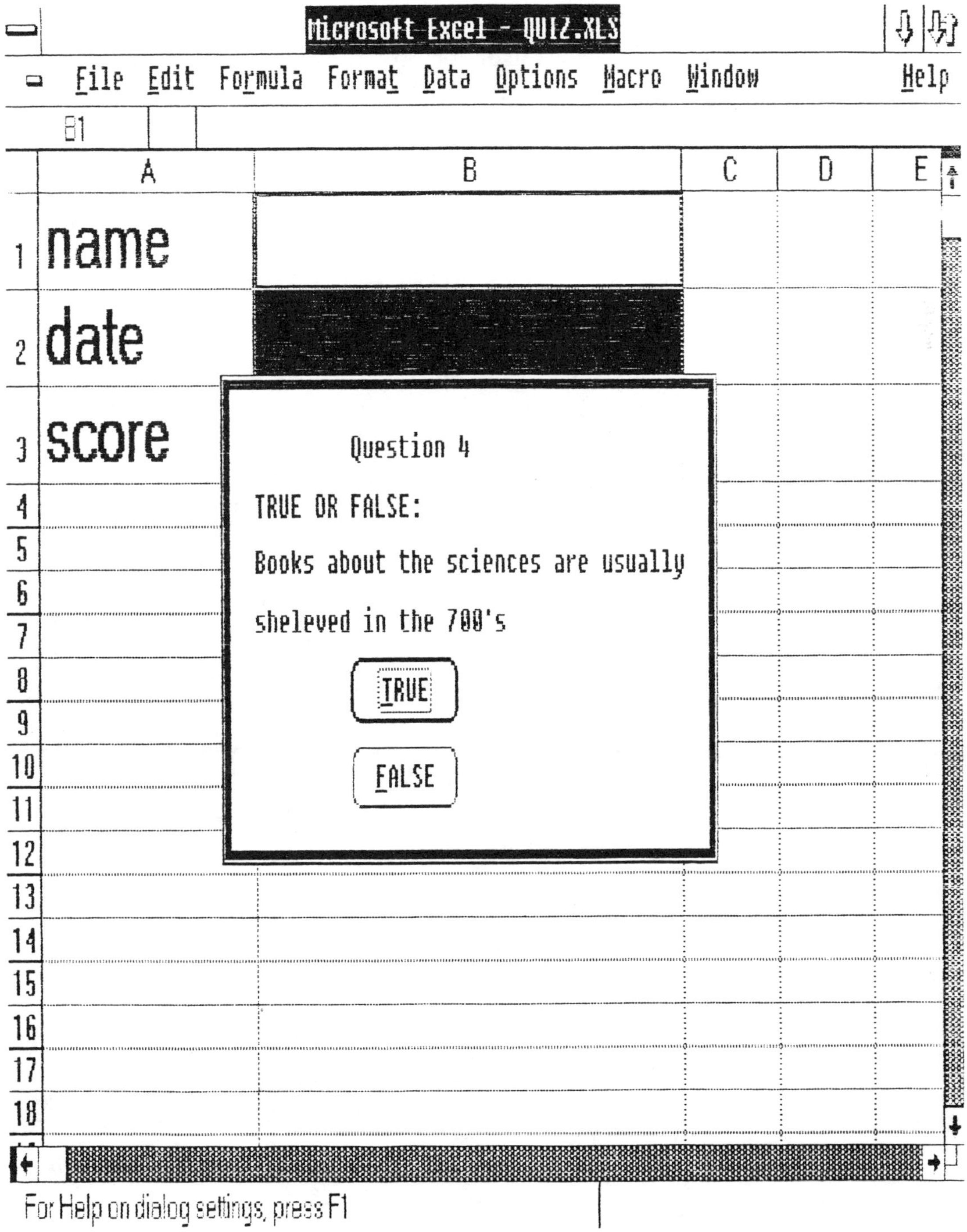
Microsoft Excel - QUIZ.XLS
File Edit Formula Format Data Options Macro Window Help
B1
A
B
C
D
E
name
date
score
Question 4
TRUE OR FALSE:
Books about the sciences are usually
sheleved in the 700's
TRUE
FALSE
For Help on dialog settings, press F1

This dialog box can then be pasted on to a blank area of the active macro sheet (ALT or /, edit, paste).

The dialog box will look like Figure 17.4. The macro code for this dialog box is displayed in Figure 17.5.

To use the dialog box, the macro uses a DIALOG.BOX() macro function:

=DIALOG.BOX(B10:H16)

The response to the DIALOG.BOX() macro function in this case will be either a 1 or FALSE in cell A11. The 1 indicates that the OK button (renamed TRUE) was chosen; FALSE indicates that the Cancel button (renamed FALSE) was chosen.

In the example, the correct response was not FALSE, and the next line of the macro evaluates the response:

=IF(A10<>FALSE,correct())

This line states that if cell A10, which is where the DIALOG.BOX() macro function is, is not FALSE do the subroutine named correct().

Question 5: Dialog Box Using Option Buttons: The fifth question also asks a true or false question using a dialog box, but instead of using the OK and Cancel buttons, option buttons are used. Once again, it is easiest to construct the dialog box using the dialog editor.

The constructed dialog box looks like Figure 17.6. The macro code for this dialog box is seen in Figure 17.7.

Once again, a DIALOG.BOX() macro function is used to display the dialog box:

FIGURE 17-5 Macro code question 4

	B	C	D	E	F	G
10		111	68	320	144	
11	5	80	12			Question 4
12	5	16	30			TRUE OR FALSE:
13	5	16	48			Books about the scien
14	5	16	66			shelved in the 700's
15	1	80	84	72		&TRUE
16	2	80	111	72		&FALSE

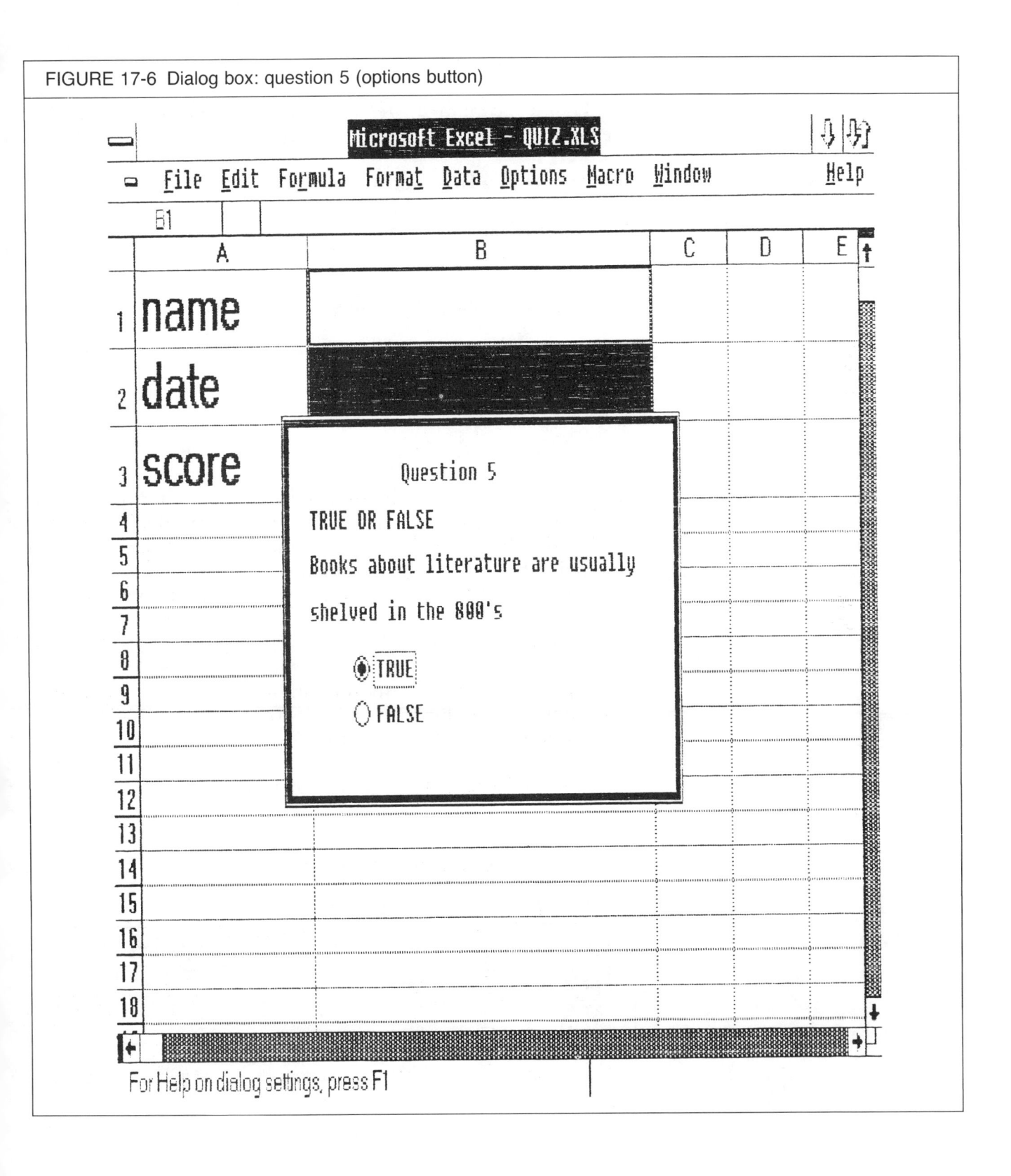

FIGURE 17-6 Dialog box: question 5 (options button)

Microsoft Excel - QUIZ.XLS

File Edit Formula Format Data Options Macro Window   Help

B1

	A	B	C	D	E
1	name				
2	date				
3	score				

Question 5

TRUE OR FALSE

Books about literature are usually shelved in the 800's

◉ TRUE
○ FALSE

For Help on dialog settings, press F1

= DIALOG.BOX(B19:H26)

Cell H24 will contain a 1 if true has been chosen and 2 if false has been chosen. The next line of the macro evaluates the response:

= IF(H24 = 1,correct())

Thus if true has been chosen, the correct() subroutine will be invoked to increase the value of the total by 1.

Question 6: Dialog Box Using a Text Box: The sixth question uses a dialog box to ask a fill in the blank question. Before the DIALOG.BOX() macro function is executed, a SET.VALUE() macro function is used to remove the previous response which would otherwise be displayed as a default:

= SET.VALUE(H35,"")

Cell H35 is where the response will be placed by this dialog box.

The dialog editor is the easiest way to create this dialog box. The displayed dialog box will look like Figure 17.8. The macro code for this dialog box is displayed in Figure 17.9.

To display this dialog box, the following function is used:

= DIALOG.BOX(B30:H35)

Once again, the textual response can have unexpected capitalization, so the macro line that evaluates the response should change the response to all lower case letters:

= IF(LOWER(H35) = "index",correct())

FIGURE 17-7 Dialog box macro code question 5

	B	C	D	E	F	G
19		111	68	320	144	
20	5	92	12			Question 5
21	5	16	30			TRUE OR FALSE
22	5	16	48			Books about literature
23	5	16	66			shelved in the 800's
24	11	0	0			
25	12	52	86		18	TRUE
26	12	52	104		18	FALSE

QUIZZES **217**

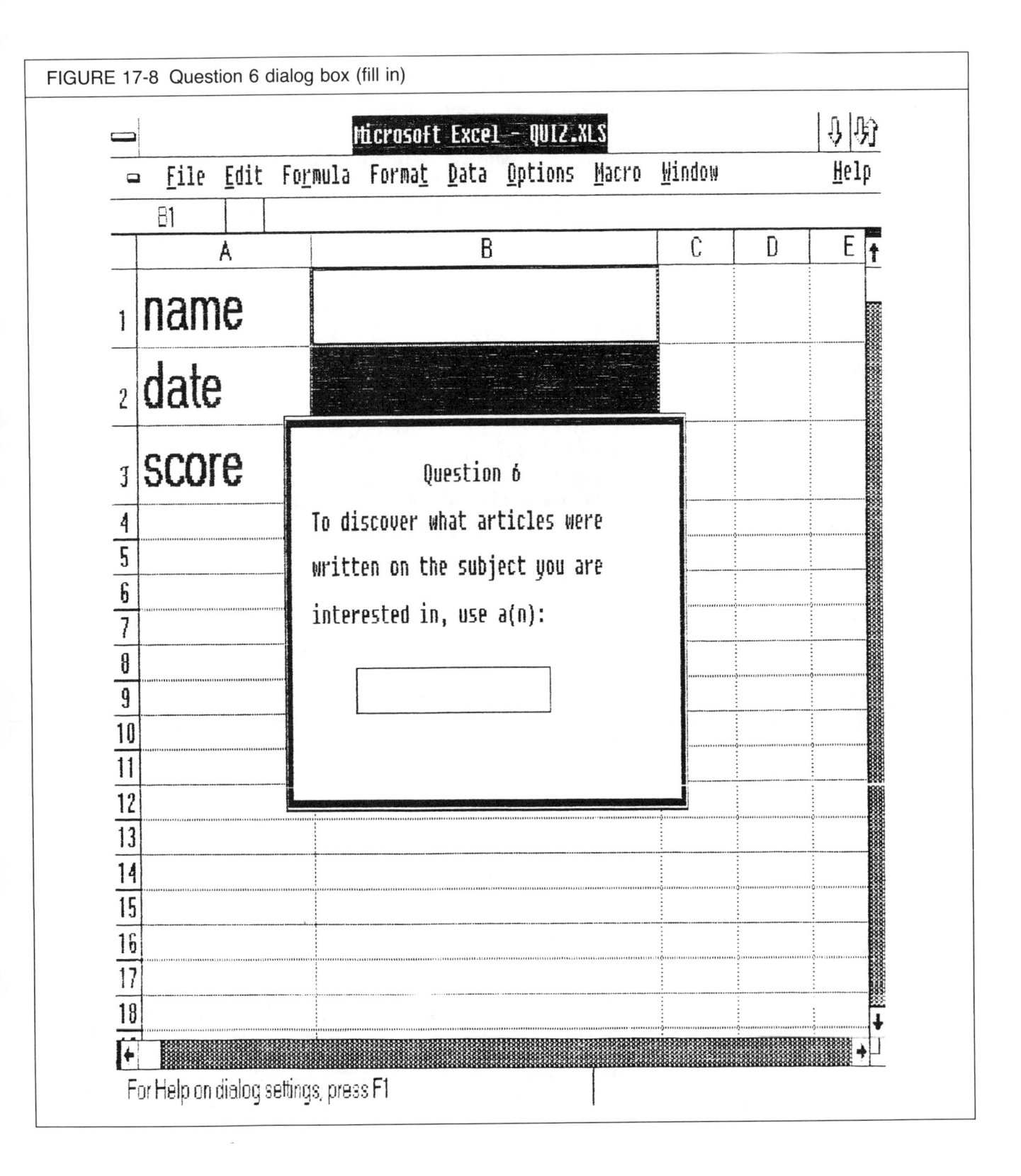

FIGURE 17-8 Question 6 dialog box (fill in)

[Screenshot of Microsoft Excel - QUIZ.XLS showing a dialog box]

Question 6

To discover what articles were written on the subject you are interested in, use a(n):

[   ]

For Help on dialog settings, press F1

Instead of the LOWER() function, an UPPER() or PROPER() function could be used; remember to modify the IF() macro function accordingly.

Question 7: Dialog Box with List Box: The seventh question uses a dialog box with a list box to answer a fill in question. The dialog editor should be used to construct the dialog box (see Figure 17.10). See the macro code for this dialog box in Figure 17.11.

When the dialog box is constructed, Excel will not be able to know where the list to be displayed in the list box is located. Once the dialog box is pasted on to the macro sheet, insert the range or name of a range in the appropriate spot. If you do not know where to insert the range or name, run the macro and Excel will post an error message, naming the cell that needs to be filled.

Construct a list somewhere on the macro sheet and then select and name it (ALT or /, formula, define name). Use this name in the macro code for the dialog box.

When the dialog box is used, the number of the response chosen will be in cell H44; the macro will have to reset this value before displaying the dialog box:

=SET.VALUE(H44,2)

The value set by Excel is not a correct one.

The macro continues with a DIALOG.BOX() macro function:

=DIALOG.BOX(B40:H45)

Cell H44 is then evaluated:

=IF(H44=10,correct())

FIGURE 17-9 Question 6 macro code (fill in)

	B	C	D	E	F	G
30		111	68	320	144	
31	5	108	12			Question 6
32	5	16	30			To discover what artic
33	5	16	48			written on the subject
34	5	16	66			interested in, use a(n)
35	6	52	93	160		

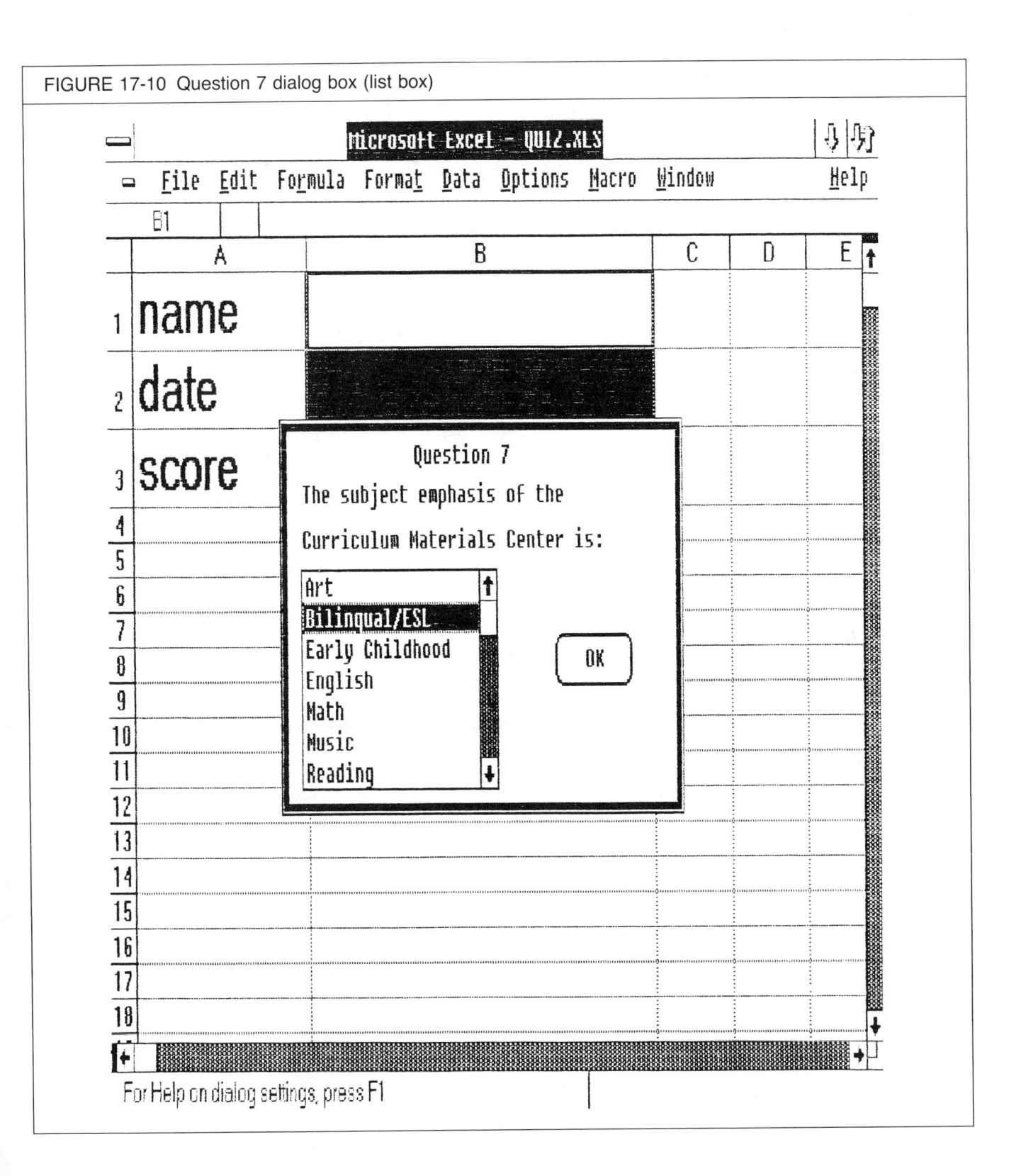

FIGURE 17-10 Question 7 dialog box (list box)

> **Question 7**
>
> The subject emphasis of the Curriculum Materials Center is:
>
> - Art
> - **Bilingual/ESL**
> - Early Childhood
> - English
> - Math
> - Music
> - Reading
>
> [OK]

The number of the correct choice in the example is 10; if it is chosen, the correct() subroutine is invoked and the total is increased by 1.

Question 8: Dialog Box Using Check Boxes: The eighth question uses a dialog box with check boxes. The dialog box asks the user to choose all the correct statements, and then evaluates the responses to the entire dialog box. Using check boxes limits the responses to each check box: true if the box is checked; false if the box is not checked.

This dialog box looks like Figure 17.12. The macro code for this dialog box is shown in Figure 17.13.

Before the macro displays this dialog box, it uses a SET.VALUE() macro function to make each of the boxes unchecked:

=SET.VALUE(H53:H57,FALSE)

Thus, when the dialog box is displayed, none of the boxes will be checked.

Then the macro displays the dialog box:

=DIALOG.BOX(B50:H58)

The response to the dialog box is evaluated using an IF() macro function in conjunction with an AND() function:

=IF(AND(H53=FALSE,H54=TRUE,H55=FALSE,
    H56=TRUE,H57=TRUE),correct())

The AND() function requires that all of the conditions listed be as specified to return a value of true; otherwise, the AND() function

FIGURE 17-11 Question 7 macro code (list box)

	B	C	D	E	F	G
40		111	68	320	144	
41	5	104	4			Question 7
42	5	12	18			The subject emphasis
43	5	12	36			Curriculum Materials
44	15	12	54	160	84	subject
45	1	220	79	64		OK

FIGURE 17-12 Question 8 dialog box (check boxes)

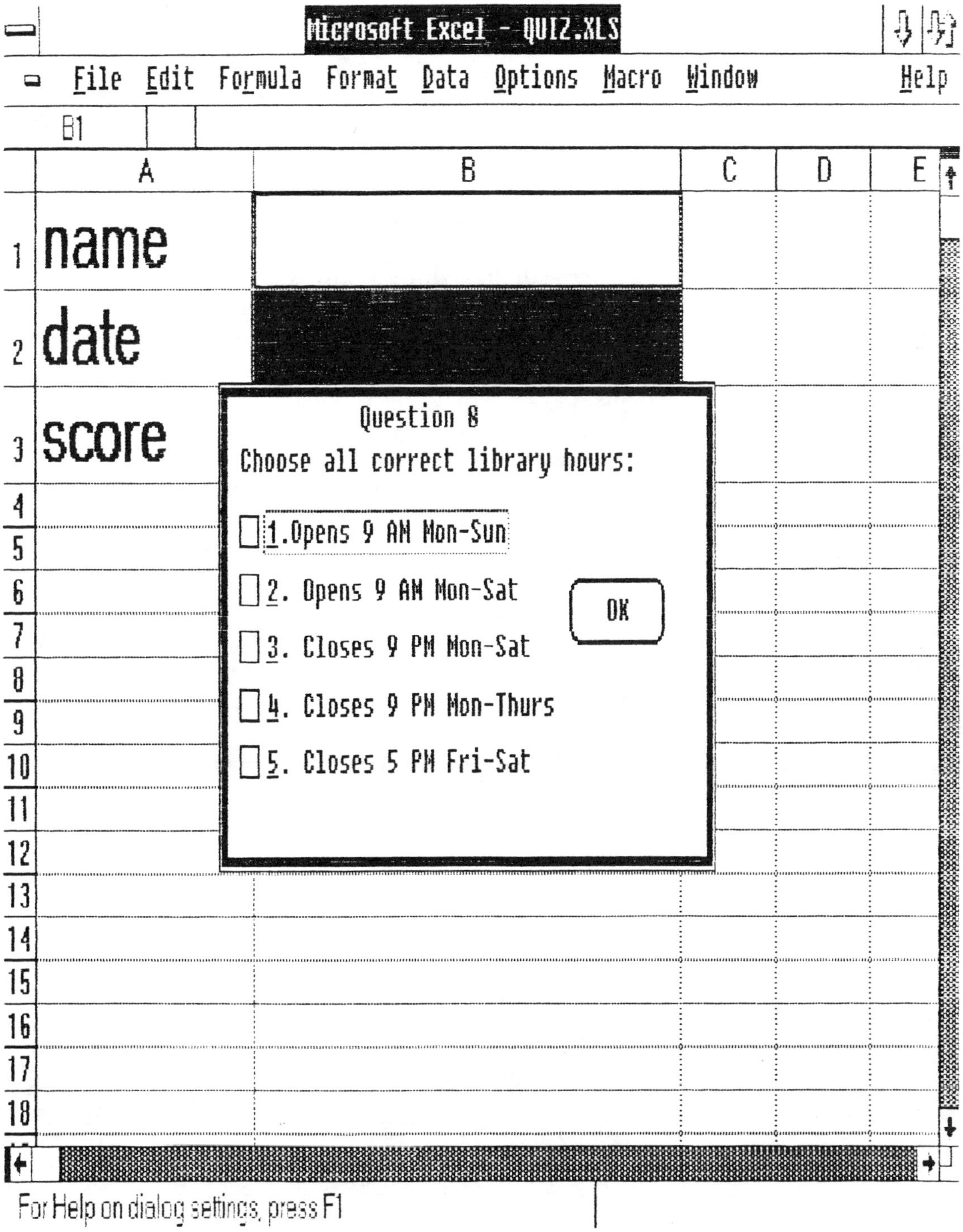

```
Microsoft Excel - QUIZ.XLS
File  Edit  Formula  Format  Data  Options  Macro  Window              Help
B1
           A                    B                     C     D    E
  1  name
  2  date
  3  score
                     Question 8
            Choose all correct library hours:

            ☐ 1. Opens 9 AM Mon-Sun
            ☐ 2. Opens 9 AM Mon-Sat          ┌────┐
            ☐ 3. Closes 9 PM Mon-Sat         │ OK │
            ☐ 4. Closes 9 PM Mon-Thurs       └────┘
            ☐ 5. Closes 5 PM Fri-Sat

For Help on dialog settings, press F1
```

will return a value of false. If the responses to the check boxes are as specified, the correct() subroutine is invoked and the total is increased by 1.

Question 9: Matching Questions Using a Dialog Box: A custom dialog box can be used to make a matching question for your quiz. The dialog editor should be used to place the items in the dialog box, but after the items are placed the macro code will probably have to be modified to have all the columns and rows parallel.

Use the dialog editor as always. Since this dialog box will have a lot of information on it, expand the borders of the dialog box by holding down the SHIFT key while using the ARROW keys. When the empty dialog box fills the entire screen, you are ready to place items.

Place the text for the directions and the first column. When you are using the text for the second column, underline one of the letters of each choice using an ampersand before it. Then be sure to create and place the associated integer edit box immediately afterwards. This will permit Excel to associate an integer edit box with the text.

At this point you can compress the integer edit box by depressing the ALT key, selecting the edit menu, and choosing the info dialog box. Edit the width to 30; this will permit the user to place up to 2 digit numbers in the integer edit box. If you decide not to do this at this point, you can make the adjustment once the macro is pasted on to the macro sheet (see Figure 17.14).

Exit the dialog editor (ALT, file, exit). Save the dialog box. When you are on a blank area of the macro sheet, paste the macro;

FIGURE 17-13 Question 8 macro code (check boxes)

	B	C	D	E	F	G
50		111	70	320	144	
51	5	88	0			Question 8
52	5	8	14			Choose all correct libr
53	13	8	34			&1.Opens 9 AM Mon-
54	13	8	52			&2. Opens 9 AM Mon-
55	13	8	70			&3. Closes 9 PM Mon-
56	13	8	88			&4. Closes 9 PM Mon-
57	13	8	106			&5. Closes 5 PM Fri-S
58	1	228	57	64		OK

FIGURE 17-14 Question 9 dialog box

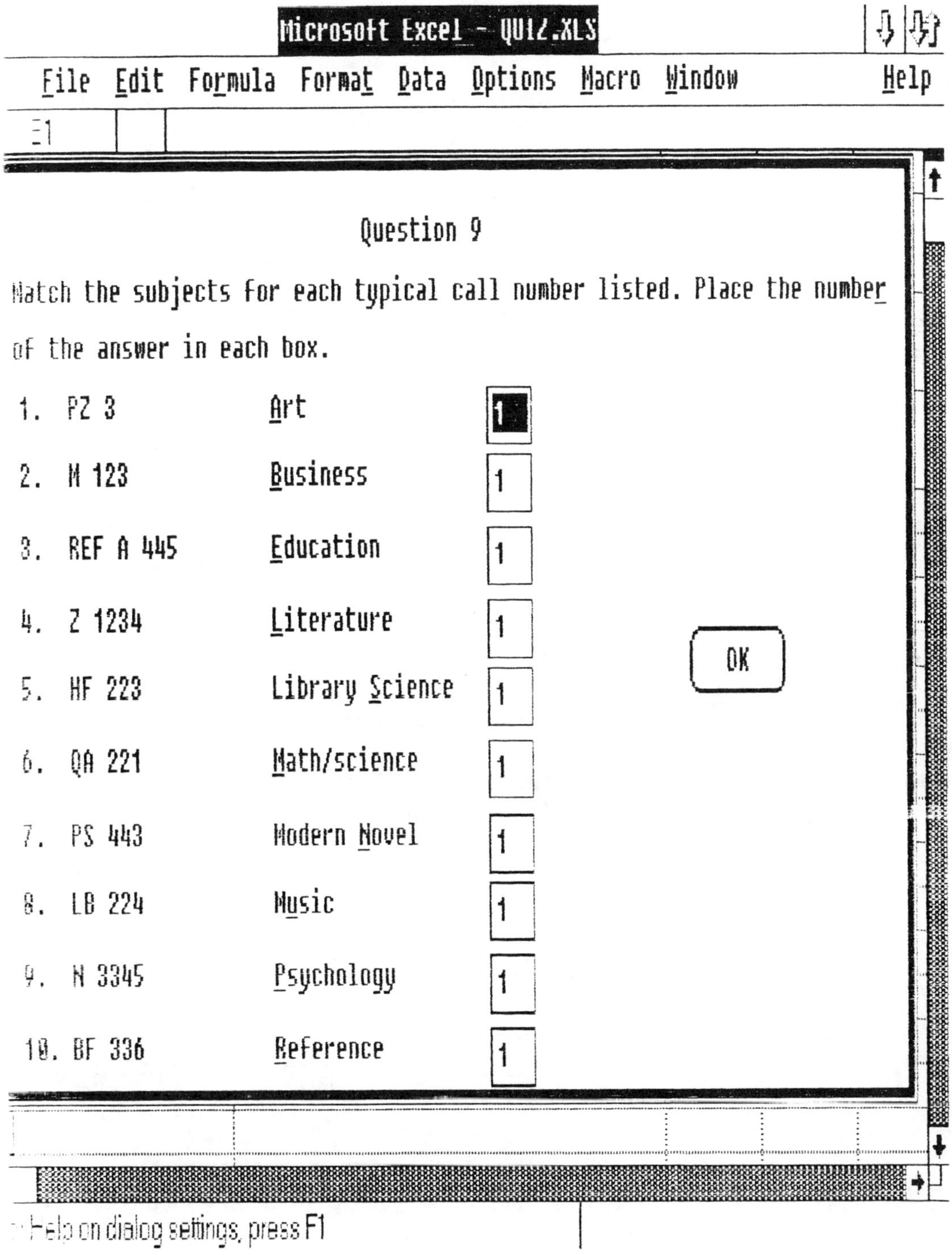

Question 9

Match the subjects for each typical call number listed. Place the number of the answer in each box.

1.	PZ 3	Art	[1]
2.	M 123	Business	[1]
3.	REF A 445	Education	[1]
4.	Z 1234	Literature	[1]
5.	HF 223	Library Science	[1]
6.	QA 221	Math/science	[1]
7.	PS 443	Modern Novel	[1]
8.	LB 224	Music	[1]
9.	N 3345	Psychology	[1]
10.	BF 336	Reference	[1]

OK

For help on dialog settings, press F1

Excel will translate the created dialog box into the required macro code.

Study the seven columns of the dialog box's macro code (see Figure 17.15): there are six filled in columns as follows:

a. The first column is used to describe the item; this column does not need to be adjusted.
b. The second column is used to describe the X position of the item. All the items on the same row on your display should have the same X position. Adjust these values as you would edit any Excel cell.
c. The third column is used to describe the Y position of the item. All the items in a column in your display should have the same Y position. Adjust these values as you would edit any Excel cell.
d. The fourth column is used to describe the width of an item. If you did not adjust the width of the integer edit boxes while using the dialog editor, you can adjust them now.
e. The fifth column is used to describe an item's height. No adjustments need to be made in this column.
f. The sixth column is used for text. All text should have been entered while using the dialog editor. If you notice any typographical errors, you can correct them on the macro sheet. In addition, if you did not underline a unique letter for each of the subjects listed in the second column, you can do that now using the ampersand.
g. The seventh column contains the initial response displayed by the dialog box and stores the user's response. It is often a good idea to change the values displayed to an incorrect answer so that the user does not only have to depress the ENTER key or choose OK to achieve a good score on the quiz.

The matching question can be handled in two different ways: either the entire question is right or wrong, or each response is judged individually.

Method One: Totally Right or Wrong: The macro will continue with a SET.VALUE() macro function which is used to set the values in the dialog box's seventh column. The seventh column displays the values in the integer edit boxes on the dialog box:

FIGURE 17-15 Question 9 macro code

	B	C	D	E	F	G	H
70		3	3	609	284		
71	5	248	12			Question 9	
72	5	20	30			Match the subjects t	
73	5	20	48			of the answer in eac	
74	5	24	66			1. PZ 3	
75	5	188	66			&Art	
76	8	330	66	30			1
77	5	24	88			2. M 123	1
78	5	188	88			&Business	
79	7	330	88	30			1
80	5	24	110			3. REF A 445	1
81	5	188	110			&Education	
82	8	330	110	30			1
83	5	24	132			4. Z 1234	
84	5	188	132			&Literature	
85	8	330	132	30			1
86	5	24	154			5. HF 223	1
87	5	188	154			Library &Science	1
88	5	24	176			6. QA 221	1
89	8	330	154	30			1
90	5	188	176			&Math/science	
91	7	330	176	30			1
92	5	24	198			7. PS 443	
93	5	188	198			Modern &Novel	1
94	7	330	198	30			1
95	5	24	220			8. LB 224	1
96	5	188	220			M&usic	1
97	7	330	220	30			1
98	5	24	242			9. N 3345	
99	5	188	242			&Psychology	1
100	7	330	242	30			1
101	5	24	264			10. BF 336	1
102	5	188	264			&Reference	1
103	7	330	264	30			1
104	1	464	141	64		OK	

= SET.VALUE(H76:H103,"!")

This command places a 1 in all the cells from H76 through H103. Not all these cells need a value, but the extra ones will not hurt the dialog box.

The DIALOG.BOX() macro function is used to display the dialog box:

= DIALOG.BOX(B70:H104)

The dialog box is displayed and each integer box has a 1 in it. If the user simply depresses ENTER or chooses OK, obviously not all the answers will be correct.

The next line of the macro uses an IF() macro function in conjunction with an AND() function: it tests whether or not all the answers are correct. If they are all correct, the AND() function returns a value of TRUE, and the IF() macro function instructs Excel to execute the correct() subroutine.

=IF(AND(H76=9,H79=5,H82=8,H85=7,H89=4,
    H91=6,H94=1,H97=2,H100=10,H103=3),correct())

Method Two: Judging the Answers Separately: Alternatively, you can judge the responses separately. If you decide to use the dialog box in this way, the SET.VALUE() and DIALOG.BOX() functions are identical to the first method. Instead of judging the responses using an IF() macro function in conjunction with an AND() function, each response is judged using separate IF() macro functions:

=IF(H76=9,correct())
=IF(H79=5,correct())

Each integer edit box is judged separately.

If you want, you can give extra credit to the person who has answered all ten parts of the dialog box correctly. After judging each of the responses, you can add an IF() macro function that uses an AND() function:

=IF(AND(H76=9,H79=5,H82=8,H85=7,H89=4,
    H91=6,H94=1,H97=2,H100=10,H103=3),correct())

Thus, if a user has correctly matched all ten subjects with the typical call numbers, a bonus is given.

Question 10: Input Type 8: A final question can be asked using the INPUT() macro function with a reference data type but this question can only be asked if your library uses the Library of Congress classification system. A reference data type asks the user to type in a combination of letter(s) followed by numbers, just like an LC number. Excel is actually looking for a cell reference; since the Library of Congress call numbers are similar, the reference data type can be called for.

```
=INPUT("A typical call number for a book about
    psychology is BF334, D45, or G445",8,
    "Question 10")
```

Since the response Excel is seeking is a cell reference, there cannot be a space between the letter(s) and numbers. The response is evaluated by an IF() macro function:

```
=IF(A26=BF334,correct())
```

The response is a cell reference, and no quotation marks are necessary.

BONUS

If you used the second method of evaluating the matching dialog box (question 9), your user can only have a score of 19. You can give a bonus to the user who has gotten all the answers correct by using an IF() macro function to test whether the total is 19; if it is, execute the correct subroutine:

```
=IF(total=19,correct())
```

PRINTING THE RESULTS

The macro can continue by printing the results of the quiz. On a blank worksheet, type the following headings in column A: Name, Date, and Score. Then format cell B2 (which will be used for the date and time) for date and time (ALT or /, format, number, and choose the date and time format or any other you think is appropriate). Format cell C2 (which will be used for the final score obtained on the quiz) for percent (ALT or /, format, number, percent). Name each of the cells in the B column using ALT or /, formula, define name: these names will be used by the macro.

You can select the six cells that will be used and choose a different font and enlarge that font to make it more visible (ALT or /, format, font). Then you are ready to continue the macro:

```
=FORMULA(A5,!name)
```

This line will place the response to the INPUT() macro function which asked for the user's name at the beginning of the macro in the named cell on the worksheet.

The next line places the date and time (or just the time if that is the format you chose) on the worksheet:

```
=FORMULA(NOW().!date)
```

Using the NOW() function will place the serial number of the date and time in the cell named date if your computer has an internal clock or you answered the DOS prompt correctly when you started the computer. Depending on how you formatted the cell, the display will show either the serial number (without formatting) or the date and/or time.

The next line will either multiply the total by .1 or .05, depending on whether you had a possible total of 10 or twenty.

=FORMULA(total*0.1,!score)

or:

=FORMULA(total*0.05,!score)

In either case, the total will be multiplied to place the percent correct in the score cell, which was formatted for percent.

Next an ALERT() macro function is used to tell the user to turn on the printer:

=ALERT("Turn on printer",2)

This ALERT() macro function only has an OK button, and when the user chooses that button or depresses the ENTER key, the macro will continue.

The next lines specify the page setup and tells Excel to print:

=PAGE.SETUP("LIBRARY QUIZ","",,,,,FALSE,FALSE)
=PRINT(1,,1,FALSE,FALSE,1)

The PAGE.SETUP() macro function has the general form:

=PAGE.SETUP(head,foot,right,top,bottom,heading,grid)

In this case, the header will be "LIBRARY QUIZ", the footer will be blank, the borders will be the default and thus do not need to be specified, and neither row and column headings nor gridlines will be printed,

The PRINT() macro function has the general form:

=PRINT(range,from,to,copies,draft,preview,parts)

In this case the range is specified as 1, which is to print the entire worksheet. Since only these six cells are used, only these six cells will be printed. The from and to options are ignored since the entire worksheet will be printed. The number of copies is one. The draft and preview options are not to be used. In terms of parts, 1 specifies the sheet; 2 would specify the notes, and 3 would specify both the sheet and the notes.

The macro ends with a RETURN() macro function. All Excel macros end with a RETURN() macro function.

NAMING AND SAVING

The macro should be named and tested. To name a macro, use ALT or /, formula, define name. After testing the macro, you can rename it AUTO_OPEN; with this name, the quiz will run whenever the macro sheet is opened.

Then save the macro sheet and the worksheet. Each must be saved separately (ALT or /, file, save or save as). Then you can hide the macro sheet (ALT or /, window, hide) and save the workspace (ALT or /, file, save workspace). When the workspace is opened, the macro sheet will be hidden and the AUTO_OPEN macro will run automatically.

FINAL CONSIDERATIONS

As the macro is written, the results from one user may be displayed on screen when another is using the quiz. You may want to avoid this problem by adding two lines to the beginning of the macro. These lines will set the value of cells B1 through B3 to blanks:

=SELECT(!B1:B3)
=CLEAR(3)

The first line selects the three cells on the current worksheet that might contain the results of another user. The second line clears the formulas from the selected cells. The result is that these cells are blank.

To add lines to the macro, you could select the cells used by the macro and use edit cut and edit paste (ALT or /, edit, cut; ALT or /, edit, paste). Instead you could use edit insert (ALT or /, edit, insert) and choose to shift cells down. Then add the lines to the macro.

You must name the macro again and save the macro sheet again. Use ALT or /, file, save: this will replace the macro sheet on disk

	A
1	start
2	=SELECT(!B1:B3)
3	=CLEAR(3)
4	=SET.VALUE(total,0)
5	=INPUT("Name: ",2)
6	=INPUT("The card catalog in this library is divided into ___ parts",1,"Question 1",,)
7	=IF(A6=2,correct())
8	=INPUT("To get help from a librarian, go to the:",2,"Question 2",,)
9	=IF(LOWER(A8)="reference desk",correct())
10	=INPUT("True or False:: The fine for overdue books is 10 cents per day per book",4,"Question 3",,)
11	=IF(A10=FALSE(),correct())
12	=DIALOG.BOX(B10:H16)
13	=IF(A12<>FALSE,correct())
14	=DIALOG.BOX(B19:H26)
15	=IF(H24=1,correct())
16	=SET.VALUE(H35,"")
17	=DIALOG.BOX(B30:H35)
18	=IF(LOWER(H35)="index",correct())
19	=SET.VALUE(H44,2)
20	=DIALOG.BOX(B40:H45)
21	=IF(H44=10,correct())
22	=SET.VALUE(H53:H57,FALSE)
23	=DIALOG.BOX(B50:H58)
24	=IF(AND(H53=FALSE,H54=TRUE,H55=FALSE,H56=TRUE,H57=TRUE),correct())
25	=SET.VALUE(H76:H103,"1")
26	=DIALOG.BOX(B70:H104)
27	=IF(AND(H76=9,H79=5,H82=8,H85=7,H89=4,H91=6,H94=1,H97=2,H100=10,H103=3),correct())
28	=INPUT("A typical call number for a book about psychology is BF334, D45, or QA55",8,"Question 10")
29	=IF(A28=BF334,correct())
30	=FORMULA(A5,!name)
31	=FORMULA(NOW(),!date)
32	=FORMULA(total*0.05,!score)
33	=ALERT("Turn on printer",2)
34	=PAGE.SETUP("LIBRARY QUIZ","",,,,,FALSE,FALSE)
35	=PRINT(1,,,1,FALSE,FALSE,1)
36	=RETURN()

FIGURE 17-16 Entire macro (10 points)

with the changed one. The workspace does not have to be saved again.

THE ENTIRE MACRO

If you decide to create the macro with ten possible correct answers, the entire macro will look like Figure 17.16.

If you decide to create the macro with twenty possible correct answers, the entire macro will look like Figure 17.17.

FINAL NOTE

If the quiz you are constructing is to be used to teach or reinforce

FIGURE 17-17 Entire macro (20 points)

	K
1	Alternative
2	=SELECT(!B1:B3)
3	=CLEAR(3)
4	=SET.VALUE(total,0)
5	=INPUT("Name: ",2)
6	=INPUT("The card catalog in this library is divided into ___ parts",1,"Question 1",,)
7	=IF(K6=2,correct())
8	=INPUT("To get help from a librarian, go to the:",2,"Question 2",,)
9	=IF(LOWER(K8)="reference desk",correct())
10	=INPUT("True or False:: The fine for overdue books is 10 cents per day per book",4,"Question 3",,)
11	=IF(K10=FALSE(),correct())
12	=DIALOG.BOX(B10:H16)
13	=IF(K12<>FALSE,correct())
14	=DIALOG.BOX(B19:H26)
15	=IF(H24=1,correct())
16	=SET.VALUE(H35,"")
17	=DIALOG.BOX(B30:H35)
18	=IF(LOWER(H35)="index",correct())
19	=SET.VALUE(H44,2)
20	=DIALOG.BOX(B40:H45)
21	=IF(H44=10,correct())
22	=SET.VALUE(H53:H57,FALSE)
23	=DIALOG.BOX(B50:H58)
24	=IF(AND(H53=FALSE,H54=TRUE,H55=FALSE,H56=TRUE,H57=TRUE),correct())
25	=SET.VALUE(H76:H103,"1")
26	=DIALOG.BOX(B70:H104)
27	=IF(H76=9,correct())
28	=IF(H79=5,correct())
29	=IF(H82=8,correct())
30	=IF(H85=7,correct())
31	=IF(H89=4,correct())
32	=IF(H91=6,correct())
33	=IF(H94=1,correct())
34	=IF(H97=2,correct())
35	=IF(H100=10,correct())
36	=IF(H103=3,correct())
37	=IF(AND(H76=9,H79=5,H82=8,H85=7,H89=4,H91=6,H94=1,H97=2,H100=10,H103-3),correct())
38	=INPUT("A typical call number for a book about psychology is BF334, D45, or QA55",8,"Question 10")
39	=IF(K38=BF343,correct())
40	=IF(total=19,correct())
41	=FORMULA(K5,!name)
42	=FORMULA(NOW(),!date)
43	=FORMULA(total*0.05,!score)
44	=ALERT("Turn on printer",2)
45	=PAGE.SETUP("LIBRARY QUIZ","",,,,,FALSE,FALSE)
46	=PRINT(1,,,1,FALSE,FALSE,1)
47	=RETURN()

rather than simply to test, the ALERT() macro function can be used to explain incorrect answers. The format of the ALERT() macro function is:

= ALERT(message,type)

CONCLUSION

After working through the first part of this book, you have learned the basic commands, formulas, and functions of Microsoft Excel. With that information, and the practical library applications detailed in the second part, you are well prepared to customize the power of Excel for your library situation.

INDEX

Absolute cell addresses, 16
Active cells, 6, 8
Active macro sheet, 192 (sample)
Add menu macro, 159 (sample)
ADD.COMMAND(), 146
ADD.COMMAND with
    ENABLE.COMMAND to
    gray it, 150 (sample)
ADD.MENU(), 151
Adding records, 60
Addition, 15
Alert message from author 4, 203
    (sample)
ALERT(), 180, 181, 193
Alignment
  of chart texts, 113
  of text, 31
Alt Shift-options, 100
Alt-C, 61, 123
Alt-D, 26, 61
Alt-Hyphen, 37
Alt-K, 123
Alt-O, 29, 119, 142
Alt-P, 144
Alt-S, 54, 119
Alt-W, 58
Alt-X, 61
AND, 174
AND(), 220
Apple Macintosh, 142
Apply names, 45
ARGUMENT, 134
Arguments
  in functions, 72
  in macro functions, 120-121
Arrange all, 35, 36 (sample), 37,
    38(sample), 82
Author 2 macro, 200
Author 3 macro, 200
Author 4 macro, 202
Author 5 macro, 202
Author macros, 196-202
Author's name dialog box, 197
    (sample)
AUTO-OPEN, 192
AUTO.OPEN, 171
AVERAGE, 73, 76
Axes of charts, 112

Backup files, 142

BEEP(), 188
Beeps
  in macros, 125, 188
  suppressing, 144
Book budgets
  charts of, 114-116
  worksheets, 78-79, 80-81
    (samples)
Book budgets with percents, 102
    (sample)
Books
  with customizing, 33-34
    (samples)
  with formulas, 103 (sample)
Books2, worksheet, 40 (sample)
Borders, 31
Box dialog box, 195 (sample)
Box macros, 166, 168, 178
    (sample)
Budgets
  charts of, 105-116
  data form for, 65
  worksheets for, 12, 13 (sample),
    14-25
  worksheets for formatting and
    formulas, 100-104

Calculation of charts, 113
Calculation of formulas options,
    100
Cancelling while typing, 6
Capitalization
  in criteria, 57
  of function names, 72
  in interactive macros, 210, 216
  of macro shortcut keys, 119
Card subroutines, 187
Card() subroutines, 189 (sample)
Catalog cards, 193-206
Cell addresses, 6
  types of, 16
Cell entry, 12
Cell formats, types of, 90, 92
Cell protection, types of, 96
Cellpointers, moving in macros,
    187
Cells
  active, 6, 8
  finding those with special
    characteristics, 84

  modifying contents of, 39
  moving to a specific, 97, 100
  naming of, 43-45
  with notes attached, 82, 84
  outlining of, 33
  protection of, 94, 96
  shifting of, 26
Changing column width, 12, 14
Chart add overlay, 112
Chart calculate now, 112
Chart delete, 112
Chart gridlines, 112-113
Chart protect document, 113
Chart select chart, 113
Charts
  alignment of text, 113
  arrows on, 111-112
  axes of, 112
    scales of, 113
  calculations for, 113
  creation of, 105-116
  customizing texts on, 110, 112
  deleting special features of,
    113
  labelling, 109
  legends, 113
  menus for, 112
  passwords for, 113
  patterns on, 113
  protection for, 113
  saving, 114
  setting default type for, 106
  styles of objects, 113
  text linked to worksheet, 113-
    114
  text location on, 110
  text size on, 111
  texts for, 113
  titles of, 107, 108
  types of, 105
CHECK.COMMAND, 152
Choose (mouse), 20
CHOOSE(), 194, 198
Circbud total with note displayed,
    83 (sample)
Circbud2, 40-41 (samples)
Circulation budget and info
    window including format,
    91 (sample)
Circulation budgets, 84, 85
    (sample), 86, 87-88
    (samples), 89

Circulation department budgets,
    data manipulation,
    records, 65, 66 (sample),
    67, 68-70 (samples)
Clear, 39
CLEAR(), 168
Click (mouse), 20
Clipboard, 156, 175, 210
Close, 37
CLOSE, 192
Close macro, 180 (sample)
CLOSE(), 180
Colors, 144
    in formats, 93
    on screen, 144
Column and row headings, display
    of, 182
Column width, changing, 12, 14
COLUMN.WIDTH, 130
Columns, insertion of, 15
Combining functions, 74-75
Command macros
    construction of, 137-139
    recording, 118-120
    running of, 121
Commands, deleting and renaming,
    152
Completed dialog box, 176
    (sample)
Computer hardware required, 3
CONTROL, 79
Control panel opening, 145
    (sample)
Control panels, 144
Control-Enter, 17
CONTROL-HOME, 12
Control-page down, up, 9, 60
Control-shift-spacebar, 15, 121
Copy, 43
Copying cells
    methods of, 17
    to other worksheets, 43
Copying formats to other cells,
    94
COUNT, 73
Count, 76-77
Country setting, 144, 146
Create names, 44
Criteria, 57, 61
Criteria name, in database
    functions, 76
Criteria range, 62-63

Cursor blink rate, 144
Custom dialog box, 155 (sample),
    175, 176 (sample), 177
Custom dialog boxes, 152-157
Custom formats, 93-94
Custom menu macro sheet, 148
    (sample)
Customization of displays, 140-
    161
Customizing books, 33-34
    (samples)
Customizing displays, 26-34

dBase files, 142
DSUM, 76
Data delete, 63-64
Data extract, 64, 165
Data find, 63
Data form, 58
Data form dialog box, 59 (sample)
Data parse, 142
Data series, 64-65
Data sort, 165
Data tables, types of, 65
Data types, 207, 208, 226
Database average, 76
Database count, 76-77
Database exact matches, 64
Database functions, 75-81
Database range, 57
Database records, finding specific,
    63
Database sum, 76
Database wildcards, 63
Databases, 57-70
    adding records to, 60
    copying specific records to a
        separate range, 64
    creating of, 57-58
    deleting records from, 61, 62
    finding records in, 61
    new records, 60 (sample)
    for periodicals holdings, 165
    of requesters, 23, 24 (sample),
        25
    restoring records to, 61
    simplifying user searching in,
        166, 168
    sorting, 62
    terms defined, 57
Date setting, 144

Date step value, 64-65
Dates
    fixing permanently, 179
    functions for, 74
        added together, 78
    in headers or footers, 52
Day of week function, 74
DCount, 76
DCounta, 76-77
Debugging macros, 137
Decide macros, 168-169
Decimal places, fixing number of,
    140
Defaults, of output, 144
Define name, 52, 55
DELETE.COMMAND, 152
DELETE.MENU, 152
Deleting, a record, 61
Department budget worksheet with
    five column headings, 13
Dialog box, 9, 10 (sample), 11,
    186-187 (sample), 223
    (sample)
    for ALERT (1), 129 (sample)
    author, 199
    code, 206 (sample)
    code for author 2, 200 (sample)
    code for author's name, 198
        (sample)
    customizing, 152-157, 175, 176
        (sample), 177, 222
    from dialog box editor, 156
        (sample)
    editor, 153-154
    formula, 196 (sample)
    with four choices (includes quit),
        205 (sample)
    installation, 144
    item types in, 153
    with list box, 218
    to locate spots on floor plans,
        184
    macro code, 177 (sample)
    for macros with question mark,
        124 (sample)
    for searching databases, 166
    title or subject, 167 (sample)
    with true and false buttons, 210,
        213
    using check boxes, 220, 221
        (sample), 222
    using option buttons, 213

INDEX

Dialog box (list box), 219 (sample)
Dialog editor, 153-154, 166, 193, 210
   menu bar for, 175
Different worksheets, switch to, 97
Directory, changing the default, 35
Directory macros with GOTO (ONKEY), 138 (sample, 139
Disabling commands, 150
DISPLAY, 170
Display dialog box, 178
Displaying formulas, 18, 19 (sample)
Displays, customizing, 26-34
DMax, 78
DMin, 78
Double click (mouse), 20
Drag (mouse), 20
Drives, changing active, 26
Dynamic data exchange, 142

EDIT, 12
Edit clear, 92
EDIT key, 12, 39
Edit paste special, 94
Edit paste special dialog box, 95 (sample)
Editing of macros, 121
ENABLE.COMMAND(), 150
END, 8-9
Enlarge macro sheet, 120
Enlarge on pull-down format menu, 149 (sample)
Entire macro, 230-231 (samples)
Equal (=) sum, 15
ERROR (), 178, 179
Error macros, 180, 181 (sample), 198, 200
ESCAPE, 132
Excel
   features of, 3-11
   features II, 90-104
Exiting data find, 63
Exiting data form, 60, 61
EXTEND, 14, 17
Extract range, 64

F1, 11
F2, 12, 47
F5, 12, 97
F6, 42
F7, 97
F8, 14, 17
Field names in database functions, 76
Fields, 57
   moving to, 60
File extensions
   for Excel worksheets, 20
   for macro sheets, 120
   for workspaces, 45
File save as advanced options, 142
File save as options dialog box, 143 (sample)
Files
   linking, 35-49
   opening macros for, 178-179
   read only, 192
   saving, 20-21
      macro for, 180
   selecting an existing, 26
Fill, 17
Find, 63
Find next, 61
Find previous, 61
Finding cells with specific contents, 84, 97
Floor plans
   drawing of, 182
   macros to locate spots on, 182-185
Font dialog box, 30 (sample)
Font selection, pull-down menu for, 157-158, 159-160 (samples), 161
Fonts
   changing of, 29
   types of, 26-27, 29, 31
Fonts pull-down menus, 160 (sample)
Footers, 52
FOR(), 185
Format, main chart, 112
Format cell protection, 94, 96
Format font, 108
Format legend, 113
Format number, compared with options workspace, 140
Format overlay, 112

Format patterns, scales, 113
Format symbols, 93
Format text, 113
Formats
   automatically recognized, 90, 92
   copying, 94
   customized, 93-94
   of files, 142
   for numbers, 92-93
   types of, 90-106
   use of colors in, 93
   using, 92-93
Formula, select special, 84
Formula bar, 6, 8, 18
   suppressing, 140
Formula find, 97, 100
Formula find dialog box, 99 (sample)
Formula goto, 96-97
Formula goto dialog box, 98 (sample)
Formula operators, types of, 71-81
Formula replace, 84
Formula replace dialog box, 88
Formula select special dialog box, 87 (sample)
FORMULA.GOTO(), 168
Formulas
   combining with functions, 74-75
   display of, 18, 19 (sample)
Freeze panes, 42
Full menus, 44, 112
Function macros, 133-137
   creating, 134-135
Functions, 75
   for macros, 120-121
   types of, 72

Gallery pull-down menus, 107 (sample)
Goto (F5), 8
GOTO(), 127, 132, 194-204
Gridlines
   changing color of, 27
   on charts, 112-113
   display of, 182, 193
   hiding and displaying of, 27-28
   printing, 52

Growth step value, 64-65

HALT(), 202
Headers, 52
Help, 11
Hidden cell protection, 96
Highlighting, 14
HOME, 12
Hour, 75

IF(), 127, 174, 200, 202
Ignore remote requests, 142
Import type 8, 226-227
Importing text files, 142
Initial chart, 106 (sample)
Initial fonts, 27
Input boxes, 209, 211-212 (samples)
  types of, 170
Input data type 4, 210
Input macro function dialog box, 131 (sample)
Input to copyright date, 201 (sample)
INPUT(), 128-133, 193, 207, 208, 226
Input() data type 1, and 2, 208
Insert, 44
Inserting a line, 26
Inserting columns, 15
Installation, dialog box, 144
Installation of Excel, 4
Integer edit box, 222
Invoiced amounts database, sorted by, 67, 69-70 (samples)

Judging the answers separately, 226

Keyboard indicator area, 8

Labelled bar chart, 110 (sample)

Labelling of charts, 108
Large worksheets, working with, 96-100
Legends of charts, 113
Letters to patrons, 46, 48 (samples)
  creation of, 46-49
  printing of, 55-56
Library map, 183 (sample)
Linear step value, 64-65
Lines, insertion of, 26
Linking files, 35-49
Linking macro commands, 170
Linking text to chart, 113-114
Linking worksheets, 42-43
List box, 184
Locked and hidden cell protection, 96
Logical data types, in macros, 210, 213
Loops, in macros, 185
Lotus 1-2-3, 4, 11, 142
Lotus Symphony files, 142
LOWER(), 77

Macro code, 225 (sample)
Macro code (check boxes), 222 (sample)
Macro code (fill in), 218 (sample)
Macro code (list box), 220 (sample)
Macro code question 4, 213 (sample)
Macro function arguments, 120-121
Macro set recorder, 119
Macro sheet, hiding, 171
Macro sheet dialog box from dialog box editor, 157 (sample)
Macro sheets
  definition of, 118
  editing, 121
  opening, 118-133
  saving, 120
Macro with ALERT(2), 125 (sample)
Macro with one input, 130 (sample)

Macro with question mark, 124 (sample)
Macros, 118-139
  to add commands to menus, 146
  automatic starting of, 181
  automatic startup of, 171
  box, 166-168
  branching in, 127, 185, 194, 207-229
  command
    creating, 118-120
    naming, 119
    running, 121
    stopping recording of, 119-120
  copying, 122-123
  creating dialog boxes for, 123, 128, 152-157
  with cancel option, 125
  debugging, 137
  decide, 168-169
  definition of, 118
  for dialog box, 168 (sample)
  documenting, 137
  enlarging, 121-122
  examples of
    added to menus, 157
    to display dialog box, 177
    for evaluating user input, 180
    for font selection, 157
    to locate spots on floor plans, 182-185
    to open a file, 178
    for printing, 227-229
    for training, 193-196, 207-231
  function
    multivariable, 135-136
    running, 135
  interrupting, 132
  last line in, 133
  looping in, 185
  moving cellpointer in, 187
  naming, 123, 135, 204
  pausing for user input to, 122-123
  for recording hours worked, 175
  for searching databases, 166-172
  second function, 135-136
  subject, 170-172
  for three fonts, 159 (sample)

INDEX

title, 169-170
with two inputs, 132 (sample)
with two message functions, 133 (sample)
types of, 118
user input in, data types, 207
user input of range in, 130
user messages in, 127-128
writing two commands on one line, 170
Make selections to change display dialog box, 126 (sample)
Maps
   drawing of, 182-192
   macros to locate spots on, 182-185
Margins, 52
Matching questions using a dialog box, 222
Mathematical symbols, 71
Menu bar, 4, 6-8
   access keys, changing, 140
Menu choice, appearance when unavailable, 150
Menus, 9, 11
   creating new, 151
   customizing, 146-150
   deleting, 152
Message area, 8
MESSAGE(), 127-128, 133, 198
Microsoft Multiplan files, 142
Microsoft Windows. *See* Windows.
Minute, 75
Mixed cell addresses, 16
Modified shelf space macro, 136 (sample)
Month, 74
Mouse
   double click, speed of, 144
   terminology for, 20
   use of, 3-4, 8, 9, 11, 26, 37, 42, 154
   in selecting ranges, 14, 18
Mouse options, 144
Move, 39
Moving
   active cells, 8-9
   to adjacent screen, 9
   to column A, 8
   an Excel worksheet, 8-9
   to END, 8-9
Moving cells, 26

Multiplan, 11

Naming cells, 43-45
Naming command macros, 119
New record, 60
NEXT(), 187
Notes
   finding cells with, 84
   reference to cells, 82, 84
NOW(), 74, 179
Number series, 65
Numbers, formats for, 92-93

ON.KEY(), 132
OPEN, 35, 192
Open macro, 178-179
Options, calculation of, 100
Options calculate document, 100
Options calculate now, 100
Options protect document, 96
Options workspace, 140-152
Options workspace dialog box, 141 (sample)
Other window, 37
Outlining cells, 33
Overlays for charts, 112

Page breaks, 55
Page setup, 52, 54, 55
PAGE-DOWN, UP, 9
PAGE.SETUP, 228
Panes, 41-42
   freezing, 42
Passwords
   for cell protection, 96
   for chart protection, 113
   limiting file access with, 142
Paste, 17, 43
Paste arguments, 72
Paste function, 72-73
Paste names, 44-45
Paste special, 94
Perd subroutine, 188
Perd() subroutine, 189 (sample)
Periodical lists, 165-172
Pie charts, 108 (sample)

Point (mouse), 20
Press (mouse), 20
Print, 52
PRINT, 228
Print area
   deleting, 52
   setting, 50, 52
Print file dialog box, 51 (sample)
Print settings, dialog box, macro sheet, 154 (sample)
Printer fonts box, 29, 30 (sample)
Printer setup, 54
Printers supported, 3
Printing, 50-56
   with macros, 227-229
PROPER(), 77
Protecting cells, 94, 96
Protecting chart specifications, 113
Pull-down menus, 6, 7 (sample), 9

Quizzes, 207-231
Quotation marks
   in ARGUMENT, 134
   around field names, 76, 78
   in formats, 93
   in formulas, 79
   in IF macro commands, 210
   in INPUT macro functions, 130, 207

Range
   filled with sequential dates or numbers, 64-65
   in formula find, 97
   in functions, 72
   input by user in macros, 130
   for list box, 218
   moving to named, 97, 100
   selection, 14
      for macro recording, 119
      summary of techniques, 18
   ways to name, 43
Ranges, selecting nonadjacent, 52
Records, 57
   adding, 60
   counting number of, 77
   deleting, 61, 62
   moving to, 60

238 USING MICROSOFT EXCEL

restoring, 61
Ref subroutine, 188
Ref() subroutine, 190 (sample)
Reference operators, types of, 71
Relative cell addresses, 16
RENAME.COMMAND, 152
Renaming commands, 152
Requesters, databases of, 23, 24 (sample), 25
Restoring a record, 61
RETURN(), 127, 133, 187, 207, 229
RETURN() macro function, 133
Row and column designations, 140
Row and column headings
   display of, 193
   hiding and redisplaying of, 29
   printing, 54
Row height, 193

Save, 20-21, 32
Save workspace, 45
Saving
   backup files, 142
   charts, 114
   a file, 20
   files
      macro for, 180
      with passwords, 142
   worksheets, 20-21
      as compatible with other software, 142
   workspace, 84
Scales, for charts, 113
Screen color preferences, 147 (sample)
Screen colors, 144
Screen settings, 144
Scroll (mouse), 20
Scroll bars, 8
   suppressing, 140
Second, 75
Second function macros, 135-136
Select (mouse), 20
SELECT(), 132
Selection techniques, 18
SELECTION(), 150
Set database, 58
Set page breaks, 55
SET.VALUE, 198, 207
SET.VALUE(), 168, 185, 216

Shading, 31
Shift cells down, 26
Shift-arrow, 14
Shift-F7, 97
Shift-F8, 14
Short menus, 44, 112
SHOW.BAR(), 146
SHOW.INFO, 170
Sorting, number of levels of, 62
Split, 41
Starting Excel, 4
Status bar, 8
   suppressing, 140
Status count, 76-77
Step value, types of, 64-65
STEP(), 137-152
Stop macro, 202
Stop recorder, 119
Stop value, 65
Styles, on charts, 113
Subject macros, 170-172, 204
Subroutines in macros, 185, 187-188, 207-229
Symbols, formats for, 93

Test macros, 181 (sample)
Text
   alignment of on charts, 113
   in customized dialog box, 153
   in formulas, 79
   importing into Excel, 142
   linked to charts, 113-114
   in macros, 208
   saving worksheet as, 142
Text alignment, 31
Text display overlap in adjacent cells, 26
Text formulas, example of, 71
Text functions, 77
Text within number formats, 92-93
Texts
   moving on charts, 110
Time, function for, 79
Time setting, 144
Timekeeping, application for, 173-181
Title macros, 169-170, 202
Titles, 54
   addition of, 26
   of charts, 107, 108

deleting, 55
Totally right or wrong methods, 224, 226
Training
   macros for, 193-196, 207-231
TRUE(), 127
Turn on/off, 20
Tutorial feature, 11
Typefaces, 26-27
Typical dialog box, 10 (sample)

Undo, 62
Undoing sort requests, 62
UPPER(), 77

Vendors, database sorted by, 65, 66 (sample), 67, 68 (sample)
Visicalc, 142

WAIT(), 188
WEEKDAY, 73, 74
What if, 65
Wildcards, in formula find, 97, 100
WINDOW, 35
WINDOW ARRANGE ALL, 82
Window arrange all, 106, 107
Window panes, 41-42
WINDOW SHOW DOCUMENT, INFO, 82
Window show info including format, 85 (sample)
Windows, 142
   changing size of, 37
   displaying multiple, 35-43
   moving, 37, 39
   use of, 3
Word processing, format, 142
Worksheets, 12-25
Workspace, saving, 84

Year, 74